SO-ATA-466

THE
CHICKASAW
FREEDMEN

Recent Titles in
Contributions in Afro-American and African Studies
SERIES ADVISER: HOLLIS R. LYNCH

The Slave Drivers: Black Agricultural Labor Supervisors in the Antebellum South
William L. Van Deburg

The Black Rural Landowner—Endangered Species: Social, Political, and Economic Implications
Leo McGee and Robert Boone, editors

"Keep A-Inchin' Along": Selected Writings of Carl Van Vechten about Black Arts and Letters
Bruce Kellner, editor

Witnessing Slavery: The Development of Ante-bellum Slave Narratives
Frances Smith Foster

Africans and Creeks: From the Colonial Period to the Civil War
Daniel F. Littlefield, Jr.

Decolonization and Dependency: Problems of Development of African Societies
Aquibou Y. Yansané, editor

The American Slave: A Composite Autobiography
Supplement, Series 2
George P. Rawick, editor

The Second Black Renaissance: Essays in Black Literature
C. W. E. Bigsby

Advice Among Masters: The Ideal in Slave Management in the Old South
James O. Breeden, editor

Towards African Literary Independence: A Dialogue with Contemporary African Writers
Phanuel Akubeze Egejuru

THE
CHICKASAW
FREEDMEN

A People Without a Country

Contributions in Afro-American and African Studies,
Number 54

Daniel F. Littlefield, Jr.

 GREENWOOD PRESS
Westport, Connecticut • London, England

Library of Congress Cataloging in Publication Data

Littlefield, Daniel F.
    The Chickasaw Freedmen.

    (Contributions in Afro-American and African studies;
no. 54 ISSN 0069-9624)
    Bibliography: p.
    Includes index.
    1. Chickasaw Indians—Slaves, Ownership of.
2. Indians of North America—Oklahoma—Slaves, Owner-
ship of. 3. Freedmen in Oklahoma. 4. Afro-Americans
—Oklahoma—History. 5. Oklahoma—Race relations.
I. Title. II. Series.
E99.C55L57   976.6'004'96073   79-6192
ISBN 0-313-22313-0 lib. bdg.

Library of Congress Catalog Card Number: 79-6192
ISBN: 0-313-22313-0
ISSN: 0069-9624

First published in 1980

Greenwood Press
A division of Congressional Information Service, Inc.
88 Post Road West, Westport, Connecticut 06881

Printed in the United States of America

10 9 8 7 6 5 4 3 2 1

For Daniel William Lewis

Contents

Illustrations

Preface

Between 1837 and the outbreak of the American Civil War, the Chickasaw Indians experienced the social discontinuity of removal from their traditional homelands in Mississippi to the Indian Territory, built a new life for themselves on the new lands, and established the Chickasaw Nation. During this period were to be found the roots of some of the most complex social problems that the tribe had to face between 1866 and 1906, when the tribal government was dissolved. One of the most difficult and perhaps the most perplexing problem of all—the posture assumed by the Chickasaw people and their government toward the persons of African descent who lived among them—grew out of the institution of slavery, which flourished in the Chickasaw Nation in the prewar years.

The history of the Chickasaw freedmen from the end of the Civil War until 1906 has been eclipsed by the story of the former slaves and their descendants among other tribes, such as the Creeks and Cherokees. Their history has also been more obscure than that of the other freedman groups in the Indian Territory, for during the time that they lived in the Chickasaw Nation they had no citizenship; they were literally a people without a country.

When the Chickasaws emancipated their slaves under the Treaty of 1866, they were given the option of adopting their former slaves as citizens of the Nation. If they did not, the United States agreed to remove the blacks from the Chickasaw country. The Chickasaws failed to adopt the freedmen, and the United States did not keep the treaty agreement. Thus the freedmen lived in the Chickasaw Nation for over forty years without civil rights or protection of the law.

Because of their anomalous state in the Indian Territory, their history has been difficult to piece together. Since they were not recognized as citizens by the Chickasaws, the Chickasaw national records contain few materials. Newspaper material is scattered and, for the most part, biased, since usually only the violent, unusual, or odd in reference to blacks was considered newsworthy. Thus I have had to rely in a large measure upon the records of the Bureau of Indian Affairs in my effort to reconstruct the history of this black frontier society in the Chickasaw Nation. Since most of the freedmen were at first illiterate, they left few records of their own during their early years of freedom. Therefore, some areas of social history are sketchy. I have generalized where I felt comfortable in doing so on the basis of available evidence. Perhaps for some readers I have not gone far enough in those generalizations, but I believe that further generalization must wait until further evidence, if it exists, surfaces.

In assimilating the scattered evidence used in writing this work, I have called upon the resources of numerous people and institutions. All cannot be acknowledged, but some deserve a special note of thanks. The basic research for this work was done during my tenure as a Younger Humanist Fellow in the Institute of Southern History of The Johns Hopkins University during the 1973-74 academic year. My thanks go to The Johns Hopkins University for supplying the physical setting for my work and to the National Endowment for the Humanities for the award that made the work possible. I also thank the archivists in the Natural Resources Branch of the National Archives for their assistance in my work with the records of the Bureau of Indian Affairs and the Department of the Interior; Martha Blaine and the research assistants of the Indian Archives Division of the Oklahoma Historical Society for their assistance in my work with the records of the Dawes Commission and the Chickasaw Nation; and Juanita Ivy, whose assistance in the manuscript preparation came at a time when it was sorely needed.

Daniel F. Littlefield, Jr.

THE
CHICKASAW
FREEDMEN

1

Backgrounds

The people known as the Chickasaws, like the Choctaws, Creeks, and Seminoles, are of Muskoghean linguistic stock and, like those tribes and the Cherokees, are known as one of the Five Civilized Tribes because of their rapid acculturation in the eighteenth and early nineteenth centuries. When Hernando de Soto made his historic expedition into the interior of the American continent in 1540, he found the Chickasaws occupying the lands between the headwaters of the Tombigbee and the Tallahatchie rivers in northeastern Mississippi. These were the lands they apparently settled after they had separated from the Choctaws, whose language they share. Their name was derived from a Choctaw phrase meaning "they left as a tribe not a very great while ago." The Chickasaws lived in settlements that consisted of small villages, a number of houses—the circular winter houses, the rectangular summer houses, sweat houses, cribs, and potato houses—in one locality. Near each family dwelling was a small plot of ground where corn, beans, peas, pumpkins, and melons were raised. The Chickasaws supplemented their vegetable diet with fish and game.[1]

Never a large tribe, the Chickasaws were nevertheless fierce and warlike. Strong allies of the English throughout the eighteenth century, they conducted predatory warfare upon the tribes of the Mississippi Valley, including the Choctaws, who were allies of the French and Spanish. The Chickasaws also successfully defended their homelands against the French and their allies as well as against the Creeks. After the American Revolution, the Chickasaws fell under American influence. In 1786, the Treaty of Hopewell recognized the Ohio River as the northern boundary of their lands, but subsequent pressure from white settlers resulted in land cessions in 1795, 1816, and 1818, the last fixing their northern boundary at the southern boundary of Tennessee.[2] During the next two decades, the

Chickasaws, like the other Civilized Tribes, received constant pressure
from the United States to give up their homelands east of the Mississippi
and take up new lands in the West.

Removal of the Chickasaws to the West was provided for by treaties
in 1832 and 1834, the execution of which depended upon the location of
suitable lands in the West. While those lands were being sought, the Chickasaws chose individual allotments of Mississippi land to use until a new
home was found, at which time the eastern lands would be sold for the
Indians' benefit. The Chickasaws were harassed and trespassed upon by
whites until 1837, when removal occurred. On January 17 of that year,
the Chickasaws signed a treaty with the Choctaws, agreeing to settle on
Choctaw lands west of Arkansas. For $530,000 paid from their tribal
funds, they were to receive all the rights of Choctaw citizens and equal
representation in the Choctaw council. Although the Choctaws and
Chickasaws could settle wherever they desired, and all lands were held
in common, a Chickasaw district was established in the western part of
the Choctaw lands, where it was assumed most of the Chickasaws would
settle.[3]

By the time of removal, the Chickasaws had given up much of their
traditional life style. Corruptive influences begun by early contact with
the French, Spanish, and British had been hastened by American contact
after the Revolutionary War. The vessels of such influence were tribal
factionalism, politically ambitious mixed-blood Chickasaws, white traders,
and missionaries. In 1801, Indian Agent Benjamin Hawkins had reported
that the Chickasaws were settling away from their old towns, establishing
and fencing their farms, raising cattle and hogs, and beginning to cultivate
cotton, to spin and weave, and to accumulate individual property, including
slaves of African descent. Missionaries, too, promoted industry and agriculture. In 1823, the Presbyterian missionaries said of the Chickasaws: "Their
previous dependence for a subsistence has, every year, become more pre-
carious: and the only alternative left is to abandon the pursuit of game,
and to turn their attention to the culture of the soil."[4]

An important by-product of the movement toward an agricultural
society was the institution of slavery. Little is known about it among the
Chickasaws east of the Mississippi. However, it is known that slaveholding
was apparently not extensive at first. The Chickasaws probably had their
first contact with people of African descent in 1540, when de Soto's ex-
peditionary force encamped in the Chickasaw country. No extensive con-

tact occurred, however, until the first two decades of the eighteenth century, when English trade flourished among the Chickasaws. Goods were carried overland from Charleston by horse or on the backs of slaves. African slavery was introduced among the Chickasaws themselves by British traders about 1750. By that time the Chickasaws well understood the concept of slavery. As the demand had grown for European trade goods, the Chickasaws had engaged in the traffic of Indian slaves, with which they purchased English goods. They preyed upon not only the Choctaws but the small tribes below them on both sides of the Mississippi and above them in the Illinois country. The Chickasaws themselves were victims of slaving raids by the Indian allies of the French. At first, slave owning among the Chickasaws was confined to whites who married natives. Some were traders, such as James Colbert, a Scot who had settled among the Chickasaws in the 1740s and who was reported in 1782 to have 150 slaves working his plantation. Others were political refugees. British loyalists such as John McIntosh, James Gunn, and Thomas Love, for instance, came to the Chickasaw country after the Spanish took control of West Florida following the Revolutionary War.[5] These men were the progenitors of some of the best-known mixed-blood families in Chickasaw history.

Little is known about the role or condition of slaves in the eastern Chickasaw country. It is certain that travelers in the Chickasaw country found them useful. But there were instances of cruelty to and violent treatment of blacks. In 1816, for example, Chickasaw Agent William Cocke reported that "several negroes" had lately been murdered in the Chickasaw Nation "in a most barbarous, cruel, and unprovoked manner." An Indian who bore a grudge against Thomas Love shot one of Love's slaves, who was riving boards in Love's yard. The Chickasaw chiefs refused to punish the killer because he was a relative of Love. A few weeks earlier Young Factor had whipped and burned to death one of his slaves.[6]

Slaves obtained from white traders or planters quickly learned the Indian language and, apparently, most were bilingual. In 1799, when the Reverend Joseph Bullen began missionary work among the Chickasaws, interpreter Malcolm McGee told him that because the whites, half bloods, and slaves spoke English, they had great influence over the Indians. He urged Bullen to begin his work among those classes, which, in turn, would "have good talks" with the Indians.

Early missionaries quickly learned the usefulness of blacks in the acculturation process. The first missionary work among the Chickasaws was

undertaken by the Presbyterians. The New York Missionary Society sent
Bullen and Ebenezer Rice to the Chickasaw country in 1799. Bullen found
the blacks' bilingualism crucial to his work and the blacks most susceptible
to his efforts. He arrived at Big Town, west of present-day Tupelo, Mississippi, on May 20, 1799, where he held "some talk by the help of a negro
who could interpret." He sought out the Scottish interpreter Malcolm
McGee, who could not read, had never heard a sermon, and was so ignorant
of the scriptures that he could not interpret. He therefore urged Bullen to
work through the whites, mixed bloods, and blacks.[7]

Everywhere, Bullen found the blacks especially receptive to his preaching. McGee's wife and blacks, understanding English, were "happy to hear."
At the home of William Colbert, about twenty slaves "dressed themselves"
and came to Bullen's room, where they prayed together. Bullen read them
several passages from the Bible and "explained to them the character and
great love of Christ, that he loves poor blacks as well as others." An "aged
negro woman" belonging to Colbert traveled thirty miles to Tockshish to
hear a sermon and told Bullen "me live long in heathen land, am very glad
to hear the blessed gospel." At his school, which he opened near present-
day Pontotoc, Mississippi, in 1800, Bullen found that his preaching made
the "most serious impressions" on the blacks, and blacks sought him out
for instructions on how to keep the Sabbath. In August of 1800, Bullen
baptized William and his four children, slaves of James Gunn. To Bullen,
William appeared "to be a true disciple of Jesus" and the children appeared
"teachable." Gunn read and prayed with his slaves and was teaching them
reading and the catechism. Wrote Bullen, "The negroes say, it is a blessed
thing to have such a master." Bullen conducted his missionary efforts
among the blacks and Indians for four years. His mission was discontinued
in 1803 when the conduct of two of his helpers turned the Indians against
the mission.[8]

It was nearly twenty years before missionary efforts were resumed. In
early 1821, the Reverend Thomas C. Stuart, under the direction of the
Presbyterian Synod of South Carolina and Georgia, began building a mission called Monroe about six miles south of present-day Pontotoc. Stations
were subsequently established at Tockshish and Martyn in 1825 and Caney
Creek in 1826. The only church, however, was at Monroe, established on
June 7, 1823. Missionary efforts in the Chickasaw Nation were transferred
to the American Board of Foreign Missions in December of 1827.[9]

These missionaries, as Bullen before them, found the blacks most susceptible to their preaching. Monroe was located in the most populous part

of the Nation. The missionaries estimated that more than 800 people lived within ten miles of the mission: "Five-eights of them are Chickasaws, and the remainder colored people of African descent, with a few white men having Chickasaw families." When the church was established, the membership consisted of the mission family and one black woman "who was the first fruits of missionary labors there." Work went slowly, only sixteen members being added until a religious revival was felt in the Chickasaw country in 1827. Between March of that year and summer of 1828, forty-two more were added, so that the membership was fifty-eight, excluding the mission family. In October, 1828, four blacks "gave satisfactory evidence of a change of heart" and were "admitted to the privileges of the church." The religious fervor continued, the meetings being well attended. Of the seventeen people admitted to church membership during the year following July 1, 1828, nine were black. A protracted meeting was held at Tockshish on July 3-6, 1829. On Saturday, four Chickasaws and three blacks were admitted to the church, and on Sunday, the Lord's Supper was administered to about one hundred persons "in the presence of a multitude of heathens." On Sunday afternoon, about thirty, "principally black people," came forward as anxious inquirers," and on the next day "a number more," including some Chickasaws, came forward.[10]

Interest in Christianity had become so great by early 1829 that many were attending who did not speak English. Therefore, a translator was regularly employed. But by the fall of 1829, it appeared that a decline in religious fervor had begun. Apprehension of removal to the West had begun to demoralize the people. But there were about twenty people, mainly blacks, who appeared to be seriously concerned about religion; of that number, the missionaries had hopes that several were Christians. The decline in fervor was more evident at a meeting held in October of 1829. However, two Indians and two blacks were admitted to the church, and at the four protracted meetings in 1830, fourteen Chickasaws and seven blacks were admitted. Between May, 1823, and September, 1831, when the Monroe church was a member of the North Alabama Presbytery, 57 of the 104 persons admitted to church membership were blacks; the remaining consisted of 23 whites and 24 Indians.[11]

With the breaking up of the Chickasaw government and the extension of Mississippi laws over the country, conditions among the people became worse, and some church members defected. In the summer of 1832, the membership stood at ninety-three, including the missionaries at Martyn. Conditions continued to get worse. In the last three months of 1832, over three hundred gallons of whiskey were brought by white traders into the neighborhood of the church; whiskey was sold at a grocery store that had been built nearby. In early 1833, four Chickasaw, one white, and two black members of the church were ousted because of backsliding. By the end of the year, it was reported that the "enemies of truth" were having too much success in their efforts "to decoy the members of the church and congregation at Tockshish and turn them aside from their steadfastness." The mission was abandoned as a lost cause in 1835.[12]

Although much of the missionary work was conducted by means of the protracted meetings called "sacramental meetings," there were regular services. The usual meeting on the Sabbath consisted of the reading of an English sermon; an explanation, through an interpreter, of free salvation through the gospel; hymns sung in Chickasaw; and a concluding prayer and exhortation. By 1829, the missionaries were holding two conferences each week, one for the Chickasaws and one for the blacks.[13] There were as well prayer meetings among the blacks and Indians. In all of these services, the blacks played a vital role.

The blacks were used as interpreters. On the day the church was organized at Monroe in 1823, a black woman named Dinah was received into the church on a profession of faith. A slave of James Gunn, Dinah had become concerned about her future during the New Madrid earthquakes of 1811 and 1812 and had tried to lead a better life. When preaching started at the Monroe mission, she became a regular attendant. She learned to read and became a reader of the Bible, carrying a New Testament around with her. Dinah was a native of the Chickasaw country, and although Chickasaw was her native language, she was also fluent in English. Because she had the confidence of the Indians, Stuart employed her as an interpreter for several years, and she was said to have delivered the missionaries' messages "with great earnestness." Dinah saved enough money to purchase her freedom and helped her husband to purchase his.[14]

Blacks seized with religious fervor also spread the gospel. One member of the church at Monroe was Sarah, a black who lived a few miles from the mission. A native of Africa, she had been taken when small to the West Indies, where she was first introduced to the gospel, but not understanding English, she was not much impressed by it. After many years of slavery in the islands, she was taken to New Orleans, where she lived a number of years among the French. She was already entering old age when she came to the Chickasaw country, the Lord, she said, leading her "by the hand, though unseen, into this land, where he revealed himself to me as a God pardoning sin." She became a regular attendant at the Monroe church but was not converted until about a year before her death in 1828. The missionaries believed that Sarah had a premonition of her death, for ten days before it occurred, she went "from house to house, exhorting sinners to flee from the wrath to come, and encouraging Christians to faithfulness in their Master's service." She died on the night that the regular monthly prayer meeting was held at her house. A "little company" of blacks had gathered for prayer, and Sarah, appearing unusually happy, asked for a favorite hymn about halfway through the service. As the company sang, Sarah got up from the bed on which she had been sitting, went about the room shaking hands with everyone, went back to the bed, lay down, and died. The missionaries estimated that she was about seventy years old.[15]

By early 1830, the missionaries had begun to look upon the blacks as a means of getting at the Chickasaws, especially the full bloods who did not speak English. Although the missionaries discouraged lay preaching among the slaves, because "of their ignorance, and for other reasons," they encouraged them as leaders in prayer meetings, such as those held at Sarah's house. In 1830, they credited the increase in the number of full bloods attending their services to the efforts of a black slave who lived ten or twelve miles from Monroe and who had "been in the habit, for two or three years, of having a prayer-meeting in his hut every Wednesday evening." At first, half a dozen blacks attended, but in late 1829, Indians began to attend, at one time numbering twenty-three among the fifty-five persons present. The services were conducted by "Christian slaves" in the "Chickasaw language." One of the slaves could read, so a portion of the scripture was read, hymns were sung, and prayers were offered. In later years, the Reverend Stuart recalled that in the fall of 1830, about half of the church members at Monroe were blacks, who generally spoke the Indian language. Because of their "being on equality" with their Chickasaw owners and because they had more contact with them than the whites had, they were used as instruments for extending a knowledge of the gospel to the Indians.[16]

Blacks figured significantly in the acculturation process in other ways. They were important in the transition of the Chickasaws to an agricultural economy. In 1836, Albert Gallatin recognized their importance when he stated that "the number of plows in The Five Tribes answered for the number of able bodied negroes."[17] As historian Arell Gibson has pointed out, by the time of removal there was the beginning of a mixed-blood aristocracy who consciously tried to adopt the ways of white planters in dress, homes, and life styles, and slavery was a part of their aristocratic pose. Slavery also provided the labor force to do the work the Indians would have been slow in doing, that is, clearing the lands and opening new fields. As time passed, slaveholding became more popular and widespread. By 1830, the Chickasaws had given up the hunt, maintained herds, and exported cotton, beef, and pork. Most of the farm labor was done by men instead of women. With profits from their goods, the Chickasaws bought not only necessities but luxury items and slaves as well.[18] Just prior to their removal in 1837, a

great many Chickasaws sold their homes, and reservations that were reserved to them under the treaties, for negroes, paid large prices for them, and emigrated west to their new homes with them, believing they were good property giving valuable considerations to the white men for them.[19]

Census rolls of Chickasaws taken west list 1,223 slaves held by 255 owners. Twenty of these 255 owners owned ten or more slaves. Of these twenty, the Colberts owned the most, but others who held large numbers were Tenessee Buynam, Rhoda Gunn, Richard Humphries, James McGlothlin, Jack Kemp, Tecumseh Brown, and A. Pitchlynn. The owners with the largest number of slaves were Pitman Colbert, who held 150, and Rodi Colbert, who held 95. Although there were a few with Indian names, most of the slaveholders were of mixed blood. There was on the roll as well a man named Jack, apparently a free black, who listed six slaves in his household.[20]

Removal resulted in further disruption of traditional life styles among the Chickasaws. But despite the drastic and rapid changes that occurred in Chickasaw society during the first forty years of the century, there were many full-blood conservatives who remained attached to and tried to preserve the traditional ways. They held tenaciously to the native religion and opposed the missionaries' efforts among the tribe. Among the full bloods in general, the Chickasaw language was retained, as were significant elements of cultural practices in such matters as religion, dress, and food.[21] These practices persisted, to a large extent, throughout the nineteenth century.

When the Chickasaws arrived in the West, they did not settle in the Chickasaw district as expected. Because they had funds from the sale of their lands in Mississippi, and because the western part of the Choctaw lands was overrun by hostile western tribes, the Chickasaws settled mainly on the Boggy and Blue rivers in the Choctaw district. In the fertile river bottoms the mixed bloods opened large plantations and began farming cotton and other crops by use of slave labor. While many were at first demoralized by removal, some invested in livestock and began building herds. The Indians to the west stole their livestock and blacks, and Texans committed depredations upon their property. As a result, in 1842, the United States established Fort Washita on the lower Washita River, and a few Chickasaws moved to the region. Although the Indian raids became less frequent, blacks continued to run away to the wild tribes, who harbored them for a while and then sold them to the Comanches. A few were brought back by the Shawnees and Delawares, who charged the Chickasaws exorbitant prices for their own slaves.[22]

Under the protection of this fort, the Chickasaws settled down to farming. The full bloods farmed small patches with their slaves; the mixed bloods raised cotton, corn, and other grains on an extensive scale, and they opened cotton gins and grist mills and developed large herds. However, the Indians between the Washita and the Red River, presumably Wichitas and Kichais, continued to be a problem. In 1843 a slave of Sloan Love, who lived near the mouth of the Washita, was wounded by Kichai arrows. Foot soldiers went after the attackers but without success.[23]

Although there was internal strife among the Chickasaws in the early 1840s, they began to settle their differences. As the population of Texas grew and with the gold rush in California, the Chickasaws found a ready market for their surplus crops among the immigrants. With the aid of missionaries they began to build schools to educate their children. As Indian depredations declined, the Chickasaws moved slowly westward into their own territory.[24] Perhaps the most unifying force was their opposition to Choctaw dominance. Although they maintained their independence in fiscal matters, the Chickasaws were outnumbered by the Choctaws three to one. Recovery from removal was more rapid among the Choctaws, and as time passed, social as well as political differences between the tribes became greater. In 1846 and 1848 the Chickasaws attempted to write a constitution. After 1848, they held regular councils in which they dealt with school and financial matters and sought separation from the Choctaw

Nation. By 1851 a third of the Chickasaws still lived in the Choctaw district. After Fort Arbuckle was established in the central part of their district, they began to move from the Choctaw Nation. Their delegation to Washington urged separation in 1851, charging that they had no effective voice in the Choctaw council and that those living in the Choctaw district were discriminated against. There was also contention over the eastern boundary of the Chickasaw district. In 1854, tension between the tribes became greater over the boundary issue, and open hostilities looked possible for a time. Agent Douglas H. Cooper had the line surveyed, to which survey the tribes agreed.[25]

The difficulties between the tribes led to the making of a treaty in Washington on June 22, 1855. The Chickasaws obtained the right to self-government in the Chickasaw district. The Choctaws and Chickasaws granted the United States a perpetual lease on their lands lying between the ninety-eighth and one hundredth meridians, from that time known as the Leased District. The $800,000 lease fee was divided between the tribes according to their population, three-fourths to the Choctaws and one-fourth to the Chickasaws. The land set aside as the Chickasaw Nation was bounded by the Canadian River on the north, the Red River on the south, and the ninety-eighth meridian on the west. The eastern boundary was formed by Island Bayou and a line running north from its headwaters to the Canadian.[26] These lands consisted of 7,267 square miles, containing 4,650,935 acres, in present-day Oklahoma, embracing Pontotoc, Johnson, Marshall, Love, Carter, Murray, Garvin, and McClain counties, the western part of Coal County, the southwestern part of Bryan County, and all but the extreme western portions of Grady, Stephens, and Jefferson counties.

In August, 1856, the Chickasaws held a constitutional convention and formally established their government. The document was lost on its way to the printer and was rewritten in 1857. Modeled after the U.S. Constitution, the Chickasaw document contained a bill of rights that guaranteed freedom of speech and religion, the right to a speedy trial by jury, and protection against unreasonable searches and seizures, excessive bail, and double jeopardy. The powers of government were divided into legislative, judicial, and executive branches. The Nation was divided into four legislative and judicial districts: Panola, Pickens, Tishomingo, and Pontotoc. Male citizens nineteen years of age and older elected representatives according to population and two senators from each district. The bicameral legislature met annually in September at Tishomingo to enact legislation. The judiciary consisted of county and district courts and a supreme court;

the executive officer of the Nation was the governor, who was elected to
a two-year term. While the Chickasaws were assembled as a constitutional
convention, they added a provision to their constitution prohibiting the
legislature from emancipating slaves without their owners' consent or without paying the owner, before the emancipation, the full value of the slaves.
The legislature could, however, in order to protect creditors, pass laws to
prevent owners from emancipating slaves. It could also require owners to
treat slaves humanely—that is, provide them with necessary food and
clothing—and to abstain from injuring them. The constitutional provision
also directed the legislature to pass laws prohibiting the introduction into
the Nation of any slaves who had committed high crimes in other countries.[27]

Until this time, the Chickasaws and their slaves had been subjected to
Choctaw laws. In 1838, the Choctaws had passed laws prohibiting cohabitation with a slave, teaching a slave to read or write without the
owner's consent, and the council's emancipating slaves without the owner's
consent. The Chickasaws now moved to establish a slave code of their own.
The legislature of 1857 passed an act that made it an offense to harbor or
clandestinely support "any runaway negro slave, or slaves, or negroes in-
dentured for a term of years." Conviction resulted in a fine of $100 to
$500, one-half of which was to go to the informer. Failure to pay the
fine would result in a sentence of six months to a year in the national
jail. The legislature also passed an act forbidding any slave to "own any
horse, mule, cow, hog, sheep, gun, pistol, or knife over four inches long
in the blade." Any such property in the hands of slaves was to be seized
and sold to the highest bidder, and the slave was to receive thirty-nine
lashes on his bare back. The law also prohibited blacks from possessing
spirituous liquors; violators received the same thirty-nine lashes. The
1857 legislature also provided for the removal of all whites known to be
abolitionists or who might thereafter advocate the cause of abolitionism
as "unfriendly and dangerous to the interests of the Chickasaw people."
Finally, the legislature forbade any black or the descendant of any black
to hold office or to vote.[28]

This last law was amended by the legislature of 1858 to deny blacks
and their descendants "any of the rights, privileges and immunities of
citizens" of the Nation and to prohibit the acceptance of a black's oath
in the courts of the Nation in cases where any persons but blacks or their
descendants were interested. The same legislature defined as murder the
willful and malicious murder of a slave or such cruel treatment of a slave

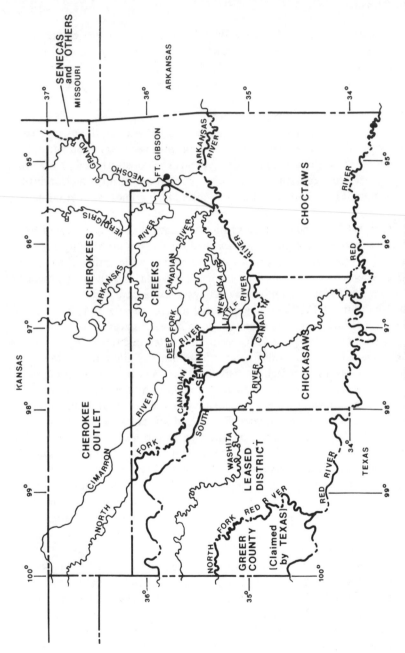

Lands of the Five Civilized Tribes, 1860

so as to cause his death. It also directed the judges of the respective
counties to order free blacks out of the Nation. If they refused to go,
they were to be seized and sold to the highest bidder for terms of one
year until they agreed to leave the Nation. Any free blacks who left
the Nation and returned were subject to the same law. The legislature of
1859 amended the language of this last act and passed an act prohibiting any person from trading with any blacks or slaves without a permit
from their owners or persons having them in charge. Violators were given
fines of fifteen to forty dollars. Any citizen of the United States found
guilty of the charge was to be arrested and taken to the agent for ex-
pulsion.[29]

It was customary among Chickasaws and Choctaws that children of slave
women were slaves even if their fathers were Indian or white. Blacks had no
rights as citizens, and free blacks were not allowed to marry Indian women,
whereas whites could intermarry and be adopted by the tribe.[30]

Although there were explicit laws forbidding free blacks to remain in
the Nation, there were exceptions to the law. A prime example was Charles
Cohee, Sr., a free man of part-Chickasaw blood, who removed with the
Chickasaws in 1837 and later acted as an interpreter. Another example was
Lydia Jackson, a free woman whose husband was a white citizen of the
United States.[31]

There is evidence as well that the slave code makes the institution of
slavery appear more severe than it was in practice in the Chickasaw and
Choctaw Nations. If slaves from different plantations married, for instance,
they lived on one farm or the other and went to their respective plantations
to work. Former slaves stated that they were allowed to do what they
pleased as long as they got their work done and did not run off. They were
allowed to visit slaves on neighboring plantations. However, there were
patrollers who enforced the slave laws. The enforcers sometimes whipped
slaves, and sometimes they asked for passes, accused blacks of staying over-
time, and beat them. Former slaves stated that their Indian masters did not
work them as hard as slaveholders in the states worked their slaves because,
one theorized, the land was so fertile that agriculture did not require much
labor. Some slaveholders had overseers, and sometimes blacks were used
as bosses.[32]

In 1906, Chickasaw and Choctaw freedmen testified that

the condition of bondage with the Indian people was less rigorous than
with whites, and more nearly approached a plane of equality. There was

therefore a larger percentage of educated freedmen in the nation than could be found in the plantation districts of the South, it being true that the house servants and many others were allowed the privileges of the Indian schools which were established.

Outside observers reached the same conclusion. Wiley Britton, serving with the Union Army on the frontier during the Civil War, made the general observation that slavery never existed among the Indians in the form it did in the states:

The worst features of slavery, such as the hard treatment imposed upon the slaves of the South was hardly known to the slaves of these Indians prior to the war. Indeed, the negroes brought up among the Indians were under such feeble restraint from infancy up that the owners and dealers in slaves in Missouri and Arkansas did not hestiate to acknowledge that Indian negroes were undesirable because of the difficulty of controlling them.[33]

Laxity in enforcing the slave code apparently coincided generally with the degree of Indian blood of the master. Most of the slave owners were mixed bloods, but some full bloods did own slaves. Lemon Butler, a former slave who had removed west with the Choctaws, said in 1872 that many of the slaves did better than their full-blood masters, whose concept of slavery was probably based more on the concept of war captives than on the concept of plantation slavery adopted by the mixed bloods. The slaves could do what they pleased, Butler said. They could leave the master's premises for as long as they liked, come back, give the master four or five dollars, and the master was satisfied. Some slaves did not work as hard as their masters. "The slave would take his gun and horse and ride and hunt all the time," said Butler.[34]

Contemporary observers presented similar observations. In 1842, Major Ethan Allen Hitchcock, on a fact-finding tour in the Indian Territory, wrote at Doaksville,

The full-blood Indian rarely works himself and but few of them make their slaves work. A slave among wild Indians is almost as free as his owner, who scarcely exercises the authority of a master, beyond requiring something like a tax paid in corn or other product of labor. Proceeding from this condition, more service is required from the slave until among the half-breeds and the whites who have married natives, they become slaves indeed in all manner of work.[35]

On the frontier, living conditions for the slaves were probably not greatly different from those of their Chickasaw and Choctaw masters. They
lived in single log cabins, while their masters had double log cabins with a
breezeway between to be used for an eating and storage area, and some
masters allowed their slaves to farm small plots of their own. Most had
adopted American-style dress. Some masters provided clothing for their
slaves, but for the most part, the Chickasaws had spinning wheels for
making the homespun in which the slaves were dressed. They made their
own shoes and sometimes made coats from buckskin. Not all of the slaves
learned the Indian language, and the "Indians who learned at all generally
learned to talk English through their slaves." In 1842, Major Hitchcock
conversed with a slave belonging to Greenwood, an old Chickasaw head-
man. Dirty and in a "tattered dress," she told him that she had formerly
belonged to Jim Adkins of Madison, Alabama, and had been among the
Chickasaws five or six years. When Hitchcock asked her if she spoke the
Indians' language, she replied, "I can *mumble* it a little."[36]

Missionaries resumed their activities among the Chickasaws in the
1840s. As church membership increased, a large number of the members
were blacks. Near the Humphries and Colbert plantations Major Hitchcock observed a church service conducted by a missionary, where, he
said, "There were about thirty-five persons present of both sexes and
colors, white, red, black and mixed, of all shades." It was later reported
that the slaves attended church with the Indians but sat in a brush arbor
apart from them. However, they could take part in the singing. Besides
hymns, the slaves sang plantation songs, probably learned in Mississippi,
such as "Steal Away to Jesus," "The Angels Are Coming," "I'm a Rolling,"
and "Swing Low."[37]

The exposed condition of the Chickasaws on the southwestern frontier
made them and their slaves vulnerable to depredations from various
sources. During the early years in the West, they had suffered attacks from
the tribes to the west. In the decade and a half before the Civil War there
were slaving raids by Texans, who stole blacks and sold them in the states.
In late 1847, for instance, a party of Texans under the leadership of Thomas
Williams and James Shannon of Red River County crossed the Red River
and took seven slaves. Four belonged to the wife of Overton Love, and
three belonged to John R. Guest, both of whom were half-blood Chickasaws. Shannon, Williams, and others made another raid on January 25,
1848, the Texans taking blacks belonging to Benjamin Love and his wife,
some belonging to orphan children, and one belonging to Ish-te-cho-cultha.

As late as 1860, the slaves had not been returned, nor had indemnity been made.[38]

Conflicts regarding slaves developed between the Chickasaws and the Choctaws. In 1846, for instance, a controversy arose between Chickasaw Pitman Colbert and Dr. John McDonna, the widower of Vicy Colbert Mc-Donna, Colbert's half sister. Colbert claimed the property, but Mrs. Mc-Donna had apparently willed it to her young son shortly before she died. McDonna sold the blacks to R. M. Jones, a half-blood Choctaw, and in 1848, Colbert tried unsuccessfully to get the Indian Office to intercede and obtain the property for him. Perhaps the best-known slave controversy occurred in February, 1857, when a party of armed Choctaw light-horse police raided the home of Edmond Pickens near Salt Springs on the Red River in the Chickasaw Nation. They captured a slave woman, Sarah, and her two children, Matilda and Alexander. Pickens had won the blacks by a suit in the Choctaw courts in 1853. Tickfunka, who had lost the suit, had nevertheless sold title to the slaves to Peter Baptiste. The Choctaw light-horse police who took the blacks in 1857 were apparently related to Baptiste. The event nearly led to open hostilities. The Choctaw and Chickasaw agent had to use his authority and promise speedy justice in the matter "to prevent Col. Pickens and a strong party of Chickasaws from invading the Choctaw district" in pursuit of the slave captors. Despite the agent's promises and the guarantees in the treaty of 1855 of indemnity for injuries, Pickens never got his slaves back, nor did he receive compensation.[39]

According to the 1860 census, 385 Choctaws owned 2,297 slaves, and 118 Chickasaws owned 917 slaves. The largest number owned by a single Chickasaw was 61, and the 10 owners who held the most slaves owned a total of 275. The average was nearly eight per owner and one to each five and one-half Chickasaws. As always, most slaves were owned by mixed bloods.[40]

Extensive holdings in slaves and the geographical location of the Chickasaws made their sympathy for the Confederate States of America almost inevitable. After the Civil War, Agent Isaac Coleman blamed the disloyalty of the Chickasaws and Choctaws on the whites who lived among them. He specifically blamed Elias Rector, an Arkansan who was serving as the Southern Superintendent of Indian Affairs, and other agents appointed by the United States. The Indians had always looked to these agents for guidance. In the spring of 1861 these appointees of James Buchanan, pro-slavery in sentiment, returned to the Indian Territory from Washington and told the tribes that there was no longer a United States government, that it had been destroyed and could not protect them, and that the tribes must join the new Confederate government "or be ground to powder." Many of these men later organized and led Confederate Indian military units.[41]

The Chickasaws and Choctaws later claimed that they "were not induced by the machinations" of Confederate agents to join the Confederacy but did so in order to preserve their independence and national integrity. Because the seceding states represented such a large part of the United States, the tribes thought that the states had a right to secede. When the war began, the United States withdrew its troops from the Indian Territory, leaving the country to the Confederates. The seceding states, the tribes said, "organized an army, took military possession of our country, and established posts and garrisons" within the limits of the nations, offering them protection. The Chickasaws and Choctaws had little choice but to join them.[42]

In January of 1861, the Chickasaws led the way in making contingency plans if the Union dissolved. They called for a council of the tribes in that event, to which the Civilized Tribes, except the Cherokees, agreed, the latter arguing that the Indians should remain neutral. Nevertheless, the council convened in February, but nothing was decided. In March the Chickasaws and Choctaws met at Boggy Depot, where they were visited by representatives from Texas. In February the Choctaws declared their sympathy for the South, and on May 25, the Chickasaws declared in resolutions that the United States had deserted them. The Chickasaws declared their independence; the Choctaws took a similar step on June 14.[43]

In February and March, 1861, the Confederate Congress had provided for the establishment of an Indian bureau and for sending an agent to the Indian Territory. Albert Pike of Arkansas was sent as special agent. Douglas H. Cooper, former agent to the Choctaws and Chickasaws, was commissioned by the Confederacy to raise troops among the Chickasaws, Choctaws, and other tribes. When federal troops were withdrawn from the Indian Territory in the spring of 1861 because of war activities in the East, Texan Benjamin F. McCulloch was given command of Arkansas, Louisiana, and Texas troops in the Indian Territory, as well as the units organized among the tribes.[44]

On June 12, the Choctaws and Chickasaws signed a treaty that guaranteed territorial integrity and representation in the Confederate Congress, control over trading activities, and the existence of slavery. The tribes placed themselves under the protection of the Confederate States and guaranteed their rights to establish military posts, courts, and postal systems and to assume the financial relations formerly maintained with the tribes by the United States.[45]

The Choctaw and Chickasaw governments decreed that anyone going north was to be killed and his property confiscated. Some of the loyal Chickasaws were arrested, and three were killed before the others started north with only the clothes they wore and the horses they rode. Governor Winchester Colbert ordered their livestock, grain, and other property confiscated and sold. Only 212 Choctaws were known to have remained loyal to the United States, 12 of the men serving in Union Army units. The number of loyal Chickasaws was uncertain, but it was known to be very small.[46]

The First Choctaw and Chickasaw Mounted Rifles was organized on July 31, 1861. Troops from that unit, Creek and Seminole units, and the Ninth Texas Cavalry were involved in the first battles in the Indian Territory late in 1861, when they tried to cut off the retreat to Kansas by the pro-Union Creeks, Seminoles, and a few loyal Chickasaws under the Creek leader Opothleyohola. Most of the military activity of the war took place in the Cherokee and Creek country in the northern part of the Indian Territory. Southern sympathizers from the Cherokee, Creek, and Seminole Nations fled their countries and went to Texas or to the Choctaw and Chickasaw Nations. They established refugee camps along the major streams but especially along the Washita and Red Rivers in the Chickasaw Nation. They lived in poverty with little food or medical attention. The loyal Chickasaws and Choctaws fared as badly as those in the Indian Territory. Life in the refugee camps at the Sac and Fox agency in Kansas was difficult for a people who had been used to comfortable homes and sufficient supplies of fresh food and clothing. Sickness was common and mortality was high.[47]

In the spring of 1863, Federal troops reoccupied Fort Gibson in the Cherokee Nation, and by the following fall there were reports that Southern sympathy was eroding among the Choctaws and Chickasaws. About three hundred had returned to the Union fold. Union leagues had supposedly been formed, and a large portion of the population were ready to throw over the Confederates if Union troops appeared. Refugees who escaped from the Chickasaw Nation that year charged that Texas troops were stationed in the Nation to watch loyalist movements.[48]

In March of 1864, overtures of peace were made to the Choctaws and Chickasaws by military authorities in the Indian Territory. Representatives of those tribes and four others met at Tishomingo in April to discuss the peace proposal. While there were many who wanted to submit, it was determined to make one more stand on the Red River. The people were discouraged. The refugees from other tribes were clustered along the Washita and Red Rivers, where they tried to make crops, and slave owners, apparently fearing loss of Confederate control of the area, had for a month been taking their slaves to the Brazos in Texas.[49]

In May, 1865, the tribes and tribal factions, including the Chickasaws and Choctaws, who had been allied with the Confederacy met in council in the Choctaw Nation and appointed delegates from each tribe to visit Washington and confer with the government. The war was over. General Douglas H. Cooper surrendered his troops in June, as did the Choctaws. The Chickasaws surrendered on July 14. Instead of asking the impoverished tribes to send peace delegations to Washington, the government sent a board of commissioners to meet the delegates at Fort Smith, Arkansas. It consisted of Dennis N. Cooley, commissioner of Indian affairs; Elijah Sells, superintendent for the Southern Superintendency; Thomas Wistar, a leader among the Society of Friends; Brigadier General W. S. Harney of the U.S. Army; and Colonel Ely S. Parker of General Grant's staff.[50]

When the meeting convened at Fort Smith on September 8, 1865, the Confederate Indians had not arrived. The loyal factions were there, including the Chickasaws Et-tor-lutkee (John Lewis), Lewis Johnson, Esh-ma-tubba, A. G. Griffith, Mahardy Colbert, and ten others; and Choctaws William S. Patton, Robert B. Patton, A. J. Stanton, and Jeremiah Ward. Cooley presented to them the President's wishes to renew alliances with the Indians. They were told that by aligning themselves with the Confederacy, they had forfeited all rights due them under former treaties with the United States and must consider themselves at the mercy of the government. The commissioners, however, assured them that the government would recognize the loyalty of those who had fought for the Union and had suffered in its behalf.[51]

The Indians were surprised by these statements. They had apparently thought that the object of the council was to make peace with their disloyal brothers. Et-tor-lutkee said, "I expected to hear something between us and the south, and wanted to hear what sort of laws you would lay down for the south; but have heard nothing." And Alfred Griffith said, "We all understand what we have come here for, but still there is some misunderstanding. How is it?"[52] Despite such questions by the Chickasaws and others, the commissioners continued their council because the Southern delegations were expected in a few days.

On the second day, Cooley made plain the penalties that the government would assess for the Indians' disloyalty. By way of new treaties, the President would insist on certain stipulations, among them that slavery be abolished and that all persons held in bondage be unconditionally emancipated and incorporated into the tribes on an equal footing with the original members or that they be otherwise provided for. Another condition was that slavery or involuntary servitude could never exist in the tribes except as punishment for a crime. The government would also require the tribes to cede some of their lands for the settlement of tribes from Kansas and elsewhere and would support a policy of unifying the Indian Territory under a territorial government according to a plan proposed in a bill then pending in Congress. Finally, no whites "except officers, agents, and employes of the government" could reside in the territory unless incorporated into the tribes.[53]

On the third day, the Chickasaw and Choctaw delegations were informed by a letter from Winchester Colbert, the Chickasaw governor, and P. P. Pitchlynn, the principal chief of the Choctaws, that the Southern delegations were on their way to Fort Smith. Meanwhile, the United States commissioners were ready to listen to anything the loyal delegations might have to say. In behalf of the Chickasaws, A. G. Griffith responded to the government's demands presented on the day before. The delegation had not been empowered by the people to make a treaty because they thought the purpose of the meeting was to settle their internal affairs. The Chickasaws were willing, Griffith said, to abolish slavery, emancipate their blacks, and make suitable provisions for them. However, Griffith did not say that they were willing to put the blacks on an equal footing with the Indians. As for the cession of lands and the abolishment of involuntary servitude, the delegates said that they were only a small part of the Nation and were not authorized to act. As for the final proposition, they wanted it to state "that no person except our former slaves, or free persons of color, now residents of the nation, will be permitted to reside in the nation or tribe, unless formally incorporated into the same," except officials or employees of the government. Similar responses were given by the Choctaw delegates.[54]

The refusal of these tribes and others to negotiate convinced the commissioners that no final treaties could be concluded until the differences

between the pro-Union and pro-Confederate factions were resolved. Therefore, they drafted a preliminary treaty to be signed by those delegates
present, rejecting treaties with all other parties, and reaffirming allegiance
to the United States. This preliminary agreement was read on the fifth day
and signed by the loyal Chickasaw delegation on the sixth. Before signing,
Lewis Johnson reaffirmed his loyalty to the United States and said,

I have heard much said about the black folks. They suffered as much as
we did. I have always understood that the President esteemed the colored
people, and we are willing to do just as our Father may wish, and take
them in and assist them, and let them help us. So I think and feel towards
them. I agree with all the wishes of my Great Father, and I expect he will
henceforth protect me. I am telling you this from the center of my heart,
and everything I say is heartfelt.[55]

When the Southern Chickasaw and Choctaw delegates arrived, they
reviewed and signed the preliminary treaty. They did so, however, with
reservations. First, they refused to assent to any control by the United
States over their internal affairs except in the question of slavery, which,
they said, was "open to further negotiation." Second, they argued that
they had in effect little choice but to join the Confederacy, which, in
1861, had military supremacy in the region.[56]

Throughout the remaining days of the meeting, the commissioners
accomplished little more than making arrangements for delegations from
both factions of each tribe to go to Washington at a later date to work out
a treaty. A joint committee of the Chickasaws and Choctaws offered
amendments and changes for the proposed treaties, but the commission
refused to accept them. Thus the council was adjourned to meet at the
call of the secretary of the interior.[57]

In October, 1865, as soon as the delegations returned from Fort Smith,
the Chickasaw legislature met. In his message to the body, Governor
Colbert told the lawmakers that emancipation of the slaves was inevitable
and urged them to pass the proper legislation at the earliest practicable
time. Meanwhile, he urged that the blacks be cared for and that they be
made useful to the community. Since there was diversity of opinion among
the people concerning the status of the blacks, he asked the legislature to
establish uniform rules regarding slaves so as "to reduce confusion in the
minds of Indians and blacks alike."[58]

The legislators ratified the preliminary peace treaty signed in Fort
Smith and passed an act to provide for amending the constitution to
abolish involuntary servitude. The legislature refused to pass a law abolish-
ing slavery because the constitution forbade it without first paying the
owners the value of their slaves. Too, the Chickasaws believed that the
peace treaty had placed jurisdiction over the matter with the United States
and that the President or other authority would free the slaves by proclamation. The legislature authorized Governor Colbert to issue a proclamation to the Chickasaws advising them to make "arrangements with
their slaves as will best subserve the interests of all concerned." By early
October many Chickasaw slaveholders had already voluntarily given their
slaves the choice of either being free or staying with and working for their
owners "for their food, clothing, doctor's bills, and the support of the
old and the young who cannot work." In his proclamation, issued on
October 11, Colbert suggested a plan of apprenticing to their former
owners all minor blacks until they were twenty-one. He also suggested
that owners provide for the aged over fifty and the infirm and hire "the
middle-aged at fair wages." Colbert argued that since it was by such a
system that Pennsylvania and other northern states abolished slavery,
he believed that it would satisfy the government's requirement that the
emancipated slaves be provided for. He hoped it would meet the approval
of the President and the nonslaveholding states.[59]

The anomalous condition in which the Chickasaw blacks found themselves in the fall of 1865 was typical of their future condition. Because
of the blacks' numbers and because of racial prejudice, the Chickasaws
did not want to adopt the blacks and would insist that they were the
responsibility of the United States. Yet the Chickasaws were not forceful
in their denial of responsibility because the labor of the freedmen in post-
Civil War years was an economic necessity. United States officials, on the
other hand, placed responsibility for the blacks squarely on the Chickasaws.
The uncertain status with which the blacks entered the Reconstruction
period unfortunately typified their existence for the next forty years.

Despite attempts by the Chickasaws to oust them, the freedmen would
tenaciously hang on to their foothold in the Chickasaw Nation. For the
most part, they identified with the Chickasaws. Slaves such as the one
Hitchcock interviewed in 1842 were representative of the acculturation
process. For decades, the blacks had been an influential channel for the

white man's ideas. Those purchased from whites had brought with them knowledge of husbandry, agricultural methods, technology, and domestic practices. The domestic activities of a slave in a Chickasaw's cabin in the Indian Territory could not fail to be influenced by her performance of those activities on the plantation of her white master in Alabama. Since many slaves had been purchased just before removal, the results of an infusion of new ideas were no doubt apparent shortly after removal. But the cultural transfer had gone both ways. By the time of removal, some families of blacks had been among the Chickasaws for generations. They knew no other language or culture. They had learned the Indian mode of agriculture and had adopted the Indians' diet, medicine, and dress. In 1837, the Chickasaw blacks were described as "picturesque looking Indian negroes, with dresses belonging to no country but partaking of all."[60] Over fifty years later the blacks of the Five Civilized Tribes were described as "picturesque in the extreme" because of the bright colors in which they dressed and because they wore "their kinky hair in knotty little braids bound with innumerable strings, feathers in their hats, and frequently immense brass ear-rings."[61] Amalgamation had also occurred before and after removal, and in the appearance of many families, the Indian blood predominated. Thus throughout the next forty years, despite the Chickasaws' rejection of them, the freedmen insisted on their right to share in the bounty of the nation to which they had blood and cultural ties.

NOTES

1. John R. Swanton, *The Indians of the Southeastern United States,* Bureau of American Ethnology Bulletin 137 (Reprint ed., New York: Greenwood Press, 1969), 116, 308, 315, 316, 337; Muriel H. Wright, *A Guide to the Indian Tribes of Oklahoma* (Norman: University of Oklahoma Press, 1951), 84, 86.

2. Swanton, 117-118.

3. Wright, 88-89; *Constitution, and Laws of the Chickasaw Nation, together with the Treaties of 1832, 1833, 1834, 1837, 1852, 1855 and 1866* (Parsons, Kans.: The Foley Railway Printing Company, 1899), 474-477, hereafter cited as *Constitution and Laws.*

4. Arrell M. Gibson, *The Chickasaws* (Norman: University of Oklahoma Press, 1971), 80-137; Benjamin Hawkins to Henry Dearborn,

October 28, 1801, Hawkins to Chiefs, n.d., and Requisition, June 24, 1797, *Letters of Benjamin Hawkins, 1796-1806,* Collections of the Georgia Historical Society, vol. 9 (Savannah, Ga.: The Morning News, 1916), 393, 177, 179; *Missionary Herald,* 20 (1824), 131.

5. Gibson, 39-40, 41, 140; Dawson A. Phelps, ed., "Excerpts from the Journal of the Reverend Joseph Bullen, 1799 and 1800," *Journal of Mississippi History,* 17 (October 1955), 261.

6. Gibson, 116; Phelps, 264; *American State Papers: Documents, Legislative and Executive of the Congress of the United States, from the First Session of the First to the Third Session of the Thirteenth Congress, Inclusive, Commencing March 3, 1789, and Ending March 3, 1815* (Washington, D.C.: Gales and Seaton, 1832-61), Indian Affairs 2: 107.

7. William L. Hiemstra, "Early Presbyterian Missions among the Choctaw and Chickasaw Indians in Mississippi," *Journal of Mississippi History,* 10 (January 1948), 11; Phelps, 262, 264.

8. Phelps, 268, 271, 274, 275, 276-277; Harry Warren, "Missions, Missionaries, Frontier Characters and Schools," *Publications of the Mississippi Historical Society,* 8 (1904), 581.

9. Percy L. Rainwater, "Indian Missions and Missionaries," *Journal of Mississippi History,* 27 (February 1966), 34, 36; *Missionary Herald,* 25 (1829), 10.

10. *Missionary Herald,* 24 (1828), 283; 25 (1829), 31, 150, 386.

11. *Ibid.,* 25 (1829), 287, 388; 26 (1830), 382; Dawson A. Phelps, "The Chickasaw Mission," *Journal of Mississippi History,* 13 (October, 1951), 233.

12. *Missionary Herald,* 28 (1832), 8, 334; 29 (1833), 132, 463; 32 (1836), 23.

13. *Ibid.,* 26 (1830), 382; 25 (1829), 287.

14. Warren, 584; Rainwater, 36-37.

15. *Missionary Herald,* 24 (1828), 284-285.

16. *Ibid.,* 26 (1830), 115; Rainwater, 37.

17. U.S. Census Office, *The Five Civilized Tribes in Indian Territory: The Cherokee, Chickasaw, Choctaw, Creek, and Seminole Nations* (Washington, D.C.: U. S. Census Printing Office, 1894), 7.

18. Gibson, 138, 140, 141, 142.

19. 50 Cong., 1 Sess., *Senate Executive Document 166,* 9.

20. National Archives Record Group 75 (Records of the Bureau of Indian Affairs), *1839 Chickasaw Census Roll.*

21. Gibson, 134, 143, 233.

22. 25 Cong., 3 Sess., *Senate Document 1,* 510-511; 26 Cong., 1 Sess., *Senate Document 1,* 470; Grant Foreman, *The Five Civilized Tribes,*

reprint ed. (Norman: University of Oklahoma Press, 1966), 101, 104-105; Gibson, 217-218, 220-221, 222; 26 Cong., 2 Sess., *Executive Document 2,* 311-312; 27 Cong., 2 Sess., *Executive Document 2,* 314-315; William H. Goode, *Outposts of Zion, with Limnings of Mission Life* (Cincinnati, Ohio: Poe and Hitchcock, 1864), 208; A. A. M. Upshaw to William Armstrong, August 25, 1842, and Upshaw to T. Hartley Crawford, September 4, 1843, National Archives Microfilm Publications, *Microcopy M234* (Office of Indian Affairs, Letters Received)-138: A16-42, U145-43, hereafter cited as *M234,* followed by the roll number.

23. Foreman, 106; Gibson, 227.

24. Foreman, 109-121; Gibson, 234-235, 242-243.

25. Foreman, 121-130; Gibson, 233, 236, 246, 248-254; 29 Cong., 2 Sess., *Executive Document 4,* 275-276; 31 Cong., 1 Sess., *Executive Document 5,* 1128-1130.

26. Wright, 90-91; *Constitutions and Laws,* 482-495.

27. Foreman, 132; Wright, 91; *Constitution and Laws,* 3-17; *Constitution, Laws, and Treaties of the Chickasaws* (Tishomingo City, Chickasaw Nation: E. J. Johnson, 1860), 22-23, hereafter cited as *Constitution, Laws, and Treaties.*

28. *Constitution, Laws, and Treaties,* 57-58, 79, 80.

29. *Ibid.,* 111, 115, 159-160.

30. 42 Cong., 3 Sess., *House Report 98,* 738-739.

31. Charles H. Burke to Wilburn Cartwright, April 9, 1928, National Archives Record Group 75, *Central Classified Files,* 95003-1922 Chickasaw 053; 59 Cong., 2 Sess., *Senate Report 5013,* 2: 1518.

32. Statements of Polly Colbert, Kisiah Love, and Mary Lindsay, in George P Rawick, ed., *The American Slave: A Composite Autobiography* (Westport, Conn.: Greenwood Press, 1972), 7: 33, 37, 192, 193, 178-179.

33. 59 Cong., 2 Sess., *Senate Report 5013,* 1: 946; Wiley Britton, *The Civil War on the Border* (New York: G. P. Putnam's Sons, 1904), 2: 24-25.

34. 42 Cong., 3 Sess., *House Report 98,* 466.

35. Ethan Allen Hitchcock, *A Traveler in Indian Territory: The Journal of Ethan Allen Hitchcock, Late Major-General in the United States Army,* ed. Grant Foreman (Cedar Rapids, Iowa: The Torch Press, 1930), 187.

36. Statement of Polly Colbert, *The American Slave,* 7: 36; Foreman, 106, 142; Gibson, 230, 231; Daniel Burton (interview), November 11, 1937, *Indian-Pioneer History* (Indian Archives Division, Oklahoma Historical Society), 51: 187, 190; 42 Cong., 3 Sess., *House Report 98,* 466; Kizzie Love (interview), October 14, 1937, *Indian-Pioneer History,* 61: 424; Hitchcock, 201-202.

37. Gibson, 233; Hitchcock, 167; Kizzie Love, 61: 424; Robert Elliott

Flickinger, *The Choctaw Freedmen* (Fonda, Iowa: Journal and Times Press, 1914), 25-26; Goode, 46, 208.

38. Statement of Kiziah Love, *The American Slave*, 7: 198. Materials relating to the slave cases are in Case 278, National Archives Microfilm Publications, *Microcopy M574* (Special Files of the Office of Indian Affairs, 1807-1904), Roll 76.

39. S. M. Rutherford to W. Medill, May 29, 1848, and A. M. M. Upshaw to Medill, May 3, 1848, *M234*-139: R254-48, U37-48; Edmond Pickens to D. H. Cooper, February 13, 1857, Elias Rector to A. B. Greenwood, April 23, 1860, and D. P. Whiting's deposition, February 26, 1857, *M234*-142: frames 340ff., 482ff., 528; H. R. Clum to Charles E. Mix, October 3, 1870, National Archives Microfilm Publications, *Microcopy M21* (Office of Indian Affairs, Letters Sent)-97: 280 (hereafter cited as *M21*, followed by the roll number).

40. Ohland Morton, "Confederate Government Relations with the Five Civilized Tribes," *Chronicles of Oklahoma*, 31 (Summer, 1953), 199; National Archives Microfilm Publications, *Microcopy M653* (Federal Population Census Schedules)-54: Arkansas Slave Schedules (Indian Country), 1860.

41. Annual Report of the Secretary of the Interior, 1865, 39 Cong., 1 Sess., *House Executive Document 1*, 208, 465, hereafter cited as *Annual Report, 1865*.

42. *Ibid.*, 529-530.

43. Ohland Morton, "The Confederate States Government and the Five Civilized Tribes," *Chronicles of Oklahoma*, 31 (Autumn, 1953), 299-300.

44. *Ibid.*, 301-302; Morton, "Confederate Government Relations," 202.

45. Morton, "The Confederate States Government," 304-305; Annie H. Abel, *The Indian as Slaveholder and Secessionist* (Cleveland, Ohio: The Arthur H. Clark Co., 1919), 74-78.

46. 42 Cong., 3 Sess., *House Report 98*, 738; *Annual Report, 1865*, 504, 208, 441.

47. Morton, "The Confederate States Government," 308-309, 313; Dean Trickett, "The Civil War in the Indian Territory," *Chronicles of Oklahoma*, 18 (December, 1940), 266-280; Annual Report of the Secretary of the Interior, 1863, 38 Cong., 1 Sess., *House Executive Document 1*, 3: 146, 301; hereafter cited as *Annual Report, 1863*.

48. *Annual Report, 1863*, 146, 295, 302.

49. Annual Report of the Secretary of the Interior, 1864, 38 Cong., 2 Sess., *House Executive Document 1*, 473, 475-476.

50. *Annual Report, 1865*, 202, 479; Morton, "The Confederate States Government," 319.

51. *Annual Report, 1865*, 481-482, 202-203, 497; Abel, *The American Indian under Reconstruction* (Cleveland, Ohio: The Arthur H. Clark Company, 1925), 189.

52. *Annual Report, 1865*, 500-501.

53. *Ibid.*, 502-503.

54. *Ibid.*, 503-504.

55. *Ibid.*, 203, 204, 511, 514-515, 518; Abel, *The American Indian under Reconstruction*, 189.

56. *Annual Report, 1865*, 529-530.

57. *Ibid.*, 532-537.

58. Abel, *The American Indian under Reconstruction*, 285-287.

59. *Ibid.*, 288-289; *Annual Report, 1865*, 541-542.

60. John E. Parsons, ed., "Letters on the Chickasaw Removal of 1837," *The New-York Historical Society Quarterly*, 37 (July 1953), 280.

61. Rezin W. McAdam, "An Indian Commonwealth," *Harper's New Monthly Magazine*, 87 (November, 1893), 891-892.

Emancipation, Reconstruction, and Post-Reconstruction Problems

2

The Chickasaws emerged from the Civil War a weakened nation. Although the Chickasaw and Choctaw Nations escaped the destruction that other tribes had suffered, much of their wealth had been in livestock, most of which had been used by the Confederate Army and refugee Indians who had fled from the Cherokee and Creek Nations. About a third of the people were destitute in 1865. However, in the summer of 1865, crops were unusually good in the Red River country, and food supplies promised to be sufficient in those areas if the estimated 6,000 refugee Cherokees, the refugee Creeks, and the estimated 1,000 refugee Seminoles, all of whom had depended on the bounty of Choctaws and Chickasaws, could be removed, for with only a few exceptions they were without money or property.

The winter of 1865-66 promised to be difficult. By fall, 2,000 Chickasaws and Choctaws were receiving rations from the government. Food and clothing were in immediate demand. Life had changed drastically for many of the leading men, who were well educated and spoke English fluently. Before the war, they had owned considerable property and led comfortable lives. Many had accumulated great wealth, especially the slaveholders, who lived in luxury by the frontier standards of the day. Before the war the two tribes had held a total of 5,000 slaves. After the war, the Chickasaws numbered 4,500 to 5,000 and had an estimated 2,000 blacks.[1] Part of the change in the life style of the Chickasaws had resulted from the abolition of slavery and the need for a new attitude toward their former slaves, now freedmen. Besides the freedman issue, the Chickasaws would find themselves beset by many other postwar problems that would determine Chickasaw relations with the United States and would shape the social, political, and economic milieu within which the freedmen carried on a forty-year struggle to acquire the right to share in the Chickasaw national domain.

Although the United States no longer considered the blacks slaves at the end of the war, the Chickasaws took no immediate action regarding them. The Choctaws, however, late in 1865, passed an act allowing freedmen to remain with their former owners until the treaty then being negotiated with the United States was ratified. Those who remained could make contracts with their former owners, before a county judge, for wages on which the two parties agreed; the former owners were considered guardians of the freedmen in such contracts. The freedmen could make contracts with Choctaws other than their former owners if they desired. Besides the wages or share of crops paid, the employer was required to clothe, pay doctors' bills, and furnish buildings and fuel for the freedmen. If the employer did not make these allowances, the council prescribed wage scales for him to follow. It also set the dates for payment of wages, as well as the hours and days of labor. The freedmen were guaranteed the same rights of civil and criminal process in the courts as the citizens of the Nation and were granted full protection of person and property. The law also forbade any former slaves who had left the Nation to return for the purpose of residing there. Finally, any former slave found moving about, not pursuing any job, could be arrested and hired out by the sheriff to the highest bidder, who would compel him to work. The proceeds from his labor would be paid to the national treasurer and used to support any freed persons who had to be provided for.[2] Perhaps not knowing what else to do with their blacks, the Choctaws apparently intended to keep them in a state of semiservitude.

Apparently anticipating some difficulty in adjusting freedman affairs, the Indian Office was receptive to the suggestion of Governors Pitchlynn of the Choctaws and Colbert of the Chickasaws that someone be appointed to regulate affairs between the blacks and their former masters. At the suggestion of Commissioner Dennis Cooley, the appointment went to Brevet Major General John S. Sanborn in October, 1865. Where Sanborn found relations between the freedmen and their former masters amicable and satisfactory to both, he was not to interfere or to disturb them. But where he found rights denied or abuses existing, he was to give immediate relief. He was to encourage freedmen to support themselves by making written contracts with persons who were willing to hire them for up to one year as laborers either for wages or as sharecroppers. Sanborn and the Indian agents were to cooperate in seeing that the freedmen were allowed to occupy lands of their own so that they could realize the profits of their own labor. He was to impress upon the Indians the justice of admitting the freedmen to rights of person and property and to the equal enjoyment of what bounty the Indian governments might later bestow. Sanborn was also to broach the idea of an equal enjoyment of civil rights, using the argument that in granting it, the Indians would be following the example of the whites, as well as increasing the strength of the Indian nation.[3] Ironically, the government was asking the Indians to do something that the whites were ultimately not willing to do.

At the time of Sanborn's appointment, rumors were rife in the Indian Territory that murder and other violence were being perpetrated upon the freedmen. In the summer of 1865 reports came to military officials that the Chickasaws and Choctaws were mistreating blacks who were attempting to travel through their territories. One man reported that he was with a party of several who had been followed and fired upon. The informant escaped, but two of his companions were killed. Blacks from other nations who went to the Choctaw and Chickasaw Nations to bring back friends met with hostility on the part of the Indians. One report came that the bodies of five murdered blacks had been seen piled together. The Chickasaws and Choctaws were accused of being determined not to let blacks pass through their country and blamed the blacks for their defeat. Freedmen complained to General H. J. Hunt, commanding the Frontier District of the Department of Arkansas, yet they were not able to testify firsthand to the murders. Hunt ascribed the rumors to the general uneasiness that gripped the freedmen. Some Indians said they were free, while others, particularly the Chickasaws, insisted that they were still slaves. Hunt took the safe route, telling them that they must support themselves and work quietly with their present owners, making contracts for wages when suitable wages were offered. For the meantime, he asked them to "keep quiet and bear the evils that attend their change in condition as well as possible." Hunt thought the freedmen "very reasonable" concerning his advice, and they seemed content with their prospects. Upon his inquiry concerning official views of the freedmen's status, Hunt was informed by Commissioner Cooley that "the constitutional number of states having ratified the anti-slavery amendment, there is not, in fact, a slave within the limits of the United States."[4] The question, of course, was whether the laws of the United States extended to the Indian Territory.

Hunt's claims were reinforced by reports of violence and lawlessness from the Choctaw and Chickasaw country. Federal troops visiting Governor Pitchlynn in November, 1865, learned that the Choctaws were having dif-

ficulty enforcing their laws because they could not keep Cherokees and
"bad white men" out of the Nation. Outlaws from the Cherokee Nation
and Texas stole cattle and committed robbery and murders. The governor
had ordered the organization of light-horse police companies in each district, but there were no regular laws in operation because people were
afraid of reprisals if they cooperated. When criminals were captured,
desperadoes released them. At Tishomingo, Governor Colbert informed
the troops that the great number of destitute refugee Indians were a
source of trouble because they stole Chickasaw cattle. The Chickasaws had
sufficient food supplies but desperately needed clothing and shoes. The
governor asked for troops to be stationed to keep down the desperadoes.[5]

   General Sanborn arrived in the Indian Territory in late 1865 with pre-
conceived ideas about the status of the freedmen of the Indian Territory.
He believed, mistakenly, that before the war the blacks of the territory
were not legal, but voluntary, slaves who had the right to leave their
owners and go where they chose. If they escaped to a free state, he reasoned, they could not have been returned by process of court. Sanborn
disagreed with Hunt, who thought that it would be disastrous to inform
the blacks that they were now free. Hunt argued that they would abandon
their homes, rush to the military posts, and become completely dependent
on the government. Sanborn, on the other hand, believed that if they were
told of their proposed rights among the Indian tribes, they would remain
where they were. If they were to be told sometime, the sooner, the better.
To Sanborn, the best course for the government was to consider the blacks
as part of the tribes to which they belonged and to give the freedmen a
choice of staying or leaving. Those remaining, he believed, should have
all the rights, interests, and annuities of Indians. Sanborn thought it important to confer upon the freedmen at once the right to hold and acquire
real estate to make them feel responsible for the contracts they made by
making their property liable if the contracts were broken.[6]

   Sanborn established headquarters at Fort Smith and made his policies
known through circulars. The first, released on January 1, 1866, directed
the Indian agents to impress upon the Indians a "correct idea" of the new
relation between them and their former slaves, stressing that the freedmen were now invested with all the rights of free men. It confirmed the
government's commitment to protect the freedmen in their persons; an
outrage committed upon a freedman was an outrage against the United
States. Sanborn instructed agents to insure fair contracts for wages be-

tween Indians and freedmen and to put in writing contracts for periods
longer than a month. Sanborn announced that the government would no
longer tolerate polygamy, which had always existed to some extent among
the Indians and had been practiced by some of the freedmen. Freedmen
would be allowed only one wife; those cohabiting at that time would be
considered legally married. Marriages that had been solemnized by Indian
custom were binding and valid, and until further provisions were made,
the agent could take the mutual pledges of couples and issue marriage
certificates. Finally, Sanborn's first circular committed the government
to removing all prejudice against the freedmen on the part of Indians.
This last point reflected the obvious naiveté of government officials in
assuming that absorption of the freedmen into the Indian tribes could be
effected without discrimination or social and racial prejudice. They were
particularly naive regarding the feelings of the Chickasaws and Choctaws.
The second circular, issued on January 2, authorized Indian agents to sign
ration returns for destitute freedmen and commissaries of subsistence to
issue rations "in case of great destitution."[7]

When Sanborn made his first visit to the Indian Territory about this
time, he saw only the Seminoles, Creeks, Cherokees, and the loyal Chickasaws under Lewis Johnson in the region surrounding Fort Gibson and Fort
Smith. He felt obligated to report to the Indian Office before he visited
the Chickasaw and Choctaw Nations because "the condition of the freedmen in these nations requires the immediate action of the government."
In general he found the freedmen the "most industrious, economical, and,
in many respects, the more intelligent portion of the population of the Indian territory." They wanted to remain in the territory on lands set apart
for their own use. The Indians generally felt the same way, he reported,
and if lands were to be set apart for the blacks, it should be done immediately because plowing and planting would begin in early March.

Apparently basing his opinion on what the loyal Chickasaws told him,
Sanborn concluded that the public sentiment concerning the freedmen in
the Choctaw Nation was "radically wrong" at that time. The majority of
opinions were against the freedmen, and there was "violent prejudice."
The public officials had acknowledged a change in the relations between
masters and slaves, but a large number of the people had not. On the other
hand, some freedmen were driven away from their former masters' farms.
One freedman was killed by his former master at Boggy Depot, and there
were rumors of "several other cases."[8]

In the Chickasaw Nation, the Indians were still holding most of the blacks in slavery and held "bitter prejudice against them all." They had passed laws for "the gradual emancipation of their slaves" and excluded those who had left the Nation during the war. This latter law was aimed particularly at those blacks who had left the country and had joined the Union Army. The same law applied in the Choctaw Nation. Lewis Johnson had told Sanford that Governor Colbert had publicly told many people before his departure for Washington that

they should hold the slaves until they could determine at Washington whether or not they could get pay for them, and if they could not then they would strip them naked and drive them either south to Texas, or north to Fort Gibson. So bitter is the feeling against the return of the negroes that have been in the federal army, that Major Coleman and myself have concluded that it is not safe or advisable for Lewis Johnson and party to return until troops are stationed at Fort Arbuckle.

Sanborn reported that many blacks had been shot down with impunity by their masters. Therefore, he advised the stationing of troops at not only Fort Arbuckle but at Fort Towson, Fort Washita, and Boggy Depot as well. Without troops, little could be done for the loyal Indians or the freedmen. With the Chickasaw and Choctaw laws what they were and the leading men absent in Washington, Sanborn felt that the best procedure was to change public sentiment, which he was attempting to do through his circulars.[9]

Meanwhile, by treaty stipulation or congressional act, the government should set aside land for the freedmen. It should be sufficient to allow one square mile for every four persons, and it should be the most fertile land in the territory since the blacks were "the principal producers." Furthermore, because of rainfall, it should be east of the ninety-seventh meridian, and it should touch the Arkansas or the Red River so the blacks could get their crops to market by flatboat; they should have access as well to prairie and timber lands. The land should be surveyed so that each freedman over eighteen years of age could homestead 320 acres with restrictions on alienation of the land. Sanborn believed that the Indians would assent to such an arrangement, "perhaps without a murmur." While the tribes unanimously opposed the establishment of a territorial government, Sanborn believed that that or a military government was necessary, for it was unthinkable that the government could leave the estimated ten or twelve thousand freedmen of the territory without any government or the protection of the law. To leave them to the laws of the Nations "would be extraordinary and anomalous." If the government would set land apart for the freedmen and erect a military or civil government over them to protect them, they would "beyond doubt," Sanborn believed, "soon become an industrious, intelligent, and happy population."[10]

In response to this report, Commissioner Cooley urged Sanborn to continue his visits to the Indian Territory and to make his role there known. He was, by every means in his power short of military force, "but with military aid if necessary," to protect the freedmen from injury or outrage. Cooley was to be informed immediately if the commander of the district failed to furnish Sanborn with troops. As for the question of land for the freedmen, Cooley asked Sanborn's advice concerning "convenient locations for such colonies."[11]

Sanborn's conclusions about conditions in the Chickasaw and Choctaw Nations were based on rumor to this point. There is some evidence that there was not as much antagonism between the Indians and the blacks as he was led to believe by Lewis Johnson and other loyal Chickasaws. A detachment of the Ninth Iowa Cavalry was dispatched to Boggy Depot on December 11, 1865, to guard supplies sent to the Indians. The troops stayed in the Choctaw Nation until February 26, 1866, and during that time the commander reported that peace and quiet prevailed and that he found the people anxious to get along with the federal government. He reported only one murder while he was there. A slave of General Douglas Cooper reported that a black man named Jackson Wright was murdered between Fort Washita and Blue Creek, but the troops had been unable to find a body or anyone who had seen one. In another incident, Jim, a black described as a "servant of Col. Leverings," was out hunting and had dismounted and was a short distance from his horse when he saw three Indians approaching. He became frightened and with a revolver and a shotgun drove the Indians away. The latter reported the incident because they were "alarmed at the attitude of the Negro toward them." Because the citizens were anxious to cooperate, the commander of the detachment believed that squads of twelve or fifteen troops at different places would be sufficient to keep the peace. And according to Matthew Gray, a licensed trader at Fort Arbuckle in the Chickasaw Nation, the Chickasaws would welcome troops to their country to help stop white men from murdering and stealing, and Gray reported the theft of horses from both Indians and blacks.[12]

Near the end of January, 1866, Sanborn visited the Choctaw and Chickasaw Nations and modified his earlier reports:

The prejudice on the part of the people of these nations against the freedmen is rapidly passing away, and their treatment of them has not been so bad and cruel as might be inferred from my former report and letters, although there is still much that is wrong and cruel.

He blamed the wrong on "improper laws" of the Nations that allowed the slave code to be considered still in force. A treaty would remedy that situation. Sanborn thought that the Chickasaws and Choctaws would agree to the settlement of the freedmen of their tribes on part of the Leased District along the False Washita, and he recommended a reservation thirty-six miles square in that area "or an equivalent tract running from the Canadian to the Red River." He recommended, first, that each male over twenty-one be allowed to enter a homestead of 160 acres, which he could not sell. Second, there were a large number of freedwomen who had had one or more children during slavery but had never had husbands. It would be difficult for them to find husbands, so Sanborn recommended that they be allowed to enter 160 acres as heads of households. Finally, four sections of every township of freedman land should be set aside as school lands. Sanborn recommended as well the establishment of a territorial government in the Indian Territory, the survey and sectioning of Indian lands, the granting of homestead allotments to individual Indians, liberal land grants to railroad companies, and the disposal of surplus lands to non-Indians. Such actions, he said, "would result in the rapid development of the country, the civilization of the Indian tribes, the enlightenment and elevation of the freedmen and the masses of all the people in the territory, and induce peace and good feeling on the part of all."[13]

Encouraged by what he found in the Chickasaw and Choctaw Nations, Sanborn believed that there was a "great improvement" in the public sentiment concerning the freedmen of the Indian Territory. Ill will and prejudice were rapidly disappearing, he thought, and most of the freedmen were finding employment at fair wages, except, of course, in the Chickasaw and Choctaw Nations. Most Indians seemed disposed to admit their rights and to treat them reasonably well. Of prime concern to Sanborn were the destitute refugee freedmen, a large number of whom were still on the Red River, where they had been taken by their masters during the war. Because most of them had no means of transportation, Sanborn asked that agents be authorized to arrange their removal to their respective nations.[14]

With the coming of the planting season, Sanborn realized the necessity of the Indians and freedmen to make as large a crop as possible to help overcome the economic destitution of the territory. In one circular, he urged the freedmen to remain in the Indian nations and cultivate the land they occupied, and he took measures to see that the Indians did not interfere with them. In another, he stressed the importance of making a large crop of corn and other cereals and encouraged the freedmen to take any land not likely to be occupied by Indians during the season and to make a crop. He asked the military officers to protect freedmen and to enforce contracts by which they owed part of the crop to Indians. Sanborn adopted these measures because he believed that the only people who would re-establish the old fields and make a crop were the freedmen. He did not want to interrupt their progress. They were working constantly and hard, and the prejudice against them seemed to him to be dying. All were reasonably well supplied with farming implements and seeds, and Sanborn expected a good crop if the season permitted it. However, in mid-April, he asked for plows to be furnished the freedmen and directed the Southern Superintendent Elijah Sells to give them "a reasonable share" of the agricultural implements under his control.[15]

By that time, few of the freedmen were calling on Sanborn for assistance. He considered relations between the freedmen and their former masters "generally satisfactory," but this generalization no doubt excluded the Chickasaw and Choctaw freedmen. During April only 150 freedmen in the entire Indian Territory applied to Sanborn for assistance, and much of that was given to those who had been taken south and were just returning to their old homes. Sanborn saw little reason to continue his commission beyond early May. Some abuses would undoubtedly require correction, and general supervision of freedman matters would be more necessary at the time the crops matured and contracts were due. But Sanborn believed that the agents, under proper instructions, could attend to and perform all of the duties that pertained to his office. Sanborn was mustered out of service on April 30, 1866, and freedman relations were put under the supervision of Elijah Sells.[16] Throughout his tenure of office, Sanborn had not been satisfied with the status of the Chickasaw and Choctaw freedmen. But there was little he could do in the face of tribal laws. He was hopeful that the treaties then under negotiation would determine the freedmen's status. The hopes that he had for a separate land for the freedmen were never fulfilled.

On April 28, 1866, the United States concluded with the Choctaw and Chickasaw tribes a treaty that profoundly affected the direction of their history for several decades to follow. The treaty officially concluded the hostilities that had existed between those tribes and the United States since 1861. Article 3 stated, in part, that for the sum of $300,000 the Indians ceded the Leased District to the United States. The money was to be held in trust, at 5 percent interest, until the Choctaws and Chickasaws passed laws

to give all persons of African descent, resident in said nations at the date of the treaty of Fort Smith and their descendants, heretofore held in slavery among said nations, all the rights, privileges, and immunities, including the right of suffrage of citizens of said nations, except in the annuities, moneys, and public domain claimed by or belonging to said nations, respectively, and also to give such persons who were residents as aforesaid and their descendants 40 acres each of the land of said nations on the same terms as the Choctaws and Chickasaws.

Upon the passage of such laws, the Choctaws and Chickasaws were to receive three-fourths and one-fourth, respectively, of the $300,000, less $100 per capita for those freedmen electing to remove from the nations.

This article further states that if such laws were not forthcoming from the Indian nations within two years from the date of the treaty, the United States would use the $300,000 for the

benefit of such said persons of African descent as the United States shall remove from the said Territory in such manner as the United States shall deem proper, the United States agreeing, within ninety days from the expiration of the said two years, to remove from said nations all persons of African descent as may be willing to remove.

Those returning after removal were to be on the same footing as United States citizens.[17]

Article 4 declared all blacks competent witnesses in civil and criminal proceedings in the Choctaw and Chickasaw courts, guaranteed them fair and equitable contracts for their labor, and required all laws to be equal in their operation upon Indians and blacks alike. Finally, as long as the freedmen remained in the Choctaw and Chickasaw Nations, they were entitled to as much land as they could cultivate.[18]

While the treaty was being negotiated, Winchester Colbert wanted to have the blacks adopted, but only three of the delegates voted for it. The delegation wanted to leave it to the people, but Colbert argued that the people had sent them there to do the best they could and that they should settle the question.[19]

Inherent in the wording of the third article of the treaty, especially since the treaty was negotiated with the combined tribes, was the idea that the Choctaws and Chickasaws must act jointly in their adoption of their freedmen. Such action would prove to be a legislative impossibility for the two nations, and the government's failure to fulfill its obligations under the treaty would leave the status of the Choctaw and Chickasaw freedmen unresolved for several decades to come. To the Chickasaws, the terms of Article 3 provided them a means by which they could be rid of the freedmen, whom they found a difficult burden and for whom they cared little.

The freedmen were only one of the major problems that beset the Chickasaws during Reconstruction. In 1865, the secretary of the interior looked forward to reorganization of the Indian Territory under a territorial government. It would be the government's responsibility to provide internal improvements necessary "to develop its magnificent resources." The tribes would make educational and religious progress, "the industry of the country" would develop, railroads would cross the country, "binding its several parts together" and to the states. The secretary urged the government to act immediately to do whatever was necessary "in paving the way for these improvements" in order to avoid difficulties that might arise in the future.[20] The secretary's grand scheme found expression in the treaties of 1866.

The treaty with the Choctaws and Chickasaws seriously weakened the Chickasaws' ability to maintain autonomy over their affairs. It gave the railroads a foothold in the Indian Territory, and the railroads, which made immediate plans to cross the territory, represented the means of opening the country to encroachment by non-Indians.

Railroad lobbyists had attended the council at Fort Smith in 1865 and were successful in inserting into the treaties with the Indians provisions for railroads to be built across the territory. Article 6 of the Choctaw and Chickasaw treaty had provided for the granting of right-of-way to railroad companies to be build railroads across Choctaw and Chickasaw lands from north to south and from east to west. The treaties had no sooner been negotiated than Congress gave franchises to two railroad companies to build lines across the Indian Territory from the east and from the north. Congress held out to the companies the promise of generous land grants along the right-of-way as soon as the Indian title was extinguished and the lands became part of the public lands of the United States. The general feeling among the Indians was that the railroads would open their lands to the kind of speculation that the railroads had caused elsewhere and that they would bring a horde of whites from the states. The north-south franchise was granted to the Missouri, Kansas, and Texas Railroad Company, which, in 1870, without tribal consent built a road from Chetopa, Kansas, across the Cherokee Nation, and into the Creek Nation. The following year the Atlantic and Pacific built a road from Seneca, Missouri, to Vinita, Cherokee Nation, on the MK&T line. Chickasaws and Choctaws differed in their opinions regarding the MK&T's progress toward their borders. There was general opposition among the Indians to the idea of land grants to the companies. Chickasaws were less receptive to the idea of railroads than were the Choctaws. The MK&T crossed only the southeastern corner of the Chickasaw Nation between Caddo, Choctaw Nation, and Denison, Texas. No more railroads were built through the Chickasaw Nation until a congressional act of 1886 put Indian lands under federal jurisdiction and granted franchises to other railroad companies. A bitter political struggle ensued in the Chickasaw Nation when the Gulf, Colorado, and Santa Fe sought to negotiate for right-of-way and building materials. The Chickasaw legislature refused to make an agreement, so Governor William M. Guy did so on his own. When the Santa Fe sought to pay for the materials, the legislature refused the money.[21]

Indian concerns regarding the coming of the railroads were realized. All along the line contractors despoiled the land of timber near the right-of-way and shipped it out of the nation. "A horde of roughs" accompanied the railroad. Whiskey was illegally brought into the territory by railroad workers and others and sold along the road. Tent towns sprang up and attracted criminals and other lawless elements, who with the disorderly construction crews disturbed the peace of the citizens. When the building boom subsided, there remained adventurers and land speculators, who with singularity of purpose, set about finding ways to extinguish the Indian title to the land, upon which depended the acquisition of large land grants to the railroad companies.[22]

Whites began to travel by rail across the Indian Territory, often exaggerated reports of the good quality of the land went out, and a clamor grew in the United States to extinguish the Indian title, allot lands in severalty to the Indians, and open the surplus lands to non-Indian settlement. The Chickasaws endorsed surveying and alloting land in 1866, but the Choctaws would not. Under the treaty, both tribes were required to act to make such changes. Apparently fearing that their nation was doomed, the Chickasaws wanted to salvage as much of it for themselves as possible. With the coming of the railroads and in the face of the outstanding freedman question, the Chickasaws allowed their country to be surveyed in 1871 and 1872 with the prospect of allotting the lands in severalty, but the Choctaws refused to allow theirs to be surveyed.[23] There the matter rested for nearly three decades.

Another way the government sought to force extinction of the Indian land title was the establishment of a grand council of the tribes in the Indian Territory. By inserting provisions for the council in the treaties of 1866, the government hoped to lead the tribes, finally, to a territorial government. When the council first met in 1870, the delegates adopted resolutions protesting the territorial bills then pending before Congress. That December, the council met at Okmulgee, Creek Nation, and adopted a constitution that organized the Indian Territory like a state with a governor, a legislature, and a supreme court. Neither the Chickasaws nor the Cherokees would approve the constitution, and the President and Congress wanted veto and appointive powers, concessions that the Indians would not make. Thus the constitution was rejected by the tribes. The council convened several more times as the delegates attempted to write another constitution. In 1875 Congress stopped appropriating funds for its expenses, for it had proved to be a forum for uniting the tribes in their resistance to the policies of the government and had been the source of numerous protests against the territorial bills introduced in Congress. Nevertheless, the council convened regularly at tribal expense until 1878.[24]

Bills providing for the establishment of a territorial government in the Indian Territory were introduced in every Congress from 1870 until the Curtis Act of 1898 extinguished the Indian title without the Indians' consent. The tribes of the territory strongly opposed these efforts to dissolve their nations, for much of the agitation for establishing a territorial govern- ment came from the railroad companies, who even went so far as to sell stock abroad on the basis of their conditional land grants. After 1879 the strong agitation for territorial bills was eclipsed by agitation for open- ing to settlement several million acres of land in the central part of present- day Oklahoma. Ceded by the Indians in the Treaty of 1866, the lands had not been assigned to any western tribes, as contemplated by the treaty. The lands were also much discussed as a possible home for the freedmen of the Indian Territory. Some whites attempted to establish a colony there in 1879, as did others under the famous "boomer" David L. Payne in 1880. Attempts to settle the unassigned lands, popularly called Oklahoma, and the Cherokee Outlet became common during the next few years. In 1885, an Indian appropriations act provided for negotiation with the Cherokees, Creeks, and Seminoles to open Oklahoma to settlement under the home- stead laws of the United States. The Creeks and Seminoles finally gave in, and the lands were opened in 1889.[25]

By the time the Oklahoma lands were opened to non-Indian settlement, the Indian nations themselves had been overrun by citizens of the United States, who squatted on the land and became known as intruders. The in- truders believed that the Indians' title was worthless except for the land actually occupied and improved by the Indians, and they were convinced that it was simply a matter of time until the land would be opened to settlement. One observer wrote in 1869, "To this class of frontiersman, an Indian reservation is a God-send." The intruders included many good people, but far more were unscrupulous, selfish, unprincipled, or indolent. Through intermarriage with citizens and economic enterprise they gained a large measure of control over the financial and political interests of the tribes. Crimes charged to Indians often resulted from the influence of corrupt, designing whites. The Indian laws were adequate for themselves but not to protect them from such whites. Intruders who infringed upon Indian rights went unpunished, because Indian laws did not apply to them. The Indian office failed to develop any system by which to punish or re- move them, although in Article 43 of the Treaty of 1866, the government had guaranteed the removal of all persons who did not have a permit to remain in the Chickasaw or Choctaw nations. Nor were governmental of- ficials always sympathetic to the tribes' dilemma. They generally held the opinion that the tribes invited the problem because in order to exempt themselves from work they hired United States citizens as laborers. And once the Americans were there, they rarely left.[26]

The Chickasaws tried to control the influx of noncitizens by requiring those employed in the Chickasaw Nation to purchase a permit to remain. An 1876 law required United States citizens who wanted to hire or rent land or seek employment in the Nation to enter into a contract with a citizen. They then gave the citizen enough money to pay their permits through the permit collector, elected in each county. The permit, necessary for every male noncitizen over 18, cost $25 per year in 1876 but was later reduced to $5. Those without permits were considered intruders, subject to removal. Merchants, traders, and physicians were required to apply to the governor for their permits. Other laws of 1876 prohibited citizens or persons holding permits to hold livestock in their names for noncitizens and required noncitizens to be of good moral character and industrious habits and to reside in the Nation two years before they could procure a license to marry a citizen. An 1879 law said that only adult citizens were allowed to make contracts with noncitizens for labor, except those employed as mechanics or clerks.[27]

Attempts to control the flow of noncitizens into the Nation failed. Although in 1877 many were forced to leave the Chickasaw Nation because of the $25 permit, land-hungry Americans continued to pour into the Nation. By 1890 farm wages were competitive with those in Texas, Arkansas, and Kansas. The land was there simply to take up and use tax-free, and the prairie lands in the western part of the Nation were excellent for grazing. More and more Texas intruders turned their attention to Pickens County, where they ran large herds. When the Chickasaws attempted to enforce their cattle tax and to remove the intruders in 1886 and 1888, they resisted the Chickasaw light-horse police, and federal troops had to be called out to maintain order.[28]

When the Santa Fe Railroad was completed from Purcell south through the Nation in 1887, towns such as Pauls Valley and Ardmore developed. Many of the noncitizens settled in these and other towns, which were disorderly, raw, unsanitary, and unorganized. In 1890, not a single town in the Chickasaw country was incorporated, although Ardmore had 2,100 people, Purcell had 1,060, Wynnewood had 398, Pauls Valley had 206, Marietta had 110, and Dougherty had 103. Few of the Indians lived in towns. Since the noncitizens had no title to the land, the buildings had a temporary look about them. There were seven newspapers supported by noncitizens and whites in the Chickasaw Nation. The noncitizens, most of them Texans and other southerners, had literally taken over the Chickasaw Nation. Figures acquired during an 1890 census of the Chickasaw Nation are staggering. The number of inhabitants of the Nation was 57,329, of whom 40,299 lived in Pickens County. Racially, the inhabitants broke down as follows: 2,941 Chickasaws; 1,282 other Indians, including 760 Choctaws and a few Cherokees, Creeks, Shawnees, Seminoles, Delawares, Potawatomis, Caddoes, and Wyandots, as well as intermarried whites and tribal freedmen; 3,676 Africans; 9 Chinese; and 48,421 whites. Nearly 91 percent of the inhabitants were of some race other than Indian![29]

Some of the noncitizens were black. Chickasaw officials had complained of black intruders as early as 1868; some of these were apparently refugees from Texas. After the Civil War several bodies of black troops were mustered out of the U.S. military service in the Chickasaw Nation; many of the former troops stayed, and blacks from the United States as well as from the Choctaw Nation were attracted to them. In 1873, it was reported that there were some discharged black soldiers staying in the western part of the Chickasaw lands and committing crimes and that there were white and black intruders along the MK&T line. The special census of the Indian territory in 1890 listed 3,676 Africans in the Chickasaw Nation in the following categories: Negroes 2,651, Mulatto 20, Quadroon 3, and Octoroon 2. Black migration increased during the next few years so that in 1897 the Chickasaws charged that there was a "multitude of colored people from the States, who have swarmed into the Chickasaw Nation, and now enjoy the gratuitous use of Chickasaw land" and that there might be more Choctaw freedmen than Chickasaw freedmen on Chickasaw lands.[30]

There is little doubt that Chickasaw politics contributed to the invasion of the Chickasaw Nation. After the war two political parties emerged: the National Party, which opposed the coming of the railroads and any change in the system of holding lands communally, and the Progressive Party, made up of most of the mixed-blood Chickasaws and intermarried, adopted whites. The controversy over the contract with the Santa Fe Railroad in 1886-87 led to a bitter election in 1888 in which the political issues were the supremacy of the rights of Chickasaws by blood and a cattle tax that mainly affected the whites. Governor William M. Guy was reelected, but the election was contested and William L. Byrd finally assumed office. The following year, intermarried whites were disfranchised, and the Progressive Party was severely weakened. In the election of 1890 Byrd was reelected because only the votes of the Chickasaws by blood were counted.[31]

With the traditionalists of the National Party in control of the Chickasaw government, the legislature now tried to deal with the intruder problem. Noncitizen intruders, black and white, greatly outnumbered the Chickasaws. The legislature ordered a census to be taken to include all noncitizens and blacks, both former slaves of the Chickasaws and all blacks from the states. On July 2, 1890, the Chickasaws complained to the President that they were overrun by intruders and asked for relief:

We are wholly unable to estimate the number of intruders now in our country, but to say the least they are very numerous, and still they come; and not knowing of any other appeal to make, we feel ourselves justifiable in applying to the head of the Great and Powerful Government from which we expect to find and get the relief so plainly promised by the grand United States Government in the year of 1866.

They asked that the United States remove all intruders. But all they could do was to make a weak plea. They were powerless to resist the onslaught, and the government had neither the means nor the desire to remove the intruders. By 1900, the number of noncitizen whites in the Chickasaw Nation was 150,000 and the number of blacks was 5,000.[32]

As the number of noncitizen residents increased in the Indian Territory, so did instances of violence and crime. The Chickasaw courts had jurisdiction over issues involving only Chickasaws, all other cases belonging to the U.S. district courts. At first the only court with jurisdiction was that for the Western District of Arkansas at Van Buren (and later at Fort Smith). Marshals of that court had to cover an estimated thirty thousand square miles. The federal court was so distant from the Chickasaw Nation that if a criminal was apprehended, it was almost impossible to convict and punish him because the hardship of traveling such a great distance had to be borne by witnesses. By the 1880s, then, there were large numbers of whites in the Chickasaw Nation virtually outside the reach of the law. Thus, very early a clamor arose to establish a federal court in the Indian Territory. Congress took the matter in hand in 1888 by giving U.S. federal courts jurisdiction over cases of murder, manslaughter, rape, assault with intent to kill, burglary, larceny, and arson in which an Indian was involved, even if the act had been committed on Indian land. In 1889 Congress gave those convicted of capital crimes the right to appeal to the Supreme Court of the United States, established a federal court at Muskogee, Creek Nation, and gave the federal court at Paris, Texas, jurisdiction over criminal cases arising in the Chickasaw Nation. In 1890, other federal courts with limited jurisdiction were established at South McAlester, Choctaw Nation, and at Ardmore, Chickasaw Nation. During the next few years, these courts took most of the power away from the Indian national courts.[33] Proponents of extinguishing the Indian land titles and opening Indian Territory to non-Indian settlement used the violence in the territory as justification for doing away with the Indian governments, which they claimed were inefficient and ineffective. In the 1890s, despite the existence of federal courts, reports of violence continued and were publicized by the Dawes Commission as an argument for extinguishing the Indian title and allotting lands in severalty.

The coming of the railroads, the influx of noncitizens, the growth of the towns, and the resulting economic development brought changes to the life styles of both the freedmen and the Chickasaws. Unfortunately for the blacks, the Chickasaws felt their autonomy threatened from all sides. The freedmen also represented a threat, but one that the Chickasaws could deal with. Their solution to the problem posed by the freedmen was simply to deny them any right to share in the Chickasaw domain.

NOTES

1. Annual Report of the Secretary of the Interior, 1865, 39 Cong., 1 Sess., *House Executive Document 1,* 205, 464, 467, 531, 205, 207, 209, 440, hereafter cited as *Annual Report, 1865.*

2. Will Nail (interview), September 9, 1937, *Indian-Pioneer History* (Indian Archives Division, Oklahoma Historical Society), 81: 176; *Constitution and Laws of the Choctaw Nation* (New York: William P. Lyon & Son, 1869), 414-417.

3. D. N. Cooley to James Harlan, October 17, 1865, National Archives Microfilm Publications, *Microcopy M348* (Office of Indian Affairs, Report Books)-14: 476; Harlan to Cooley, November 18, 1865, and Circular 1, January 1, 1866, National Archives Microfilm Publications, Microcopy *M234* (Office of Indian Affairs, Letters Received)-836: I1382-65, I56-66, hereafter cited as *M234,* followed by the roll number.

4. Annie Heloise Abel, *The American Indian under Reconstruction* (Cleveland, Ohio: The Arthur H. Clark Company, 1925), 273; General H.

J. Hunt to Cooley, November 28, 1865, *M234*-836: H1323-65; Cooley to Hunt, December 15, 1865, National Archives Microfilm Publications, *Microcopy M21* (Office of Indian Affairs, Letters Sent)-79: 23 (hereafter cited as *M21*, followed by the roll number); and National Archives Record Group 393 (Records of the United States Army Continental Commands, 1821-1920), Frontier District, *Seventh Army Corps and Department of Arkansas, Letters Received, 1865-66.*

  5. Report of Sergeant H. T. Holmes of an Expedition through Indian Territory, District of Arkansas, *Letters Received, 1863-65,* Bureau of Freedmen and Inspection Reports, 1864-65, Box 1: H1865.

  6. General John Sanborn to Cooley, December 26, 1865, *M234*-837: S101-66.

  7. Circular 1, January 1, 1866, and Sanborn to Harlan, January 10, 1866, *M234*-837: I56-66, S91-66.

  8. *Report of the Secretary of the Interior* (Washington, D.C.: Government Printing Office, 1866), 283-284, hereafter cited as *Annual Report, 1866.*

  9. *Ibid.,* 284.

  10. *Ibid.,* 285.

  11. Cooley to Sanborn, January 30, 1866, *M21*-79: 217.

  12. Lieut. W. R. Bryce to Lieut. Col. Craig, February 26, 1866, Department of Arkansas, *Letters Received, 1863-65,* Bureau of Freedmen and Inspection Reports, 1864-65, Box 1: B1866; Matthew Gray to Hunt, February 8, 1866, District of the Frontier, *Letters Received,* G1866.

  13. *Annual Report,* 1866, 286.

  14. Sanborn to Cooley, January 29, 1866, *M234*-837: S89-66.

  15. Sanborn to Major Pinkney Lugenbeel, April 7, 1866, Circular 6, March 27, 1866, and Sanborn to Cooley, April 10, 1866, *M234*-837: S216-66, S203-66, S216-66; Cooley to Elijah Sells, April 17, 1866, *M21*-80: 41.

  16. *Annual Report, 1866,* 287; Harlan to Sells, April 30, 1866, *M234*-837: S237-66.

  17. 50 Cong., 1 Sess., *Senate Executive Document 166,* 2; *Constitution, and Laws of the Chickasaw Nation, together with the Treaties of 1832, 1833, 1834, 1837, 1852, and 1866* (Parsons, Kans.: The Foley Railway Printing Company, 1899), 496-497, hereafter cited as *Constitution and Laws.*

  18. *Constitution and Laws,* 497-498.

  19. 42 Cong., 3 Sess., *House Report 98,* 581.

  20. *Annual Report, 1865,* 210.

  21. *Report of the Secretary of the Interior* (Washington, D.C.: Government Printing Office, 1869), 515, 541, hereafter cited as *Annual Report,*

1869; Annual Report of the Secretary of the Interior, 1870, 41 Cong., 3 Sess., *House Executive Document 1,* 4: 756, hereafter cited as *Annual Report, 1870;* Joseph B. Thoburn and Muriel H. Wright, *Oklahoma: A History of the State and Its People* (New York: Lewis Historical Publishing Company, 1929), 2: 475, 481, 482; Muriel II. Wright, *A Guide to the Indian Tribes of Oklahoma* (Norman: University of Oklahoma Press, 1951), 93-94.

22. Annual Report of the Secretary of the Interior, 1872, 42 Cong., 3 Sess., *House Executive Document 1,* 5: 622, hereafter cited as *Annual Report, 1872;* Annual Report of the Secretary of the Interior, 1871, 42 Cong., 2 Sess., *House Executive Document 1,* 5: 982, hereafter cited as *Annual Report, 1871;* Angie Debo, *The Road to Disappearance* (Norman: University of Oklahoma Press, 1941), 197, 199.

23. *Report of the Secretary of the Interior* (Washington, D.C.: Government Printing Office, 1868), 739, hereafter cited as *Annual Report, 1868; Annual Report, 1870,* 4: 755; 49 Cong., 1 Sess., *Senate Report, 1278,* 2: 278, hereafter cited as *Report 1278;* Arrell M. Gibson, *The Chickasaws* (Norman: University of Oklahoma Press, 1971), 296.

24. "Journal of the General Council of the Indian Territory," *Chronicles of Oklahoma,* 3 (April, 1925), 33-44; "Journal of the Adjourned Session of the First General Council of the Indian Territory," *Chronicles of Oklahoma,* 3 (June, 1925), 120-140; "Okmulgee Constitution," *Chronicles of Oklahoma,* 3 (September, 1925), 216-228; Morris L. Wardell, *A Political History of the Cherokee Nation, 1838-1907* (Norman: University of Oklahoma Press, 1938), 209; *Annual Report, 1872,* 5: 621; *Report 1278,* 2: 279.

25. *Annual Report, 1868,* 739; *Annual Report, 1871,* 5: 987; Wardell, 260, 297, 301-306.

26. *Annual Report, 1872,* 5: 617; *Annual Report, 1869,* 515; *Annual Report of the Commissioner of Indian Affairs to the Secretary of the Interior for the Year 1877* (Washington, D.C.: Government Printing Office, 1877), 107-108, hereafter cited as *Annual Report, 1877; Annual Report of the Commissioner of Indian Affairs to the Secretary of the Interior for the Year 1883* (Washington, D.C.: Government Printing Office, 1883), 88-89, hereafter cited as *Annual Report, 1883;* Annual Report of the Secretary of the Interior, 1874, 43 Cong., 2 Sess., *House Executive Document 1,* 5: 381, hereafter cited as *Annual Report, 1874; Annual Report of the Commissioner of Indian Affairs to the Secretary of the Interior for the Year 1876* (Washington, D.C.: Government Printing Office, 1876), 64, hereafter cited as *Annual Report, 1876; Annual Report of the Commissioner of Indian Affairs to the Secretary of the Interior for the Year 1884* (Washington, D.C.: Government Printing Office, 1884), 99, hereafter cited as *Annual Report, 1884.*

27. *Constitution and Laws,* 134-135, 142-144, 148-149, 229-231.

28. *Annual Report, 1877,* 110; *Annual Report of the Commissioner of Indian Affairs to the Secretary of the Interior for the Year 1889* (Washington, D.C.: Government Printing Office, 1889), 211; *Report 1278,* 2: 281, 282; U.S. Census Office, *The Five Civilized Tribes in Indian Territory: The Cherokee, Chickasaw, Choctaw, Creek, and Seminole Nations* (Washington, D.C.: U.S. Census Printing Office, 1894), 11, 13, 19, 51; hereafter cited as *The Five Civilized Tribes.*

29. Gibson, 284; *Five Civilized Tribes,* 51, 8, 9-10, 13, 4-5. For the most thorough study of the origins of the non-Indian population in the Indian Territory, *see* Michael F. Doran, "Population Statistics of Nineteenth Century Indian Territory," *Chronicles of Oklahoma,* 53 (Winter, 1975-76), 492-515.

30. Letter of Cyrus Harris, January 19, 1868, National Archives Record Group 393, *District of Indian Territory, Letters Received, 1867-68,* Bundle E, B90-1868; Gibson, 291; 55 Cong., 1 Sess., *Senate Document 157,* 8-9; A. Parsons to Commissioner, May 17, 1873, *M234*-180: P112-73; *Five Civilized Tribes,* 5.

31. Wright, 93-94.

32. *Constitution and Laws,* 262, 273-274; Gibson, 285; *Annual Report of the Secretary of the Interior for the Fiscal Year Ended June 30, 1898* (Washington, D.C.: Government Printing Office, 1898), 156-157.

33. *Annual Report, 1874,* 5: 321-322, 382; *Annual Report, 1876,* 63; *Annual Report, 1877,* 108; *Annual Report, 1883,* 87-88; *Annual Report, 1884,* 99; *Annual Report of the Commissioner of Indian Affairs to the Secretary of the Interior for the Year 1887* (Washington, D.C.: Government Printing Office, 1887), 115; *Report 1278,* 2: 279, 292-293; Wardell, 309-310; *Five Civilized Tribes,* 21-22; *Annual Report of the Secretary of the Interior for the Fiscal Year Ended June 30, 1897* (Washington, D.C.: Government Printing Office, 1897), 142-143; Gibson, 294.

3

Freedom without Rights

The political and economic problems faced by the Chickasaws during the forty years following the Civil War helped to form the social milieu in which the Chickasaw freedmen struggled to establish their right to a home in the Indian Territory. The legal base for that right was the stipulations of the Treaty of 1866 regarding adoption of the blacks. Unlike the other tribes, the Chickasaws and Choctaws were given an alternative. If they did not enact legislation to adopt their freedmen within two years, the United States agreed to remove the blacks from Chickasaw and Choctaw lands and to make them citizens of the United States, using the $300,000 received for the Leased District in the freedmen's behalf. The two tribes saw the treaty stipulation as a means of getting rid of the freedmen, whom they liked less as time passed and whose political power they feared. Soon after the treaty it became apparent that the Chickasaws would not pass adoption legislation. Their stand on the issue would prevent the Choctaws from adopting their blacks because the treaty required joint action by the tribes. Although the Choctaws urged action, it would be several years before they received permission to separately adopt their freedmen. The Chickasaws would never give in. In 1866, the Chickasaw freedmen began forty years of freedom in the Chickasaw Nation without any rights whatsoever except the right to occupy and work the land, to which they had no title.

On November 9, 1866, the Chickasaw legislature unanimously recommended that the United States retain the Chickasaws' share of the $300,000 for the benefit of the freedmen and remove them from the Nation. To put pressure on the freedmen to go, on the following day the legislature directed Governor Cyrus Harris to order all intruders and refugees out of the Nation, which directive he shortly followed.[1]

The freedmen had anticipated this Chickasaw policy. On September 23, a group who had left the Indian country after the treaty had asserted their

right to the $100 per capita under the treaty stipulations. Doubting that
the Indians would adopt them, they suggested that the Choctaw and Chickasaw freedmen be removed to Sevier County, Arkansas. On December 8,
a committee claiming to represent 1,500 freedmen in Pickens County expressed to Agent Martin W. Chollar a desire to remove from the Nation
because of unfriendly and bitter feelings toward them. In exchange for
land on Cash Creek, about one hundred miles southwest of Fort Arbuckle
in the Leased District, they would give up their part of the $300,000 if
the United States would provide transportation and supplies for a new start.
Chollar consulted Governor Harris, who approved the freedmen's proposal.
Harris wanted to get rid of these and intruder blacks as well. He asked the
agent's advice concerning cases where black intruders and refugees refused
to leave the Nation or to procure permits to remain in accordance with his
recent proclamation. Harris was also unsure of the Nation's right to try
any freedmen violating its laws, since the blacks were not considered citizens; yet he was not sure that the laws of the United States extended over
them. Although 292 signatures appeared on the freedmen's petition, no
attention was given to it, perhaps because it was discredited by the Chickasaw delegates to Washington.[2]

Although the petition had been signed as well by some of the loyal
Chickasaws, delegates Holmes Colbert and G. D. James denied that those
Chickasaws had any complaints. As for the other signatures, the numbers
were no doubt swelled, they charged, by "negroes and others" who had
no claims as Chickasaws. They claimed to recognize only the name of
Mitchell Beams, the interpreter who was half black and half Choctaw.
Colbert and James charged that the petition was the work of "contractors
and speculators" who were using the "destitution of Indians" as a means
of aggrandizing themselves.[3]

In Agent Chollar's patronizing view, the freedmen had to prove that
they were "civilized" in order to reach their goals. He told them that to
be worthy of freedom, they must demonstrate the capability of self-
government and "good behavior." They should not expect the "wild-
ness of unlimited freedom" but should emulate the "conduct, order,
and industry of the white man." The situation was peculiar. Under the
protection of the U.S. government, they were residents of a nation under
the "protectorate" of the United States; thus to get along agreeably with
the Chickasaws and among themselves was a necessity. Chollar encouraged
them in industry and honesty and advised them to give the Indians "no
cause" to dislike them. He urged them, for instance, to give up the practice

of polygamy that persisted and that he called "a relic of barbarism" discarded by the educated Indians. Its continued practice would teach immorality to their youth. He urged them to give up all manners "except
such as are recognized by the civilized world": "Do right, be industrious,
get the good will and respect of the people you live among and you will
thus obtain an approving conscience, and the good opinion of the government which has done so much for you."[4]

Another year passed without further action by the Chickasaws. As the
deadline for adoption legislation approached, the Chickasaws asked the
government twice during the first few months of 1868 to remove the
freedmen under the terms of the treaty and of the Chickasaw legislative
act of 1866. June 10 was the date by which the Indians were to have
adopted the freedmen, after which, under treaty stipulations, the government had ninety days to remove the freedmen. On June 10, the Chickasaw
and Choctaw freedmen met in council at Boggy Depot, Choctaw Nation,
and drafted a petition for their removal "at an early day." The Chickasaw
act of November 9, 1866, made it plain that the Chickasaws did not want
them, and the time stipulated in the treaty had passed. The freedmen asked
that the $300,000 be used as the government saw fit for their benefit and
that a delegation be permitted to go to Washington. James Squire Wolf,
Squire Butler, Isaac Anderson, and Anderson Brown were selected to confer with the Choctaw and Chickasaw agent and with the commissioner of
Indian affairs. Upon receipt of their petition Secretary of the Interior O. H.
Browning asked Congress to provide for the early removal of the freedmen,
to designate a place to settle them, and to appropriate funds for their removal.[5] Congress, however, took no action.

The status of the freedmen was as uncertain as ever. A conflict had
arisen between authorities of the United States and the Chickasaw Nation
regarding criminal jurisdiction over blacks. The Indians doubted their
authority to try the freedmen, whom they did not consider citizens of
their nation. Chickasaw commissioner Holmes Colbert wanted the question submitted to the U.S. attorney general for a decision, but the acting
secretary refused to do so. On August 17, Colbert and Sampson Folsom,
attorney general for the Choctaw Nation, again asked removal of the freedmen, since neither tribe had adopted their freedmen and since both wanted
the freedmen removed. This plea was echoed by some government officials
and Chickasaws. A growing "lack of sympathy" was developing between
the Chickasaws and Choctaws and their freedmen because the Indians began
to feel that the freedmen had been forced upon them by the Treaty of 1866.

Conflicts were more frequent between freedmen and Indians, and "quite a number" of freedmen had reportedly been killed. On September 26, 1868, L. N. Robinson, head of the Southern Superintendency of the Office of Indian Affairs, sought removal of the freedmen to a reservation and suggested that the government locate all freedmen of the Indian tribes together. They wanted, he said, education, instruction in the mechanical arts, and a small plot of land per person. It was unreasonable to expect more generous action by the Indians than by the former slaveholders in the South. Therefore, Robinson suggested that lands west of the Chickasaw lands between the Red and Canadian rivers be set aside and that freedmen of other tribes in the Indian Territory be persuaded to join the Chickasaw and Choctaw freedmen.[6]

Agent Chollar, too, urged removal of the freedmen "to some public lands, where they can have homes of their own and found a prosperous colony." He said of them:

These freedmen are by far the most intelligent and self-reliant of any of their race that have come under my observation, and were they to have a fair chance in life, would solve the problem of their capacity for self-government. They have been waiting patiently the action of the government in their behalf, and have at last become uneasy and dissatisfied.

Justice, he said, dictated their speedy removal to lands west of the Seminole Nation. Otherwise, he expected "more serious difficulties and complications."[7] But Congress made no appropriations for the removal, and the department could not act. Indian Office officials put off such inquiries and refused to issue any instructions. In November, 1868, Sampson Folsom presented suggestions for modifying the 1866 treaty to provide homesteads for the Chickasaws, to give them all the rights of citizenship, and to include suffrage for the freedmen. Folsom suggested allotment of land to each citizen and freedman without the right of alienation (that is, sale), and he requested that a delegation of freedmen be permitted to meet with the government at the same time as the Indians in negotiating the matter.[8]

In February, 1869, the government brought delegates James S. Wolf, Mahardy Colbert, and Anderson Brown for the Chickasaw and Choctaw freedmen to Washington, where they submitted a memorial to Congress, urging the government to fulfill the treaty stipulations by removing their people and paying their removal expenses. Since the Choctaws and Chicka-

saws had failed to adopt them within two years, they remained in the
Chickasaw Nation without the protection of the law. They wanted the
$300,000 paid to them per capita so they could afford to remove and begin
a new life in a new country, "thus leaving them entirely free to elect their
homes outside of said Choctaw and Chickasaw nations, as other freedmen
are permitted to do." But nothing was accomplished by this mission. The
commissioner could say only that he could furnish them no satisfaction or
"definite information." Until Congress acted, the Indian Office could do
nothing. Not only did the delegation fail, but Congress failed to appropriate
money for their expenses. The secretary of the interior had to draw money
from provisions set aside for Indian delegations in order for them to get
home.[9]

At this time the government proposed to appoint a commission to determine the Choctaw and Chickasaw freedmen's condition. The Choctaws,
afraid of secret or exclusive consultations with the freedmen, asked that
the interviews with the commission be held in those districts with the
heaviest freedman population and that due notice be given to allow the
governor and other headmen of the tribe to be present. Captain George
T. Olmstead, Jr., the new Chickasaw and Choctaw agent, was directed
to hold open, public, and impartial investigations of the freedmen's condition and report their wishes, to report the Indians' sentiments and the
cause of their failure to comply with the treaty, to investigate Arkansas as
a possible place to which to remove the freedmen, and to find where the
freedmen preferred to go if they left the Chickasaw Nation. Olmstead
called a large meeting of the Choctaw and Chickasaw freedmen at Boggy
Depot on August 28, 1869. Among the three hundred people who attended
were Governor Cyrus Harris, Choctaw Chief Allen Wright, and representatives from all parts of the two nations except the neighborhood of Fort
Smith. Among the latter were the leading black men from every farm,
plantation, and neighborhood, in short, the most influential freedmen
of the two Nations. They were asked to express their desires to remain
or to remove and, if the latter, where they wished to go. A black preach-
er from the Choctaw Nation had gone to Liberia, and Allen Wright thought
that it would be good for them all to go. He had talked to an agent of
the American Colonization Society and discussed it with the freedmen.
He told them at the convention, "Now it seems that everybody is against
you, and would it not be better if I were to advise you to leave the country and go to Liberia, where there is a home provided for the freed people?"

In response, the freedmen declared unanimously for remaining in the Indian country.[10]

In his annual report for 1869, Olmstead reasoned that the freedmen had so declared in order that they might remain under the protection of the United States. He reported that the Choctaws favored having them remain, but that the Chickasaws awaited action by the government. Olmstead suggested the negotiation of a new treaty. If the freedmen could not remain, he favored removal to Arkansas or elsewhere. In 1870 he reported that the unsettled condition of the freedmen had made some of them dissatisfied. But those with energy and labor, he said, lived "as well as the Indians, and are better able to take care of themselves than the majority of their race in the Southern States." He said that they were not badly treated by the Indians but that it would become more incompatible with their interests to become Chickasaw citizens and live under the Indian laws.[11]

Olmstead's report differed greatly from that given a few months earlier by S. N. Clark, special agent for the Bureau of Refugees, Freedmen, and Abandoned Lands. Ordered in late 1869 to investigate the condition of the Chickasaw and Choctaw freedmen, he reported early in 1870 that of the estimated population of seventeen thousand in the two nations, forty-five hundred were freedmen. Clark argued the injustice of Article 3 of the Treaty of 1866, which applied only to the freedmen who were residents of the nations at the time of the treaty. He noted that half of the freedmen had been refugees from the territory at that time. Many men had not been mustered out of the army, some women and children had escaped to the Seminole country and to Kansas, and many slaves had been taken to Texas by their masters. Clark charged that Article 4, guaranteeing that freedmen should be considered "competent witnesses" in all civil and criminal suits in the Chickasaw and Choctaw courts, had steadily been violated. He also charged that "about all attempts at agriculture" had been made by the freedmen, that the fruits of their labor were enjoyed by "rebel Indians and mean whites," and that protection of persons and property had generally been denied.[12]

Clark's report included a letter from S. S. Mitchell of the Chickasaw Nation, who claimed that the freedmen generally agreed that they could not live in the Indian nations under Indian laws. According to Mitchell, they preferred to go to the Leased District if the government would give them a year's rations and farming implements and retain the $300,000 as a permanent investment for them. He believed that the Chickasaws would agree to all except the money, and that many of the freedmen would remain in the nations if they had the protection of the U.S. government. They feared citizenship in the nations because they felt that they would have no rights in the Indian courts. Clark's report also included the resolutions passed by a convention of the Chickasaw and Choctaw freedmen at Scullyville, Choctaw Nation, in September of 1869. They resolved that, since the Chickasaws and Choctaws had refused to fulfill the treaty, they no longer regarded the treaty stipulations concerning them of any force, that they were full citizens of those nations with all the rights, privileges, and benefits of citizens, that they could claim no territory as theirs but the territory in which they resided, that they favored allotment in severalty, that they favored the opening of the territory of white immigration and the sale of surplus lands, and that they would elect three men as delegates to Washington when the need arose.[13]

The resolutions cited by Clark had come after a good deal of effort on the part of the freedmen. They had held a mass meeting on February 16, 1869, but Congress had adjourned before they could draft a petition. Then the leading freedmen from different parts of the Indian Territory went to Valentine Dell, editor of the Fort Smith, Arkansas, *New Era*, asking his advice. Dell urged them to hold a convention and declare the 1866 treaty null and void, claim citizenship, declare in favor of sectioning the country, and appeal for the protection of the U.S. government. The freedmen asked Dell to go to Washington for them, since they had no money, but he could not because of the current session of the Arkansas State Assembly, in which he was a senator. However, the freedmen took Dell's advice and planned two meetings for September 25, one at Scullyville in the east and one at Armstrong Academy in the west.[14]

The convention was held at Scullyville and the resolutions drawn, but the one scheduled for Armstrong did not come off. The Indians in that region were determined to prevent the freedmen from meeting to discuss their condition. They threatened the life of any freedman who attempted to go, tore down the posters announcing the meeting, and arrested some of the leading men among the freedmen as they made their way to the convention. On November 27, at the request of James Ladd and Richard Brashears, Dell asked Lemon Butler at Armstrong Academy to notify the men of his area of a convention to be held in December. On December 7, U.S. Commissioner James O. Churchill at Fort Smith signed a warrant for the

arrest of Ladd and Brashears. Based on information from the Chickasaw
and Choctaw agent, the charges said that Ladd and Brashears "did, in the
month of November, 1869, send messages, circulars, and letters to individuals in the Indian country with intent to disturb the peace and tranquility
of the United States." Brashears was arrested and taken to Van Buren,
Arkansas, to appear before the commissioner. On the way, Brashears sought
Dell's help and advice; Dell went before Churchill, who found no grounds
for arrest and ordered Brashears released.[15]

The executive committee of the freedmen, consisting of William Ed-
wards, Thomas Blackwater, J. Kearney, Brashears, and Ladd called another
meeting at Scullyville on January 15, 1870, at which time they reaffirmed
their resolutions of the previous September and passed another set of resolutions. They condemned as "unwarranted, unjust, and tyrannical" the
action to prevent their meeting and called the arrest of Brashears "a most
outrageous and flagrant violation" of his rights as a free man. They were
now less inclined than ever to leave their native land, and more than ever
they claimed the protection of the government, equal rights with the Indians, and the need to open the territory to white settlement. They declared that those who served in the army but were out of the territory
when the Treaty of 1866 was signed should have their rights, and they
authorized Ladd, Brashears and N. C. Coleman to act as delegates for
the Chickasaw and Choctaw freedmen in Washington. If they were unable to travel to Washington, then Dell was to be their representative.[16]

Finally, they asked the removal of Olmstead as agent to the Chickasaws and Choctaws. Part of their opposition to Olmstead no doubt resulted from his official lack of sympathy for them. He reported in 1870
that the rumors of their bad treatment were "almost entirely without
foundation," and he urged that if nothing was done for them at the next
meeting of the Choctaw council, the government should remove them.[17]
Olmstead was replaced by T. D. Griffith.

By late 1870 obvious differences existed between the Chickasaws
and Choctaws concerning the status of the freedmen. The Choctaws tended
to be more tolerant of the blacks than the Chickasaws. In January, 1871,
the freedmen became agitated when the Chickasaws required a one-dollar
permit for each freedman to stay within the Nation. Agent Griffith, however, believed that the permit law conflicted with Article 4 of the 1866
treaty, which guaranteed equal operation of all laws "on Choctaws, Chick-

asaws, and negroes," and he urged Governor W. P. Brown not to enforce
the law.[18]

There were other unsettling aspects of the freedmen's condition in the
Chickasaw Nation. In his annual report for 1871, Griffith pointed out the
difficulty of prosecuting offenses against or by the Chickasaw freedmen
in the United States court at Fort Smith, Arkansas. Also, to allow them
to remain in the Nation was unfair to both the Chickasaws and them,
since the blacks had no educational funds. Yet they were averse to removal,
and the Chickasaws needed their labor. However, he felt that if removal
was best, the Seminole cession in the central part of the Indian Territory
would be a "fine country for them," and schools could be established
with the interest from the $300,000 trust fund.[19]

That October, Griffith was directed to take a census of the Chickasaw
and Choctaw freedmen. Early in 1872, they were reported three thousand
strong, contented and doing well because they were "getting a living."
However, they had no equal rights and could be driven off the land. Many
were bilingual, hard working, and "more provident than many of the Indians." But they were without money and education, and they were not
organized. And it was feared that unless the government acted in their
behalf, they might "run on for years and largely increase, making it much
more difficult to effect a change."[20]

On January 23, the Choctaw freedmen petitioned Congress to become
citizens not of the Choctaw Nation but of the United States, since the
Choctaws had refused to adopt them and they had gone four years beyond
the adoption deadline without education and protection of life and property. With Daniel C. Finn of Little River County, Arkansas, as their
attorney, they asked Congress to appoint a special agent to help them
select homes and to protect them and the Chickasaw freedmen against
speculation in land.[21]

Such action by the freedmen caused some stirrings in Congress, which,
in turn, made the rest of the freedmen uneasy about removal. For the
most part they denied that there was any enmity toward them or that they
wanted to remove. Instead, Griffith insisted that they wanted to remain in
the Nations, "even under all the disadvantages of their present condition."
However, they did insist on the need for well-defined rights. Because their
rights were so vague, they were not encouraged to make permanent improvements, and without them they were "but hewers of wood for others,"

Griffith said. They needed education but could not hire suitable teachers.
Said the agent,

It would cost something to establish a school system for them and carry
it on until they could do it themselves, but they will do all in their power
to aid, and it will be cheaper to educate them than to allow them to grow
up as they are now growing, in ignorance.[22]

In the summer of 1872, a committee of the House of Representatives
visited the Indian Territory to investigate reports of fraud upon the Indians.
Although not specifically charged to do so, the committee examined the
condition of the freedmen. They celebrated the Fourth of July at a barbecue held by Choctaw and Chickasaw freedmen at Old Boggy Depot, Choctaw Nation, and noted how orderly, temperate, and well dressed the blacks
appeared. They heard testimony from Indians and freedmen alike. Winchester Colbert, former governor of the tribe, told the investigators that if
the government would allow them $400,000 or $500,000 for the Leased
District, they would adopt the freedmen and give them a portion of the
money to educate their children. Indians and blacks alike testified to the
good feelings between the races, but R. M. Jones, a Choctaw, felt that the
good feelings were bolstered by the belief that the United States protected
the blacks and that if they should come under Indian rule, the Indians
might oppress them. Blacks, too, wanted to remain in the Indian country
but under the protection of the United States.[23]

Colbert told the investigating committee that he had favored adoption
of the blacks from the start. He blamed his stand on the freedman issue
for his failure to be elected to public office since the war. Now, he said,
those who had been so bitterly opposed to what he was trying to do for so
long had begun to think that it was better to adopt the blacks.[24]

Early in 1873, it appeared momentarily that the problem of the Chickasaw freedmen was about to be solved. Alarmed by the influx of black intruders, and apparently afraid that they might not be able to separate their
freedmen from other blacks as time passed, the Chickasaws made a move
toward adoption. In January, the Chickasaw legislature passed "An Act to
adopt the negroes of the Chickasaw Nation." Approved January 10, it
provided that all "negroes belonging to the Chickasaws at the time of the
adoption of the treaty at Fort Smith, and resident in the nation at the date
thereof, and their descendants, be adopted, in conformity with the third
article of the treaty of 1866." This adoption was on the provision that the

proportional part of the $300,000 be paid to the Chickasaw Nation; that
the freedmen should not be entitled to any part of it, nor to any benefit
from the principal and interest of invested funds, nor to any share in the
common domain except the forty acres provided by the treaty, nor to any
privileges or rights not conferred by the treaty; and that the adopted freedmen be subject to the laws of the Chickasaw Nation, just as if they were
Chickasaws. Commissioner H. R. Clum, believing that it was in the best interests of the Indians and the blacks for the freedmen to remain where
they were, recommended to the secretary of the interior that Congress
extend the time by which the Indians could adopt the freedmen, apparently hoping to give the Choctaws time to act. On February 10, Secretary
Columbus Delano recommended to Congress that it pass legislation to
extend the time for execution of the treaty to July 1, 1875. The papers
were sent to the Committee of Freedmen Affairs, but no action was taken.[25]
Thus Congress failed to seize the one opportunity the Chickasaws were to
offer to resolve the freedmen issue.

The logic of arguments such as those of Winchester Colbert and the
Choctaw Peter P. Pitchlynn may have been behind the Chickasaw move to
adopt the blacks. Since 1866, they had feared a black colony in the Leased
District. They were afraid that thousands of blacks from the states would
flock there if the freedmen were there, and in a few years the colony would
reach "formidable dimensions." In that case, "more lands and other advantages" would be required for them at the expense of the Indians. Pitchlynn and Colbert asked

If they remain among us, outnumbering them as we do, can they do us any
harm? While their services as laborers will be of importance and value for
years to come, removed and established as a separate colony, they may do
us and our brethren of the other adjacent tribes irreparable injury.[26]

While the Choctaws and Chickasaws debated the question and the U. S.
Congress pondered it, the condition of the Chickasaw and Choctaw freedmen worsened. They were supposedly free men, but they were without
equal rights and privileges, including those of property ownership and
educational facilities. In an attempt to better their lot, the Chickasaw freedmen met on November 15, 1873, and chose delegates to Washington. Early
in 1874, they sent King Blue and other deputies to lay their case before U.S.
officials. With letters of introduction from the Indian Territory, Blue ob-

tained an interview with Commissioner E. P. Smith, who, in his recommen-
dation of Blue to Secretary Delano, called the Chickasaw freedmen

the only colored people in the United States whose rights are at present
abridged on account of race or color. They are represented as the most industrious and hopeful element of civilization in the Nation and are very
desirous of educating their children, but being without means and without a voice, in their government, they are liable to be left in ignorance
and subject to a degree of oppression inconsistent with their rights as
men.[27]

That spring, Congress attempted to pass Senate Bill 680, "An Act for
the relief of certain persons of African descent in the Choctaw and Chickasaw Nations." Hated by the Choctaws and Chickasaws, the bill stated that
since the Indians had not adopted the freedmen and since the latter were
anxious to remain in the Indian nations, all persons of African descent
under the Treaty of 1866 were entitled to all rights, privileges, annuities,
moneys, and public domain. Therefore, it authorized the secretary of the
treasury to issue bonds of the United States, payable in twenty-five years
in gold coin and bearing 5 percent interest payable semiannually, for the
sum of $300,000, the money to be held in trust for the Chickasaws and
Choctaws.[28]

In presenting the bill to Congress, acting Secretary B. R. Cowan called
the freedmen a people who were "desirous to learn, anxious to secure to
themselves homes in severalty, and, above all, anxious to remain in the
country where they now live, and which is the only home they have ever
known." None would leave the country voluntarily because they had a
strong attachment to the soil, but the Choctaws and Chickasaws refused
to adopt them because of strong prejudice against them. Cowan admitted
that the proposed legislation might "not be exactly in accordance with
the letter of the treaty," but it was "simply a matter of justice to this
class" of industrious citizens of the nations.[29] The Choctaw delegates
protested the bill on May 2, 1874, a protest approved by D. O. Fisher,
the Chickasaw delegate.

Secretary Delano believed that the freedmen were as "meritorious, to
say the least, as the average Choctaw and Chickasaw population" and that
they had

probably done as much toward securing the wealth possessed by said
nations *per capita* as the average Choctaw and Chickasaw population.

Under these circumstances, their condition is not simply anomalous;
it is unjustifiable, oppressive, and wrong, and ought to be remedied.

In arguing for Bill 680, Delano blamed this condition on Choctaw and
Chickasaw failure to fulfill treaty agreements. He argued that the income
from the invested $300,000 would be sufficient to give the freedmen a
share in the annuity and denied the validity of the Indians' argument
that the Indians should not be required to give the freedmen equal rights
to the public domain, since the Americans had not been required to
make like concessions to their former slaves. The freedmen, Delano argued,
were responsible in large measure for the wealth of the Chickasaws and
Choctaws. On June 12, the Choctaws again objected to Bill 680, saying
that they would have conferred citizenship on the freedmen but for the
blacks' preference for U.S. citizenship and their unwillingness to be put
on the same footing as Choctaw citizens.[30]

The Choctaws and Chickasaws found support in some territorial newspapers. For instance, the *Cherokee Advocate,* the official newspaper of
the Cherokee government, said that the refusal of those tribes to adopt
their freedmen was used as a "pretext" by Congress to force the blacks
upon them. The $300,000, it claimed, was "in consideration of a riddance"
of the freedmen, and the failure to adopt them constituted a forfeiture of
the money. The editorial concluded, "The whole effort is an attempt of
sympathy, excited by an exaggerated representation of the condition of
the freedmen in those nations to establish a common property in the
public moneys and domain of those Indians."[31] Such rhetoric was not
needed, for Senate Bill 680 failed to pass.

The same logic that had been used by proponents of Bill 680 was
used by proponents of House Bill 3505 during the early months of 1874.
They argued that since the Indians had made no move toward giving the
blacks their rights, it was up to Congress to do so. Opponents, led by
J. P. C. Shanks, argued that the proposed bill violated the treaty of 1866.
Shanks did not advocate removing the blacks, for he thought that they
ought to be citizens of the Indian nations. However, he did not want to
achieve that end by an open violation of the treaty. To pass the bill would
be to force upon the Chickasaws and Choctaws "a people they are not
willing to receive into their tribe. We attempt to force upon their farms
and upon their lands," Shanks argued, "these negroes whom they do not
want. We attempt to force upon these Indians a division of their property
without their consent." Representative Benjamin Butler, who introduced

the bill, argued that the government had the "right to do anything it pleases with anybody within its jurisdiction." As for treaties, Congress interfered with them every day. Despite treaty stipulations, Butler said, Congress could organize the Indian Territory under a territorial government without the Indians' consent. But, countered one opponent, "if we do we are responsible in the eyes of God and of all civilized nations for having violated our plighted faith, and this bill, to my mind, looks in that direction." To that Butler replied, "I cannot spend the whole day over the rights of a few negroes and the fancied rights of a few Indians." The bill passed by a large margin.[32]

From the Indians' point of view, matters were not going well regarding the freedmen. In 1874 Commissioner Edward P. Smith argued that there was "no reason in justice or equity" why the freedmen should not be treated by the government as a constituent part of the Indian nations:

They are orderly, industrious, and eager for the education of their children, and yet are obliged to expend their labor upon farms to which they have no title, and which once well improved are not infrequently taken from them. Their children grow up in ignorance, in sight of schoolhouses which they may not enter.[33]

That same year, the Chickasaws and Choctaws lost their agent when the government established the Union Agency for the Five Civilized Tribes at Muskogee. The Chickasaws and Choctaws now had to travel farther to do business with the government, and they lost the advantage of having an agent to look after their needs alone.

In the wake of congressional attempts to force the blacks upon them, the Chickasaws once more pressed for their removal. In January, 1875, Governor B. F. Overton directed the Chickasaw delegates to Washington to request removal of "all persons of African descent, not lawfully permitted, beyond the limits of the Chickasaw Nation." Union Agent G. W. Ingalls, however, observed Overton's "unfriendly spirit" regarding the freedmen and prevailed upon Delegates Ah-it-to-tubby and D. O. Fisher not to press the point because the department opposed it and because it would result in "the displeasure not only of the department but of members of Congress, who were their friends." Plans were being made to send a special commissioner to the Indian Territory during the following summer, and Ingalls suggested that any such commissioner be instructed to counsel the

tribal authorities to treat the freedmen more liberally and to agree on legislation in their behalf to be placed before the next Congress.[34]

The Honorable J. P. C. Shanks was appointed to investigate and report
on the status of the Choctaw and Chickasaw freedmen. He arrived in Muskogee, Creek Nation, on September 10, 1875, and went directly to Tishomingo, where the Chickasaw national council was in session. Regional newspapers expressed the hope, upon his arrival, that "the vexed question"
would finally be settled. He urged the Chickasaws to adopt the blacks as
the best possible solution. Both the Chickasaw and Choctaw legislatures
appointed commissioners to confer on "the Negro Question." They met
during the last week in October but failed to come to any agreement. In
his report to the secretary, Shanks opposed removing the freedmen and
recommended that the United States "take measures to secure their recognition as full citizens" in the Choctaw and Chickasaw Nations. Again,
however, the government did not act.[35]

Shanks had some local support for his recommendations. However, the
conclusions had other bases. The Choctaw social critic who wrote under
the pen name of "Tuskahoma" made a plea to the public:

Let the council adopt the freedmen of the Choctaw and Chickasaw nations
and ask the government to confirm payment of the $300,000 with the pro-
vision that all negroes not formerly belonging to the Choctaws and Chickasaws conform to our laws governing persons not citizens of either tribe.[36]

But there was the rub, particularly for the Chickasaw Nation, which at the
time had the greater number of black residents. Great numbers of freedmen from the United States had come to the Indian Territory following
the Civil War, so that by 1875 it was virtually impossible, in many cases,
to tell which freedmen were entitled to rights in the Indian lands and which
were not. And the problem grew more acute as time passed.

When the Chickasaw legislature convened in September of 1876, Governor Overton dwelt on the freedmen for some time in his annual message.
He made clear the main obstacle to solving the problem: the state of the
freedmen would likely remain the same since, under the treaty, joint
action was required on the part of the Chickasaws and Choctaws. He told
the legislature,

I have twice consulted Governor Cole on the subject, asking cooperation
in demanding their removal by the President, but he positively refuses to

act in that direction, claiming that we have the right to enact such laws
as would compel the negroes to take the oath of allegiance to our respective
governments, and become amenable to our laws, without having any of the
privileges and immunities of citizenship conferred upon them. But the most
ignorant can see how utterly foolish such a position is.[37]

Thus the difference between the stands taken by each tribe was aired: the
Choctaws would somehow keep their freedmen while the Chickasaws would
somehow remove theirs.

Overton reported to the legislature that the freedmen themselves were
anxious to have the matter settled. They had met with him twice, asking
what course to pursue. He had referred them to the legislature and expected
the present legislature to receive a memorial from a representative of the
freedmen. Overton urged the legislators to hear their complaints and to
"act to a speedy adjustment of this most difficult question." However, he
appealed to the body not to admit the freedmen to citizenship under
Article 3, for, he said,

If you do, you sign the death-warrant of your nationality with your own
hands; for the negroes will be the wedge with which our country will be
rent asunder and opened up to the whites; and then the grand scheme
so artfully devised by the treaty of 1866, will have been effected, and the
ends of the conspirators attained.[38]

The alternative to adoption was removal. In response to Overton's appeal,
the legislature passed "An Act confirming the Treaty of 1866," in which
it expressed consent to the "sectionizing and allotment of the lands in
severalty," authorized the United States to keep the Chickasaws' share of
the $300,000 held in trust under the treaty, and asked the government to
remove the freedmen from the Nation. On the following day the legislature
provided for the election of commissioners to confer with their counterparts in the Choctaw Nation and to work out a plan for removing the freedmen and their descendants from the nations and for keeping them out.[39]
Such action was futile because of the divergent philosophies of the two
nations.

Meanwhile, the condition of the freedmen remained peculiar. Without
the rights and privileges of the tribesmen, they were deprived of participation in school funds; thus, education was provided for only a few of their
numbers. Its provision came from the federal government, which by 1877

maintained five schools in the Choctaw and Chickasaw Nations. The freedmen were also without the protection of the United States except in criminal cases. That summer, the Chickasaw freedmen appointed Isaac Alexander and King Blue as their representatives to visit Washington on their
behalf. Their plight was made worse by their population increase since the
Civil War. In 1878, there were an estimated twenty-six hundred unadopted
freedmen in the Chickasaw Nation and four thousand in the Choctaw Nation.[40]

In March, 1879, the Chickasaws and the Choctaws appointed commissioners to confer on the freedman question. They met in Caddo with representatives of the United States on April 14. The Choctaws remained steady
in their attempts to urge adoption of the freedmen. The joint commission
agreed on an election to be held throughout the Chickasaw Nation to determine the sentiment of the people regarding adoption. Governor B. C.
Burney called an immediate election so that the legislature would know
how to act that fall. However, in some counties, Burney's right to order
such an election was questioned, and the people were not allowed to vote.
Therefore, when he delivered his annual message to the legislature on
September 1, he said,

I cannot, with authority, tell you what the people of the Chickasaw
Nation desire in this matter, but would recommend some definite action
on your part in regard to it. Justice to ourselves and the Negro demand
this. It has already been suffered to go unattended to too long. Whatever
your action may be on the subject, it will be met with my co-operation.[41]

Although for some time the Choctaws had indicated a willingness to
adopt their freedmen, after a fashion, the Treaty of 1866 required joint
or concurrent adoption by both nations before adoption would be valid
in either. The Chickasaws could not be persuaded to act. Thus, at its
regular session in 1880, the Choctaw council adopted a memorial to Congress, asking that legislation be passed enabling them to adopt their freedmen independently. The council provided for the registration of the Choctaw freedmen in anticipation of adoption.[42] But action was long in coming.
A Senate bill was introduced but never reported.

Ironically, the educational deprivation of the Choctaw and Chickasaw
freedmen provided the means by which the Choctaws were finally allowed
to adopt their freedmen and thus break the social and political stalemate

that had existed for seventeen years. In early 1882, federal officials received appeals by the freedmen for educational opportunities and relief from privation due to the drought of 1881. Congress appropriated $10,000 for Chickasaw and Choctaw freedmen education for one year. The money was to go to schools maintained by the American Baptist Home Mission Society and the African Methodist Church for the maintenance of the schools, which, at that time, numbered only thirteen. This small appropriation by no means covered the expenses of those schools, and the number of schools was insufficient.[43] The money, appropriated out of the $300,000 held in trust for the tribes, was to be divided, three-fourths going to the Choctaws and one-fourth to the Chickasaws on the basis of population. Each tribe was given permission to adopt the freedmen independently; in that case, the tribe's share would be paid to the tribe; otherwise, it would go to the missionary societies.[44]

Meanwhile, the Department of the Interior continued to consider relocation of the freedmen on unoccupied lands west of the Five Civilized Tribes. Since the war, the Leased District had been considered a possible location. Now attention turned toward the Oklahoma Lands, an area in the center of the Indian Territory unoccupied by any Indian tribe. The Creek and Seminole treaties of 1866 had ceded these lands, among others, as possible homes for western Indians and freedmen.[45] In late 1880, Kansan David L. Payne and some followers tried to establish a colony in the Oklahoma Lands; Payne was arrested and taken to Fort Smith for trial.

At the May, 1881, term of the U.S. District Court for the Western District of Arkansas, Judge Isaac Parker ruled in UNITED STATES v. D.L. PAYNE that the language in the Seminole treaty of 1866 indicated particular freedmen to be located on the western lands. At the time, Parker argued, the government desired to protect the rights of former slaves of the Indian tribes, fearing that the tribes would not. The government thought that it might become necessary to settle them in a colony by themselves. It planned for that contingency in the Seminole treaty. Thus, concluded Parker,

Colored persons who were never held as slaves in the Indian country, but who may have been slaves elsewhere, are like other citizens of the United States, and hence have no more right in the Indian country than other citizens of the United States.[46]

In June of 1882 inquiries came from Congress for a report on public lands in the Indian Territory as a potential region for settling the blacks of the United States. Impetus for the inquiries came at the request of blacks of Kansas and elsewhere, who wanted a land where they could organize communities of their own. At a convention in Parsons, Kansas, they had drafted for congressional consideration a bill to allow them to settle on the Oklahoma Lands. Commissioner of Indian Affairs Hiram Price, like Judge Parker, argued that the language of the treaties of 1866 clearly indicated that only those freedmen formerly associated with the Indian tribes had rights in the territory. The treaties clearly did not refer to the freedmen of the United States. In Price's opinion, colonization schemes such as that advocated by the Kansas group should be condemned.[47]

During the summer of 1882, concerned Chickasaw freedmen sent inquiries to the Indian Office regarding their status in the Chickasaw Nation and the right of the Chickasaws to require them to buy permits to remain in the Nation. On September 16, the freedmen met in convention on Soldier's Branch in the Chickasaw Nation "to consider the better administration to their present situation and condition." With Captain Harper as president and D. M. Grayson as secretary, they resolved to make the Chickasaw Nation their permanent home and to urge a settlement of their status. They asked the Chickasaw legislature to adopt them under the seventh section of the Chickasaw constitution of August 18, 1856. Meeting with them were also some of the loyal Chickasaws, who, with the freedmen, decided to send delegations, including King Blue and Chickasaw Fletcher Frazer, to Washington in January of 1883.[48]

The Chickasaw legislature went into session on September 1, but it took no action toward adopting the freedmen. The Choctaw legislature would not convene until November 1, but there was no action anticipated because they believed that their act of 1880, expressing their willingness to adopt their blacks, had exempted them from the provisions of the appropriations act of May 17, which took funds from the Choctaws to support freedman schools. Therefore, Commissioner Hiram Price drafted a bill that he wanted Union Agent John Q. Tufts to present to the Choctaw legislature. Aimed at nullifying all legislation that had previously excluded the freedmen, the bill gave to all freedmen, formerly held in slavery and resident in the Nation at the date of the treaty at Fort Smith, and their descendants all the rights of suffrage and citizenship except a share in annuities, moneys, and the public domain. It gave all freedmen forty acres of land on the same terms as the Choctaws and Chickasaws held their land. It guaranteed the blacks all of the rights to civil and criminal processes in the national courts and guaranteed full protection of life and property. They were also given educational privileges and facilities equal to those of the Indians as far as neighborhood schools went. Finally, all blacks who elected to remove from the nations would receive $100 per capita. Those who did not elect to become citizens and did not remove would be declared intruders and would be on the same footing as citizens of the United States.[49]

The Choctaws failed to act at their regular session in 1882. The freedmen therefore continued to agitate for a settlement of the matter. In January of 1883, three freedmen and one Chickasaw went to Washington to urge adoption of the freedmen as Chickasaw citizens. In February a delegation of freedmen from the various Five Civilized Tribes went to Washington and asked to be settled in the Oklahoma country. They asked for an appropriation of $25,000 for the purpose and an allotment of 160 acres to each head of family, 80 to each single person over 21 years of age, 80 to each orphan under 21. Their request was presented to Secretary H. M. Teller, who in turn sent it to the Senate; however, the Senate failed to act.[50]

The Indian Office began to make contracts for the education of the freedmen under the act of May 17, 1882. Early in 1883, the Chickasaws protested, denying that they knew about the act or had been notified of the intent of the Indian Office to make the contracts. They asked Commissioner Price to defer action until the Chickasaw legislature met to deliberate and act.[51]

This unilateral action by the Indian Office was evidence that the government was determined to press the freedman question. It apparently moved the Choctaws to action. Chief J. F. McCurtain called a special session of the Choctaw council late in the spring of 1883 to deal with the freedman issue. He asked the blacks to send a commission to consult with the council. The result was that on May 21, the chief signed an adoption bill passed by the council. The law first declared that all persons of African descent, resident in the Choctaw Nation on the date of the Treaty of 1866, and their descendants were entitled to all rights, privileges, and annuities, including the right of suffrage, as citizens of the Choctaw Nation, except in moneys and public domain. Second, it guaranteed them equal rights of civil and criminal process in the national courts. Third, it guaranteed the protection of property; each freedman was entitled to forty acres of land to be selected and held under the same title and terms as Choctaws. Fourth, it guaranteed equal educational privileges and facilities. Fifth, it granted each freedman a $100 per capita payment. Sixth, it provided that all who refused to become citizens and did not remove from the Nation would be considered intruders. Seventh, intermarriage with a Choctaw freedman did not entitle one to citizenship, and such intermarried persons were subject to the permit laws. Finally, a freedman could hold any office of trust or profit in the Nation except principal chief or district chief. On May 22, 1883, Chief McCurtain signed a registration bill that allowed sixty days for the enrollment of the freedmen.[52] It was not, however, until March 3, 1885, that a congressional act appropriated the $52,125 Choctaw share of the balance of the $300,000.

The adoption act was not entirely popular with the Choctaw freedmen. In early May they had met at Brazil and resolved not to become citizens and asked the government to remove them. This action was no doubt instigated by J. Milton Turner, a well-known black lawyer from St. Louis, who attended the meeting. Turner, who had been involved in efforts to make the Oklahoma Lands a black colony, had good reason to persuade the freedmen that removal was the best policy. In June the Choctaw freedmen met in Red River and Towson Counties to protest being adopted by the Choctaws until they understood exactly what it meant. They wanted to remain in the Choctaw Nation but under the protection of the United States government, and they wanted to take part in the final negotiation of their status. Of particular concern to them were clauses regarding school privileges, their exclusion from certain offices, intermarriages, and the forty-acre limit on land holdings. Rather than give up their "present citizenship" with the United States and "become a partial citizen of an inferior tribe," they wanted the country divided equally among the inhabitants. They vowed not to become Choctaw citizens unless they were equal in every way.[53]

Enrollment of the Choctaw freedmen went slowly, and therefore their final adoption as Choctaw citizens was delayed for two years. The matter of taking testimony, proving citizenship, and disproving fraud was a difficult and tedious one. By summer of 1885, registration was completed in the three districts. In the first, 66 were registered as citizens, 77 were registered for removal, and 3 were doubtful cases. In the second, 1,237 were registered as citizens, 8 for removal, and 18 as doubtful cases. In the third, 1,718 were registered as citizens and 6 for removal.[54]

At its regular session that fall, the Choctaw council approved the registration, and a certified copy of the list of citizens was forwarded to the commissioner of Indian affairs. Those who registered as citizens represented some two hundred black families. A number of others wanted to register but were unable to prove citizenship; the federal government and the Choctaws agreed to give these people $150 per family and a reasonable time to remove. All of those who either were not qualified for or were refused citizenship became intruders and were to be removed by the military if necessary. There were six hundred families of these latter.[55]

Of those who qualified as citizens, about one-fifth were voters. This fact had far-reaching implications in Choctaw politics. Nevertheless, in April of 1886, Governor Edmond McCurtain issued a proclamation declaring the citizenship of all freedmen who had registered as bona-fide citizens under the registration act and instructing them to vote in all future elections as did the Choctaws by blood.[56]

During the next few years, the quality of life improved for the Choctaw freedmen. They now had access to the political process and to the judiciary of their nation. But most important, they had access to the common schools by which they could educate their youth. The Chickasaw freedmen no doubt watched with envy as they saw their Choctaw counterparts enter a new era of freedom. Whatever hopes they may have entertained for a change in their own status were not to come to fruition for over two decades, during which they endured their anomalous status of freedom without rights. During that time they were plagued by uncertainties created by the Chickasaws' wavering between ignoring the freedmen and asking the United States to remove them and United States officials' wavering between fulfilling the treaty obligations by removing the blacks and insisting that the Chickasaws provide for them. One thing was certain by 1885: the Chickasaws would not adopt the freedmen.

NOTES

1. Cyrus Harris to the President, June 8, 1868, National Archives Microfilm Publications, *Microcopy M234* (Records of the Office of Indian Affairs, Letters Received)-142: frame 454, hereafter cited as *M234*, followed by the roll number; 50 Cong., 1 Sess., *Senate Executive Document 166,* 2,

hereafter cited as *Document 166; Annual Report of the Commissioner of Indian Affairs to the Secretary of the Interior for the Year 1887* (Washington, D.C.: Government Printing Office, 1887), LX, hereafter cited as *Annual Report, 1887;* 42 Cong., 2 Sess., *House Miscellaneous Document 46,* 8, hereafter cited as *Document 46.*

2. *Document 46,* 7, 8; *Document 166,* 3, 14; *Annual Report, 1887,* LX; 54 Cong., 1 Sess., *Senate Document 182,* 110, hereafter cited as *Document 182.*

3. Holmes Colbert and G. D. James to Commissioner of Indian Affairs, received January 10, 1867, *M234* 142: frame 75.

4. Martin W. Chollar to the Freedmen of the Chickasaw Country, September, 1867, National Archives Record Group 75 (Records of the Bureau of Indian Affairs), *Letters Sent by the Choctaw and Chickasaw Agency, 1867, 1870-73,* 8.

5. Letter of Harris, January 19, 1868, National Archives Record Group 393 (Records of the United States Army Continental Commands, 1821-1920), *District of Indian Territory, Letters Received, 1867-68,* Bundle E: B90-1868; Harris to the President, June 8, 1868, *M234*-142: frame 454; N. G. Taylor to O. H. Browning, July 20, 1868, National Archives Microfilm Publications, *Microcopy M348* (Office of Indian Affairs, Report Books)-17: 378, hereafter cited as *M348,* followed by the roll number; 40 Cong., 2 Sess., *Senate Executive Document 82,* 1-4. Those signing the petition were James Squire Allen, Edmond Clarke, Jack Brown, Isaac Alexander, Henry Ro-shi-ka, Byington Colbert, Isam Love, Richard Ro-shi-ka, Caesar Nelson, Richard Stevenson, Phillip Stevens, Henry Johnson, Watson Brown, Smith Brown, John Scott, Francoisa Chake, Sampson Dick, Jack O'Dair, Squire Butler, Ben James, Mose (no surname), King Blue, Bartlett Franklin, Nathan Cochran, Jack Blue, Isanue Flint, Joshua Love, Henry Harris, Nathan Madison, Henry Crittenden, Sam Freeney, Henry Garven, Joseph Morris, Ned Shoals, Soloman Pytchlynn, Elijah Harris, and Anthony McKinney. *See also, Document 166,* 15; *Document 182,* 110.

6. *Document 46,* 9; *Document 166,* 15; *Report of the Secretary of the Interior* (Washington, D.C.: Government Printing Office, 1868), 736, 740, hereafter cited as *Annual Report, 1868;* L. N. Robinson to Charles E. Mix, September 26, 1868, *M234*-838: R349-68.

7. *Annual Report, 1868,* 736, 740; J. D. Cox to Taylor, March 16, 1869, National Archives Microfilm Publications, *Microcopy M606* (Office of the Secretary of the Interior, Letters Sent)-9: 314; Taylor to J. W. Leavenworth, March 18, 1869, National Archives Microfilm Publications, *Microcopy M21* (Office of Indian Affairs, Letters Sent)-89: 344, hereafter cited as *M21,* followed by the roll number.

8. *Document 46,* 10.

9. Mehardy Colbert, et al. to the Senate and House of Representatives, 55 Cong., 1 Sess., *Senate Document 157,* 20-21; *Document 166,* 3, 15; *Annual Report, 1887,* LXI; *Document 182,* 110; E. S. Parker to Cox, April 26, 1869, *M348*-18: 315; *Document 46,* 11.

10. Report of the Secretary of the Interior for 1869, 41 Cong., 2 Sess., *House Executive Document 1,* 3: 850-851, hereafter cited as *Annual Report, 1869;* 42 Cong., 3 Sess., *House Report 98,* 564, hereafter cited as *Report 98.*

11. *Annual Report, 1869,* 408; *Document 46,* 12, 13; Annual Report of the Secretary of the Interior, 1870, 41 Cong., 3 Sess., *House Executive Document 1,* 1: 753, hereafter cited as *Annual Report, 1870.*

12. 41 Cong., 2 Sess., *Senate Executive Document 71,* 1-3.

13. *Ibid.,* 3-4.

14. 45 Cong., 3 Sess., *Senate Report 744,* 157, hereafter cited as *Report 744.*

15. *Ibid.,* 155, 158-159.

16. *Ibid.,* 155-157, 160.

17. *Ibid.,* 160; *Annual Report, 1870,* 1: 753; *Document 166,* 15.

18. T. D. Griffith to W. P. Brown, January 21, 1871, *Letters Sent by the Choctaw and Chickasaw Agency, 1867, 1870-73; Document 46,* 13.

19. Annual Report of the Secretary of the Interior, 1871, 42 Cong., 2 Sess., *House Executive Document 1,* 5: 987; *Document 182,* 110-111.

20. *Document 46,* 14-16.

21. *Ibid.,* 1-2. This petition was drawn up in December of 1870 and was signed by several hundred freedmen, their marks witnessed by J. D. Layne, justice of the peace of Little River County, Arkansas. Blacks and Indians alike complained of Finn's efforts in 1870 to get the freedmen to sign petitions for their removal from the Choctaw and Chickasaw Nations. Some of the freedmen apparently believed that Finn was up to no good. Lemon Butler, an influential Choctaw freedman, went to Agent Olmstead, who promised to investigate and have Finn arrested, but nothing happened. *Report 98,* 462, 463, 465.

22. Annual Report of the Secretary of the Interior, 1872, 42 Cong., 3 Sess., House Executive Document 1, 5: 622.

23. *Report 98,* 461-463.

24. *Ibid.,* 581.

25. Douglas H. Cooper to H. R. Clum, January 23, 1873, and Harris to the President, January 10, 1873, *M234*-180: frames 439, 442; Clum to Columbus Delano, January 30, 1873, and February 4, 1873, *M348*-22: 234, 245; 42 Cong., 3 Sess., *House Executive Document 207,* 1-3; *Document 166,* 3, 16; *Annual Report, 1887,* LXI.

26. *The Vindicator,* August 27, 1873; *Address by P. P. Pitchlynn, Principal Chief of the Choctaw Nation and Winchester Colbert, Governor of the Chickasaw Nation to the Choctaws and Chickasaws* (Washington, D.C.: Joseph L. Pearson, 1866), 6.

27. J. D. Malin to E. P. Smith, March 7, 1874, and Albert Parsons to Smith, February 26, 1874, *M234*-181: frames 324, 453; Smith to P. P. Pitchlynn, March 30, 1874, *M21*-116: 510; Smith to Delano, March 30, 1874, *M348*-24: 239. It should be noted that in matters of education, the Choctaw freedmen fared better than their Chickasaw counterparts. A number of freedman schools were established at Scullyville and Doaksville, and the one at Boggy Depot, destroyed by fire that year, was rebuilt at federal expense. *The Vindicator,* July 24 and December 8, 1875.

28. *Report 744,* 325-333.

29. *Document 182,* 114.

30. *Report 744,* 322, 325-333; *see also* 43 Cong., 1 Sess., *Senate Miscellaneous Document 118,* 1-3 and *Document 182,* 114-115.

31. *Cherokee Advocate,* June 27, 1874.

32. *Congressional Record,* 43 Cong., 1 Sess. (May 27, 1874), 4296-4298.

33. *Document 182,* 111.

34. B. F. Overton to Ah-it-to-tubby and D. O. Fisher, January 7, 1875, Overton to the President, February 15, 1875, and G. W. Ingalls to Smith, March 12, 1875, *M234*-182: frames 144, 148, 151, 154.

35. *The Vindicator,* September 18 and 25, October 27, and November 3, 1875; *Document 166,* 3-4, 16; *Annual Report, 1887,* LXI; see also, *New York Times,* September 13, 1875.

36. *The Vindicator,* June 12, 1875.

37. *Oklahoma Star,* September 28, 1876; *The Vindicator,* September 20, 1876.

38. *Oklahoma Star,* September 28, 1876.

39. *Document 166,* 4, 16; *Constitution, and Laws of the Chickasaw Nation together with the Treaties of 1832, 1833, 1834, 1837, 1852, 1855 and 1866* (Parsons, Kans.: The Foley Railway Printing Company, 1899), 120-121, hereafter cited as *Constitution and Laws; Annual Report, 1887,* LXI; *The Vindicator,* October 18, 1876.

40. *Annual Report of the Commissioner of Indian Affairs to the Secretary of the Interior for the Year 1877* (Washington, D.C.: Government Printing Office, 1877), 111; S. W. Marston to J. Q. Smith, July 25, 1877, *M234*-868: U145-77; *Report 744,* III; *Indian Journal,* August 11, 1877.

41. *Document 166,* 4, 16; *Annual Report, 1887,* LXI; *Indian Journal,* April 10 and November 13, 1879; *Cherokee Advocate,* September 24, 1879. The Choctaw delegation consisted of E. T. Perry, S. S. Stanley, S. Williams, C. E. Harkins, and J. P. Folsom.

42. *Indian Journal,* July 5, 1883.

43. *Congressional Record,* 47 Cong., 1 Sess. (February 17, 1882), 1240; Thomas Greenwood to Commissioner of Indian Affairs, March 18, 1882, National Archives Record Group 75, *Letters Received,* 5712-82; *Document 182,* 110; *Annual Report of the Commissioner of Indian Affairs to the Secretary of the Interior for the Year 1882* (Washington, D.C.: Government Printing Office, 1882), 89.

44. *Document 166,* 4, 16; *Annual Report, 1887,* LXII; *see also Annual Report of the Commissioner of Indian Affairs to the Secretary of the Interior for the Year 1883* (Washington, D.C.: Government Printing Office, 1883), 89 (hereafter cited as *Annual Report, 1883)* and *Document 182,* 109.

45. *See* Berlin B. Chapman, "Freedmen and the Oklahoma Lands," *The Southwestern Social Science Quarterly,* 29 (September, 1948), 150-159.

46. 55 Cong., 1 Sess., *Senate Document 157,* 7-8; 47 Cong., 1 Sess., *Senate Miscellaneous Document 117,* 5, hereafter cited as *Document 117.*

47. *Document 117,* 1-5; *Cherokee Advocate,* June 30, 1882.

48. Hiram Price to Willburne Gaines, August 31, 1882, and Price to E. McClain, August 22, 1882, National Archives Record Group 75, *Letters Sent,* Civilization 164: 533, and Land 170: 518; Captain Harper to Secretary of the Interior, September 16, 1882, *Letters Received,* 23315-82.

49. Price to Tufts, October 10, 1882, *Letters Sent,* Land 170: 693.

50. *Indian Journal,* January 11 and 18, 1883; 48 Cong., 1 Sess., *Senate Executive Document 51,* 1-3; this same request was sent to Congress in January of 1884, but, as usual, there was no action on the bill. *Congressional Record,* 48 Cong., 1 Sess. (January 14, 1884), 397.

51. John E. Anderson and Jocelyn Brown to Price, March 6, 1883, *Letters Received,* 4420-83.

52. *Indian Journal,* July 5, 1883; *Document 166,* 4; *see also Annual Report, 1883,* 89.

53. *Indian Journal,* May 5 and 10, 1883; Green Gunn, et al. to Commissioner, June 9, 1883, *Letters Received,* 11488-83; 49 Cong., 1 Sess., *Senate Report 1278,* 2: 296.

54. *Indian Journal,* August 13, 1885.

55. *New York Times,* November 20, 1885.

56. *Indian Journal,* August 13, 1885, and April 15, 1886.

4

Freedman Life in the Chickasaw Nation

The coming of the railroads to the Chickasaw Nation was the beginning of great economic and social change. The Missouri, Kansas, and Texas Railroad had touched only the southeastern corner of the Nation, but the Sante Fe, completed in 1887, ran north and south through the middle of the Nation, providing shipping points for livestock and cotton. During the following decade, cotton was a significant cash crop. Shipments from Ardmore alone rose from 800 bales in the 1887-1888 season to 25,000 in the 1893-1894 season.[1] This dramatic rise came from an increase in the number of acres put into cultivation by immigrants from the states, who rented from the Chickasaws or freedmen or simply, as intruders, occupied the land. Until this great influx of foreign population, the freedmen had lived rather isolated lives among the Chickasaws.

Although at times some factions of the Chickasaw freedmen had advocated removal from the Nation, most had emotional and cultural ties to Chickasaw lands, and many had blood ties to the Chickasaw Nation. For the most part, they lived like the poorer classes of Chickasaws. During slavery, they had been a means of Chickasaw acculturation. Blacks obtained from whites had brought into the Chickasaw home cultural traits of the American slave society and of the whites as well. Missionaries had found them useful media in their efforts to Christianize the Chickasaws. After the Civil War, they had set about making a life for themselves as free people. With the onslaught of immigrants from the United States, there was a corresponding infusion into freedman society of social attitudes and practices of American blacks. Large numbers of the blacks who came to the Nation settled in the towns, but many sought out the freedman communities. Although there were some instances in which the newcomers wished to have little association with the Chickasaw freedmen, the two groups mingled

Chickasaw Nation, circa 1898

freely, often intermarrying.[2] The close association of these two groups, the startling economic changes, and the great influx of whites after 1887 brought about great changes in the life style of the Chickasaw freedmen.

For several years after the Civil War, many freedmen remained as share-croppers on the plantations of their former owners. In some areas, however, hostilities existed. Panola County, which lay between the Washita River and Island Bayou, had a large black population before the war, but after the war the blacks were forced to leave because their former masters, mostly mixed bloods, apparently threatened to kill them. In the fall of 1865, Chickasaws were allegedly so cruel that by early 1866 hardly a freed-man could be found in the county. The freedmen drifted from there into Pontotoc County in the north-central part of the Nation. By 1886 Pon-totoc County was about half black, while few blacks remained in Panola County. Indians greatly outnumbered the freedmen in Pickens County, which lay west of the Washita. In Tishomingo County, which lay between Panola and Pontotoc, there were about two-thirds more Chickasaws than freedmen. There were large settlements of freedmen at Wynnewood, on Spring Creek on the Lower Washita, at Cross Roads near Blue, and at Bur-neyville, Pauls Valley, Colbert, Stonewall, and Fort Arbuckle. Some Chick-asaw freedmen resided at Caddo, Choctaw Nation, and there was a settle-ment of them on the south bank of the Canadia River south of Sacred Heart Mission to the Potawatomis. In general, most were in the cotton country, that is, the bottoms of the Washita, Red, and Canadian rivers and their tributaries. Where they settled to themselves and farmed, they did well, but there was a tendency to "flock to villages," where, the Indians charged, they would not work, had no idea of contracts or bargains, and were given, in some cases, to stealing.[3]

Most of the freedmen made their living from the land, which varied in character in different parts of the Chickasaw Nation. The western part of the Nation was prairie land, in the center of the Nation were the Ar-buckle Mountains, and the eastern part of the Nation was hilly and heavily timbered with pine, oak, ash, hickory, pecan, and bois d'arc (osage orange). The western part was a cattle-raising region, while the eastern part was a land of small farms. The best farming lands were in the bottoms of the Red, Canadian, and Washita rivers and their tributaries.[4]

The agriculture practiced in the Chickasaw Nation was diversified. Corn was the major grain crop. Because of overproduction and an increase in the production of cotton, production of corn decreased in the last two decades of the century. The fertile Washita Valley was prime corn land. In 1866 one farmer raised 100,000 bushels on his farm. In 1890 some Washita valley farmers raised eighty bushels per acre; fifty bushels was a fair yield. A little wheat and some oats were raised. There were a few orchards, melon raising was extensive, and there were two crops of potatoes each year. Popular vegetables included cabbage, tomatoes, and sweet potatoes. The major cash crop was cotton. In prewar days, slaves produced a bale or more of excellent quality cotton per acre. After railroads came and the number of whites greatly increased in the Chickasaw Nation, Ardmore became the market center for an area that reached from Fort Sill east to the Washita and south into Texas. In the 1887-88 season, for instance, 835 bales were marketed from there, and during the next two seasons, 3,500 and 17,000 bales were marketed, while smaller towns handled from 500 to 5,000 bales each year. Livestock production included hogs, beef cattle, Angora goats, a few sheep, and a hardy horse that was a cross between American horses and Indian ponies.[5]

Everyone occupied what was known as a permit or an improvement, which he owned as long as he stayed there. No one could improve land within 444 yards of anyone else's improvements. The balance of the land was public domain. One's improvements went to his heirs, and he could sell them. Fences could be joined only by mutual consent. Freedmen could locate wherever they chose. Lemon Butler, a former Choctaw slave, testified in 1872 that the freedmen could choose their own places and improve the amount of land they thought they could cultivate without rent or share of the crop. They were, however, permitted to rent other places than the one on which they lived. Their improvements ranged from half an acre to well over one hundred. The blacks owned livestock of various kinds. Some had only a single family milk cow, and others owned large herds of cattle, some of which were probably work oxen. Few had large herds of horses or mules; most had only a team or two of work animals. Some had only a single mule or horse, which probably doubled as means of transportation and of cultivating the vegetable and corn patches. Most families raised a number of hogs, some owning herds that numbered over a hundred. Pork was a large part of the meat diet of the freedmen, and the fat was necessary for cooking. The freedmen lived in single- or double-log cabins with dirt floors and mud-and-stick chimneys; in 1891 they estimated the value of their homes from $200 to $2,000.[6]

Despite their access to the land, the freedmen were poor, and they lived with uncertainty. Droughts in 1877, 1878, and 1879 caused crops to fail

and destitution to be more widespread than usual. In early 1882 they suffered as a result of a drought during the 1881 crop season. They lacked provisions and clothing because cotton was their only large cash crop.[7]

There were other uncertainties as well, despite rapid economic progress
during the postwar years. In 1873, Agent Albert Parsons reported that they
were improving farms and accumulating property. In 1874, Commissioner
Edward P. Smith said that the freedmen were "orderly, industrious, and
eager for the education of their children, and yet are obliged to expend their
labor upon farms to which they have no title, and which once well improved
are not infrequently taken from them." That same year, It was reported that
"Many of the freedmen have doubtless made improvements on the lands
which they and their fathers occupied but not possessed."[8]

Although the freedmen occupied the land, their improvements were not
guaranteed security under the Chickasaw law. The law forbade one person to
make improvements closer to another than 444 yards or face confiscation
of his improvements and a fine. It was also unlawful to cut trees within the
same distance of a settler. This law was often ignored in relation to the freedmen. In 1880, G. W. Dallas, a teacher in the Choctaw Nation for the Baptist
Home Mission Society, wrote,

The blacks go and settle them places and the Indians, whenever they feel
disposed, will come and cut timber, clear up the land and fence in what
belongs to the black man's claim. The black man has to submit or move to
another place to be treated perhaps in the same manner.

Intermarried whites sometimes moved in and made claims on land improved
by freedmen, and the Indians often built fences through the freedmen's
fields. The blacks had no redress in the Chickasaw courts against the Chickasaws or their lessees ("boomers") because they were not citizens. However,
after the establishment of the U.S. court at Ardmore, the freedmen sometimes found themselves in court defending their right to possession against
the whites.[9]

Disputes over improvements sometimes led to violence. In 1893, for
example, deputy U.S. Marshal E. H. Scrivener was hired by Al Nelson to
fence a tract of land near Pauls Valley. Inside the fenced area was a black's
cabin, which Scrivener claimed the owners had agreed to sell. Another
cabin, also occupied by blacks, was said to belong to an Indian. Scrivener
and his men were armed with Winchester rifles as they worked near the
house of freedman Dan Jackson. Jackson's "vicious" dog allegedly "both-

ered" them, and Tom Noah, a worker, shot it. The blacks then armed themselves and shot at some of the workmen. Scrivener arrested Albert Samson
for carrying a pistol and, with Noah, whom he deputized, went in pursuit
of Ben Brown and Ben Jackson, for whom he had warrants. When Scrivener
and Noah caught up with the blacks, a gunfight ensued; Brown's and Jackson's horses were shot from under them, but they escaped. Later, someone thought to be these same blacks, hid near Tom Noah's house, trying to
kill him. Noah, who rented from Scrivener, shot at the blacks, and a warrant was sworn out for his arrest. The blacks also continued to harass
Scrivener. In February, 1894, freedman Tom Alexander was charged with
cutting Scrivener's fence.[10]

Bad blood continued between Tom Noah and the blacks. In July, 1894,
he shot and killed Alex Franklin, who allegedly threatened to kill Marshal
Scrivener, apparently over a land dispute. Noah left home and hid out because he was "afraid that the gang of negroes" who lived near him would
kill him. Said the local newspapers, "The negroes are a hard set, so we learn,
and it would be a good thing if more of them were transported to the other
shore in the same manner." Noah surrendered to Scrivener at Fort Arbuckle
the following month, claiming that he had shot Franklin in self-defense
while trying to arrest him. Noah was described as "a gentleman who stands
high as a law abiding citizen," while Franklin was described variously as "a
negro tough and desperado," "a notorious negro horse thief," and "a des-
perate and notorious thief." But there is some evidence that the "official"
story was not the whole story. It was reported that white friends of Alex
Franklin "threatened the life of Deputy Marshal Scrivener should he ever
go over in that part of the country."[11]

That fall, it was reported that King Blue, an important leader of the Chickasaw freedmen, had led a raid upon the farm of George H. Traux, a white
man and postmaster at Stonewall. The exact purpose of the raid was not
reported, but there were reports of similar kinds of harassment of Indians
and whites by blacks in the eastern part of the Chickasaw Nation. Since
land disputes were the major source of difficulties between blacks and
whites in the Nation, it is most probable that land was in question in these
cases. In 1895 a double killing over a land dispute occurred on Winters
Creek about thirteen miles east of Chickasha. It seems that Bob Carter, a
black, owned improvements that he had rented to a white man named
Estes on the condition that Estes would make further improvements in
return for use of the land. Carter claimed that Estes was not making the

improvements agreed upon, so he took a group of blacks to the property and spent a day, in Estes' absence, making improvements. That afternoon, Carter and his workers went to the house, where they found Mrs. Estes, her father, her brother, and another white man. A gunfight ensued. Carter was killed, another black was fatally wounded, and one of the whites was wounded.

The Chickasaws objected to the freedmen's opening more farms than they could cultivate and refused to issue permits to American laborers that the blacks wanted to hire. Some freedmen got around the problem by having Indians secure permits for them, and those who engaged laborers sometimes had their workers arrested by Chickasaw officials. In 1885, the Chickasaws made a move to require freedmen from the states who had married Chickasaw freedwomen to purchase permits. There were even threats that the freedmen themselves would be required to obtain permits to remain in the Nation.[12]

Some freedmen did not work the land and pursued other means of livelihood. A few were mechanics. Some had trades, and others hired out as laborers at competent wages. Simon Love of Pickens County, besides owning a good fenced farm, over one hundred head of cattle, and ten to fifteen horses, had a ferry boat that operated across the Red River. After the towns sprang up and the noncitizen population rapidly increased, blacks who cast their lots with the towns found work as waiters and porters in depots, business establishments, hotels, barber shops, and laundries; as laborers in cotton gins and compresses; as construction workers; and as barbers, lunch-stand operators, boardinghouse and restaurant owners, saloon keepers, and dance-hall owners. Others were laundresses, charwomen, and prostitutes. Many blacks in the western part of the Chickasaw Nation worked as cowhands for Chickasaw or white ranchers who ran large herds on the fine grasslands. Many blacks were every bit the range-seasoned cowboys that their Chickasaw or white counterparts were. They were tough, and like most men on the frontier, resorted to firearms to settle their disputes. In 1884, at a large spring roundup on Rock Creek near White Bead Hill, the crew was made up of blacks and whites. Charles Stevenson became involved in a dispute with the white roundup boss. Both men drew their pistols, Stevenson firing first. Others got into the gunfight so that it was soon a shootout between whites and blacks, a dozen or more joining each side. When the fight was over and the smoke cleared, Stevenson was the only cowboy injured. While most blacks in

Singing Waiters, Park Hotel at Sulphur, Chickasaw Nation, circa 1900. Courtesy of Photograph Archives, Division of Library Resources, Oklahoma Historical Society.

the cattle industry worked as ranch or roundup hands as Stevenson did, a few maintained ranches of their own.[13]

In many ways the freedmen's life style was not much different from that of others on the frontier. Shortly after the war, for instance, they fell victim to attacks and harassment by Indians from the west, particularly the Comanches. Although there were some instances of wealth, for the most part their existence was poverty ridden and isolated. Travel was impossible when water was high because there were few bridges or ferries. There were no improved highways, and what roads existed turned to mud in wet weather. They had little protection against contagious diseases such as cholera and smallpox. Hydrophobia was common. They suffered as well from diseases such as asthma and dysentery. There were few physicians for them, fewer still for those who resided outside the towns. Thus, they relied on herbal medicine. Dog fennel, butterfly root, and life-everlasting were boiled and made into a syrup for treatment of colds, pneumonia, and pleurisy. Pursley weed (squirrel physic) was boiled into a syrup for chills and fever. Snakeroot was steeped for a long time and mixed with whiskey for chills and fever. Balmony and queen's delight were boiled for "blood medicine." For hydrophobia, the mad stone was applied. Oil springs, thought to have curative value in the treatment of rheumatism, were located on the lower Washita, and chalybeate springs, thought to have medicinal value, were found elsewhere in the Nation.[14]

Diseases that could not be explained were sometimes thought to result from voodoo magic or witchcraft. In 1891, Henderson Carter, a Choctaw freedman, killed his brother because he said that his brother and a voodoo doctor had twice tried to give him medicine against his will for the purpose of putting him under a spell. Carter became ill and died while he was in jail. Before he died, he attributed his illness to "voodoo charms" used against him by his dead brother. In 1895, Louisiana Fisher, a black woman, was murdered by an Indian in the Choctaw Nation while she was gathering snakeroot for medicine. It was generally believed by both Indians and blacks in the community that she was a witch, and murder had been attempted on her at least once before. Belief in such practices was also common in the Chickasaw Nation. Native doctors, who were thought to have magical powers, still practiced, and medicine dances were held as late as the mid-1890s. There was also apparently a widespread belief in witchcraft, a trial regarding the practice taking place in the Chickasaw Nation in 1888.[15]

Diet was simple. The freedmen raised a variety of vegetables, but corn was a staple. They ate all sorts of Indian dishes made from it. *Ta^n fula* (commonly called "Tom Fuller") was boiled corn that had been pounded in a wooden mortar. *Ta^n fula hawushko* was fermented hominy that was eaten as a soup. Sometimes hickory-nut meats were added to it. *Pishofa* was pounded corn that was cooked, then mixed with pieces of fresh pork or beef, and cooked once more. "Tom-budha" was green corn cooked with fresh meat and seasoned with tongue grass or pepper grass. *Paluska* (corn bread) and *Paluska hawushko* (sour bread) were common dishes. Ash cakes (*Paluska holbi*) were dough rolled in corn shucks or cabbage leaves and put in hot ashes to bake. The cakes were sometimes sweetened with molasses. Other dishes included *bunaha* (boiled corn bread with beans) and *walakshih* dumplings flavored with wild grapes). Like the rest of the population, the freedmen supplemented their diet by hunting. In 1879, the freedmen stated that they used to get most of their meat from the woods but that lately, because game population had declined, they had not averaged a deer or turkey apiece in a year. However, they continued to take small game such as passenger pigeons, oppossums, racoons, and squirrels. They took fish from the streams. Near the end of the territorial period, they sometimes found themselves in trouble with the law for obtaining fish through the old Indian method of poisoning the streams, which had been outlawed. In the woods, they gathered and dried wild berries and grapes and took honey from colonies of wild bees.[16]

Most holidays observed by the freedmen were apparently adopted from the whites. In 1872, for instance, they celebrated the Fourth of July by holding a barbecue that was attended by blacks, whites, and Indians. In 1877, missionary teacher G. W. Dallas reported that Thanksgiving was new to the freedmen.[17]

There is no evidence that during the Reconstruction the Chickasaw freedmen observed Emancipation Day, as did the other blacks of the Indian tribes. Throughout the last quarter of the nineteenth century, Cherokee, Creek, and Seminole freedmen faithfully observed August 4 as Emancipation Day. Why that date was chosen is uncertain; it was neither the date of President Lincoln's proclamation nor the signing, ratification, or proclamation of the treaties with the tribes in 1866. In the 1890s, after the influx of a large number of black noncitizens into the Chickasaw Nation. Emancipation Day was observed in the Nation on June 19. The celebrations were heavily attended. In 1895, for instance, blacks from Ardmore,

Berwyn, and adjoining neighborhoods met six miles north of Ardmore, and in 1896 they met in Roff's pasture near Ardmore. The people began to gather about ten in the morning, and by eleven the shady groves on the meeting ground were filled with people, visiting and playing games. About half past one in the afternoon, the meal was served. The main course was the beef that had been slowly barbecuing for several hours. After lunch, oratory was in order. After the welcome address, various speakers, white and black, mounted the speaker's stand. Local businessmen, physicians, preachers, and teachers were the main speakers. The common theme of the speeches was the advancement of the race. In 1896, for example, a rousing speech was given by Professor T. S. E. Brown, the black teacher of the subscription school for blacks in Ardmore. With his speech punctuated by cheers, he told his listeners that the Caucasians had had over 1,800 years to put themselves where they were while the freedmen had had only thirty. He told them about many black men who had attained a high level of education and had become wealthy, and, pointing at his black listeners, concluded, "You've made no mean record in these 30 years."[18]

The freedmen's forms of entertainment were greatly influenced by the presence of large numbers of blacks from the United States and were like those forms common on the frontier. There were dances, picnics, barbecues, and public gatherings at which the people were harangued by local orators. In the 1890s, when the baseball craze hit the Indian Territory, black teams were formed in towns like Burneyville and Ardmore and drew crowds at their matched games. There was also musical entertainment. In 1892, for instance, Ardmore boasted of having the "only colored band" in the Indian Territory.[19]

After the coming of the railroads, traveling shows such as Terry's Big Uncle Tom's Cabin Tent Show with "colored-jubilee singing," Mahara's Colored Minstrels, the Nashville Students, and the Georgia Minstrels drew crowds in the railroad towns such as Purcell and Ardmore. For weeks before the coming of the stage groups, newspaper advertisements announced their appearance at the local opera house. On the day of the show, the troupe held a street parade or a brief musical concert on the street in order to draw crowds for the night's performance. Anyone who did not have the admission price could get a brief, and no doubt tantalizing, view of what he was missing. Sometimes, huge crowds gathered and followed the parading troupe through the streets. On stage, the all-black Nashville Students entertained the crowds with their solos, duets, quartets, dances, impersonations, and comic routines. The crowds were amazed by the men's quartet's imitation of a calliope, Al Watt's stick dancing and old man character routine, Smith and Johnson's banjo song and dance routine, Ida Lee Wright's serpentine dance, John Stewart's slack-wire performance, and P. W. Lowery's coronet solos. It was said of James White, the comedian, that if a white man had possessed his ability, he would have been ranked a star in the minstrel world.[20]

The Nashville Students were alleged to be rivaled only by the all-black Richards and Pringle's Georgia Ministrels. When Billy Kersands performed his "local hits," he was unintelligible to the whites in the audience and applauded loudly by the blacks. In 1896, the Ministrels played to a crowd of about 200 blacks in Ardmore. The audience liked the show, but the local white editor complained about the "sameness about all negro minstrel shows." He concluded that "people are by them like some folks are about the circus, they always go to take the children, they don't care anything about seeing them, but then the little folks like them."[21]

There were, as well as these nationally known groups, itinerant companies that set up tents at various points in the Chickasaw Nation. These carnivals often employed blacks and sometimes had as their purpose the fleecing of the frontier people. There were instances, too, in which black itinerant showmen were run out of town.[22]

The railroads also made it possible for circuses to play the squalid little railroad towns of the Chickasaw Nation. When the circus cars arrived, town and country folk gathered in large numbers and crowded the streets to watch the parade and the crews set up the tents. That was the only show those without the admission fee would see, but what a sight unfolded before the eyes of those who got inside the tent! In 1893, for instance, Sells and Renfrow's Monster Museum and Three Ring Circus dazzled the railroad townspeople with its fine lady riders, aerialists, gymnasts, acrobats, bicyclists, knights in arms, ladies dressed as princesses, male and female jockeys, and "open dens of savage brutes": elephants, lions, tigers, hyenas, bears, wolves, leopards, and panthers. In the tents the people watched William Dutton perform forward and backward somersaults on the back of a running horse. They watched Charles Watson, the "greatest six horse rider in the world." An added thrill for the entire town was a grand balloon race and a double parachute jump by Misses Annie Bell Holton and Lillie Rice. In 1894, the Howe and Cushing circus with its "freaks and curiosities" filled its tents. The crowds were thrilled by Miss Blanche Reed, the bareback rider; the McCree Brothers, the acrobats; and Miss Agna Barrington, the "strongest woman in the world." In 1895, the Paris Hippodrome visited Ardmore. The crowd watched as the Martell family performed their antics on bicycles. Francis Reed, the child bareback rider, turned somersaults on the back of a beautiful snow-white horse. Minnetti, the "iron-jawed lady," hung by her teeth from a leather strap. In the air, trapeze artists Harry King and Paul Devene and Lorenze and Lotta performed their daring feats, while the Livingston family did their acrobatics. And Theodore Baretta, the clown, made the people laugh.[23]

Churchgoing became widespread among the Chickasaw freedmen and served as a social outlet. As slaves, the blacks had been very responsive to the teachings of missionaries in the Chickasaw country in the 1840s and 1850s. During that time, the slaves attended church with the Indians. After the Civil War, the freedmen usually did not attend Indian churches, although they were permitted to do so if they wished. However, their children were forbidden to attend the Indian Sabbath schools. The blacks could form their own churches and hold their own Sabbath schools, but most attended churches organized by white missionaries. In the Sabbath schools, missionaries taught the freedmen to spell and read, gave Bible narrations, and taught singing. Some settlements had freedman preachers who preached regularly at their little churches. Despite the missionaries' efforts, in 1878 the Reverend G. W. Dallas, a black Baptist missionary, reported on the freedmen: "They are not heathens, and yet they are substantially without religion." In the late 1870s and early 1880s mission societies received financial aid from the U.S. government and became quite active in freedman education. However, the aid was withdrawn, and after the missionary presence declined, the blacks lamented the lack of anyone to preach the gospel to them.[24]

In isolated communities where the freedmen had no preachers, they carried on the best way they could and, if descriptions of services among the Choctaw freedmen can be accepted as a parallel, they made innovations of their own in church services. In good weather they gathered for their Sabbath or midweek prayer meetings. If the deacon was present, he read out two lines of a hymn, and the people sang them and continued the process until the hymn was finished. If the deacon was absent, an elder would ask someone to "line out" or "raise" a hymn that "the old folks" could sing. If the one who started the hymn could not carry on, someone else could pick it up at the end of two lines and "line it out"

for the rest. If anyone who could read was present, a lesson was read
from the Bible. Next, the people went "down to pray," asking God to
"come this-a-way" to "walk in, and take a front seat." Some prayers
were repetitious, and some were chanted. If someone got the floor to
say "a few remarks" and talked too long for the people's taste, someone
started a hymn to bring him down. If that did not work, one of the congregation might simply tell him to shut up and sit down. At the end of
the service, they sang another hymn and went home. At the Sabbath
service, the deacon "lifted the collection." In this part of the service
the deacon announced how much was needed, and the people brought
their offerings forward and placed them on the pulpit or a nearby stand.
From time to time the deacon announced how much had been collected.
Meanwhile, the people sang, the song punctuated now and then by the
deacon's announcements and joyous shouts of members of the congregation. Sometimes the services turned into what the freedmen called
"feelin' meetin's," with people shouting and sometimes falling into
swoons. Sometimes the freedmen did not understand church structure
and claimed to be elders or other officials without having the sanction
of the church.[25]

As the number of noncitizen blacks increased in the 1890s, the number of black churches multiplied, mainly in the towns. Baptists and Methodists were the most commonly represented sects, both groups having a
church in towns like Ardmore. During the 1890s, A. R. Norris and H. Y.
Hunt served as pastors of Ardmore's AME Church, and Felix Jones served
as pastor of the black Baptist Church, which, in 1895, claimed 160 members. These two churches were the setting for a number of revivals. In
1893, "Sin Killer" Griffin, of Bonham, Texas, held an extended revival
and organized a charitable organization aimed at self-help. In 1894 Felix
Jones, of Texarkana, who styled himself the "Black" Sam Jones after
the well-known evangelist, held a successful revival. The Baptists liked
Jones so well that they made him pastor of their church. Under his direction and influence the people built a new church building in 1895. Revivals were not only religious affairs but social ones as well. Benefit socials,
suppers, and picnics as well as baptisms in the local millpond or some
local stream were also important social affairs related to the church.[26]

Affairs were not always harmonious in the black churches. Despite
Felix Jones's popularity among the black Baptists of Ardmore, he had

his problems. In 1895 he testified in federal court against Curley Eubanks, who ran a gambling house and saloon in east Ardmore. Curley's
wife subsequently left him, and he blamed Jones. He apparently spread
rumors that Jones had been dispensing his affections among the women
in his church and swore vengeance against Jones. He stuck a pistol in
his belt and went to Jones's boardinghouse and called him out to talk.
But Jones was apparently aware of Eubanks' intent. He took the pistol
away from Eubanks and whipped him with it, for which action he was
promptly hauled before the local U.S. commissioner and fined. The dea-
cons of the church came to Jones's defense, published a statement exon-
erating him of any wrongdoing with the sisters of the church, and branded
Eubanks as the ringleader of a "dirty gang" and owner of "dives" and
"hell holes."[27]

    The black Baptists in the Chickasaw Nation seemed less responsible to
any regional Baptist Association than members of other sects were to their
administrative organizations. They were congregationalists in the most
literal sense of the word. Dissatisfaction in church affairs often led to a
breakaway faction setting up its own church. Members of the New Hope
Missionary Baptist Church, established in 1893 in Chickasha, became embroiled in a controversy in 1895, and a faction broke away, solicited contributions from the local populace, built a small building, called it Mount
Eagle, and placed it under the leadership of William Stephen. New Hope
deacon and exhorter M. T. Jackson went to press with a statement that
New Hope was the "only true colored church" in Chickasha. Despite
this assertion, the church felt it necessary to advertise its "good singing"
and the preaching of the Reverend H. F. Fields to entice people to attend. The Mount Eagle Church countered with an entertainment consisting of singing, an old-folks concert, comic acting, an old slavery sermon,
declamations, and ice cream and cake. The local newspaper editor advised
the factions to "read their Bibles, cultivate a spirit of meekness and for-
giveness and be one church and stop trying to follow the example of their
white brethren in dividing churches."[28]

    The controversy between these Baptist factions in Chickasha was not
a violent one. But because the church was a basic social outlet in the black
communities, personal conflicts arose at church-related activities and sometimes ended in violence. "Disturbing a religious worship" was a common
charge brought against blacks from various parts of the Nation. In the

opinion of the federal judge at Paris, Texas, many such disturbances occurred because the preachers were men who were incapable of leading services.[29]

Missionaries who came to the freedmen were often shocked at what they observed in the freedmen's domestic affairs. For instance, polygamy was common among the Indians before the war and was practiced by some of the freedmen after the war. The government had prohibited it among the freedmen after the war, and in 1876, the Chickasaw legislature passed laws against its practice by Chickasaw citizens. In 1878, Dallas reported that "a very large portion of them live without wedlock, and the older people are extremely reluctant to receive any notions of its necessity." For the freedmen, marriages were difficult to legalize. Because they were not Chickasaw citizens, they could not obtain marriage licenses. In some cases the ministers who married couples maintained records of the ceremonies.[30]

Intermarriage with Chickasaws was rare. As the freedman delegates to Washington said in 1884,

There may be a few of such cases, but as a general rule, we of African descent do not intermarry with Chickasaws; we intermarry amongst ourselves, and we do not wish to be either forced or induced by any custom, law or power to abandon our social habits of life and fall into new ways.

If a freedman married a Chickasaw, however, he became a citizen and could sue or be sued in the courts. The Chickasaws recognized few such cases. In the special census taken by the United States in 1890, in the category of the Chickasaws were listed 122 "Negro Chickasaws" and nine "Mulatto Chickasaws." The tribal custom that status was determined by the status of the mother prevailed. If the mother was Chickasaw and the father black, the offspring were considered Chickasaws. Still, the Chickasaws claimed to have "preserved their blood pure and uncontaminated" by the African strain, the degree of purity being at least as high "as in any other southern community." The blacks had been their slaves and were regarded as former slaves were regarded in the South, except that, according to the Chickasaws, they had been treated better. While the Chickasaws would not go so far as to say that there had been no marriages between them and the blacks, they insisted that a "practical unanimity" of sentiment was against it. Those who ignored the custom were socially ostracized. Their marriages were not considered legal, and their children were considered illegitimate.[31]

While it was generally claimed that the Chickasaws were racially pure, miscegenation was apparently common and probably widespread. There were notable instances of intermixing that even the casual observer could not ignore. Charles Cohee, a prominent leader of the freedmen in the 1890s, was of mixed blood. He was born in 1858 the son of Charles Cohee, Sr., a free man, part Chickasaw and part African, who had come west with the Chickasaws in 1837. His wife, Mary, too, was supposedly mixed African and Chickasaw. Charles Sr., who lived on the Blue River, supposedly looked like an Indian and always attended the council of the Chickasaws on the Blue and at Post Oak Grove, where he acted as an interpreter. He had long, "quite strait" hair. His mother was supposedly part Chickasaw, and his grandfather was understood to be James Colbert, a Chickasaw leader in Mississippi, whose daughter Lydia was Cohee's mother. The freedmen descendants of Lanie Stevenson claimed that she, also, was the daughter of James Colbert. Her sons Dick and Joe Stevenson were born about 1829 and son Dave was born in 1857. They were slaves of Holmes Colbert. From these sons came a large number of freedman descendants. There were other similar cases.[32]

In the first decade of the twentieth century there were many freedman claimants to Chickasaw blood. In 1906, for instance, Harriet Spears swore that she was five-eighths Chickasaw, her father being one-half and her mother three-quarters blood. Bettie Ligon alleged that she was the daughter of Bob Love, a Chickasaw, and a "mixed breed slave woman named Margaret Ann Wilson." Jesse McGee, a Chickasaw, lived as common-law husband to Dora McGee and was the father of her nine children. In 1907 two thousand persons claimed to have Indian blood. Granted, these claims were made in an effort to obtain a greater share in the wealth of the Chickasaw Nation, which was then being dissolved. But most of them no doubt had merit. Racial intermixture was apparently the basis of social distinctions among the freedmen. Some of the mixed-blood freedmen, who as a rule spoke Choctaw, would not associate with the others.[33]

For the most part the Chickasaw freedmen spoke English. In 1878, it was reported that all of the estimated 2,300 Chickasaw freedmen could speak the language. Bilingualism was common among the blacks during slavery times, but the extent of it in later years is unknown. Slaves who

had been purchased from the whites apparently picked up the Indian
language rather quickly. In Mississippi, missionaries had used blacks as
interpreters of their messages. While in the West instances of their use as
interpreters were rare, they did exist. Charles Cohee, Sr., for example,
who removed with the Chickasaws in 1837, interpreted in Chickasaw
councils. In late 1866, Jack Blue acted as interpreter for U.S. commissioners who traveled through the Chickasaw Nation. In 1871, the loyal
Chickasaws had as their interpreter a freedman named King.[34]

The freedmen were socially segregated from the Chickasaws. In 1872,
freedman Lemon Butler testified that in general the Indians remained
separate from them and refused to put the blacks on a level of equality.
Some would eat and drink with the blacks, but others would not. According to Butler, the full bloods did not make as much distinction between
themselves and the freedmen and would sleep with them, he supposed, if
they would allow it. The mixed bloods, however, would not associate with
them. Likewise, the full bloods made good neighbors, but the mixed bloods
did not. The Indians thought the freedmen a "very excitable people,"
who were "governed by passion and temper" and who fought "a good deal
among themselves." Social segregation, of course, was not absolute. Mixed
crowds were common at public gatherings and entertainment events. The
number of Afro-Chickasaw mixed bloods indicates that Chickasaw men at
least had liaisons with the black community. Indians frequented the "dives"
in the black sections of the towns; in outlying areas, violence between
blacks and Indians sometimes erupted as a result of personal feuds.[35]

The Choctaws and Chickasaws had few difficulties with the freedmen,
but that was not the case with blacks from the United States. It was mainly toward this latter group that racial violence was directed. Most of the
white noncitizens in the Chickasaw Nation were from the Southern states
and brought with them their old biases. Confederate veterans' organizations were active in Ardmore and other towns. In "Little Dixie," as the
region later would be called, racial prejudice against blacks ran high among
the white population. When crimes were committed, blacks were "naturally"
suspected; blacks seen doing anything "unusual" were often arrested on
"suspicion." If blacks could not convince local whites that they had business in the area, they were asked to leave town. Fistfights were common on
the streets of the towns. If the fight was between two blacks, a crowd
gathered to enjoy the spectacle and to cheer the fighters on. When the com-
batants were white and black, tensions ran high, and the conflict threatened

to spread to the onlookers. Blacks in the southern part of the Chickasaw
Nation frequently had their religious services disturbed by whites. The crime
was so common that in 1894 the judge of the United States court at Paris,
Texas, called attention to it and said, "It is an outrage to decency for a
man to disturb negro congregations." In 1891, a crowd of drunken white
men burned a black church east of Colbert and fired their Winchesters into
the cabin of Aaron Hogan, wounding five of the occupants, one of whom,
a young girl, died later. Three men were arrested and charged at the court
in Paris with assault and murder.[36]

The white noncitizens wanted the blacks to remain "in their place."
If whites taunted blacks and they fought back, the whites became enraged.
A "proper respect" toward whites was expected of blacks. In 1895, for
instance, Simon Brown and his wife Joe were arrested at Center and fined
ten dollars for "cursing and otherwise abusing some white ladies." In November of that year some "ladies" were taking a Sunday stroll in Pauls
Valley when a black man and three women companions came along in a
carriage. Because the "ladies" did not get out of the road quickly enough,
he drove his team upon them and narrowly missed hitting them. That evening a number of Pauls Valley men took the black to the outskirts of town
and flogged him. They warned him and the women he was with and others
to leave town. To emphasize the message, that night the men rode through
the black section of Pauls Valley and fired shots into the house occupied
by the blacks. Said the editor of the *Pauls Valley Enterprise*,

There are some people this community can spare, and these negroes were
of that order. There was a rumor that an attempt would be made to drive
all the negroes out, but we have a large quota of true southrons in our
midst, and who know the darkies as a race, more thoroughly than any
other people, and they are too fair minded to endorse so extreme a measure.

In Ardmore that same year, Sam Smith received the approval of the local
newspaper editor when he pummeled a black who had addressed him too
familiarly with "Hello, Sam." In 1896, William Binks, a black barber at
Ardmore, was fined $300 and sentenced to six months in jail for disturb-
ing the peace and using "obscene and defamatory language" about some
local officials and the "white ladies of the city." And in late April, 1897,
a masked vigilance committee warned all blacks to leave Davis. Two

months later, it was reported that as a result of the warning not a black
man remained in the town.[37]

The noncitizen whites in the Chickasaw Nation watched the development of neighboring Oklahoma Territory with concern. By the mid-1890s
it was obvious that statehood was in the future of the Indian Territory.
The question was whether the two territories would become a single state.
In the Choctaw Nation, there was much support for separate statehood,
mainly because of racial attitudes. Great numbers of blacks had migrated
to Oklahoma from the Southern states and elsewhere. Some blacks had
been elected to political office, and it appeared for a number of years
that the territorial legislature might reject the idea of segregated schools.
Newspaper editors in the Chickasaw Nation spoke out against single statehood because of the school issue and set the goal "of making a glorious
white man's state out of the Indian Territory, free from the contaminating
influences of social equality of negro and white children in the public
schools." When the national Anti-Lynch League spoke out for protection
for black men, the editors demanded protection for white women. Black
men did attack and rape white women in the Chickasaw Nation.[38] It is
interesting to note, however, that despite the rhetoric and the intense
racial prejudice, lynch law did not prevail. Although the rope was spoken
of in some cases, there were no lynchings. Suspects were routinely taken
to the U.S. court at Paris to be tried for crimes that, in Texas, probably
would have been punished by a mob. The reason was, no doubt, that
criminal acts in the Chickasaw Nation were under federal jurisdiction.

Also, despite the rhetoric concerning racial purity, there were more
social and sexual liaisons between the races than the white editors wished
to admit. Black prostitutes were no doubt frequented by men of all races
in towns such as Ardmore. Such liaisons were more acceptable than those
between white women and black men, but those, too, existed in the Chickasaw Nation. Early in 1895, a white prostitute called "Widow" Bessen
outraged white Ardmoreites by seeking her patrons among the blacks.
She was warned to leave town by a "committee of citizens" but failed to
do so. On February 26, the "committee" attacked her house, ripping
off the windows, doors, porch, and part of the outside walls. They did
not have to enter the house; demolition of the outside achieved their
desired end. At about the same time, J. T. Brown, a black, was charged
in Ardmore with adultry with Rosa Davis, a white woman. Miss Davis,
aged 17, testified that she had been held against her will at Brown's house

for several weeks, where she had had sexual intercourse with several men. She said that she had escaped once but had been brought back. As testimony proceeded, however, it became apparent that Miss Davis had willingly remained with Brown. She had accompanied Brown to a picnic held by the local blacks and had met a young white schoolteacher whom she had known in Arkansas and whose later testimony confirmed that she was willingly cohabiting with Brown. In March of 1896, a young white woman attracted considerable attention in Gainsville, Texas, when she stepped off a train from the Chickasaw Nation and was joined by a black man who had ridden in the same train but in the Jim Crow car. They spent the night in a local black boardinghouse and tavern and the following day boarded separate coaches for Colbert. A few days later they returned and took the train north to Ardmore. Rumors circulated that they had been recently married in Kansas, and while she was in Gainsville, the woman told the curious citizens that she taught an Indian school near Ardmore and that the man taught a black school near Berwyn, apparently Dawes Academy.[39] Such instances were viewed by the whites in the Chickasaw Nation as dangerous examples. And their reactions to such situations threatened to cause their racial hatred to spill over to the Chickasaw freedmen.

In general, the whites considered the Territory-raised blacks "well behaved." Still, they opposed social equality for them, even with the Chickasaws. In the 1890s, editors attacked what they considered the Dawes Commission's attempts to establish "an equality of rights" between the Chickasaws and their freedmen and to establish "an exclusive Indian State" on the lands of the Five Civilized Tribes. Such attempts would "play smash with things" in the Chickasaw country. The editor of the *Chickasha Express* wrote in 1895:

It is a pity that such tom foolery has to be endured, but just so long as we have an eastern man at the head of the government who insists on putting 'Down Easters' on such important commissions we can expect nothing else. Give us a western man for president next time, who will put practical men in such places and the Indian question will soon be disposed of.[40]

It was no wonder that the whites became concerned when outsiders—either white or black—agitated among the Chickasaw freedmen. The incident of the black teacher and the white woman must have increased suspicions regarding activities at the Dawes Academy, near Berwyn. The school, established by the Chickasaw freedmen in the 1880s, was taught in 1895 mainly by "northern ladies" who, according to the whites, sowed "the seeds of equality . . . among the young people" and fostered it among the older ones. So the blacks in the neighborhood became "sassy," especially those from the states. Racial tensions, which had been rising for some time, flared at Christmas, 1895. On Christmas day, a black named Veal, allegedly drunk, came to the Berwyn post office and became embroiled in an argument with the postmaster. The postmaster threw him out of the post office, and Veal went about the street trying to buy a gun and cursing the postmaster. The latter, meanwhile, had gotten his own pistol and followed Veal into the street, where he pistol-whipped him. All was quiet that night, but the next day three blacks came to town, armed with hickory clubs, which they used on the first white man they met, Kin Hardy. Whites rushed to Hardy's rescue, and more blacks appeared on the scene, shooting as they came. After a battle with clubs and guns, the blacks retreated. A number of people were wounded, among them one black who had shot himself in the leg when he tried to pull his pistol from his pocket as he ran. All other shots, however, missed their marks. Ed Colbert, the local Indian policeman, and other citizens disarmed all of the blacks who remained in town, and whites who lived near Berwyn armed themselves with Winchesters and went to town for the night. For several days the whites were unnerved as they awaited a new attack from the blacks, voting to fight back and "to submit no longer to the impudence and insults of the negroes." The blacks gathered at Dawes Academy for an "indignation meeting." After a few days, tensions eased, and no arrests were made. The editor of the *Daily Ardmoreite* believed that the skirmish would furnish "campaign literature" for the republican press from Kansas to Maine: "They can now harp about the oppressed negro being subject to mobocracy at the hands of the whites of the south. Let them rave but negro impudence will not be tolerated just the same."[41]

Throughout the nineteenth century, the Chickasaw freedmen lived without civil rights in the Chickasaw Nation. In the Chickasaws' eyes, the freedmen were technically intruders because the Chickasaws never adopted them. The fourth article of the Treaty of 1866 had guaranteed that the laws would be equal in their operation upon the Chickasaws and freedmen and that no distinction would be made at any time regarding the blacks. In 1884, the freedmen acknowledged that the Chickasaws had treated them with

kindness and had protected them from injury. Nor could they complain
that any special laws had been made affecting them differently or unequal-
ly. However, because the Chickasaws refused to pass any laws to adopt
them, the freedmen could not enjoy an equality of the laws that existed.
They could not bring suit, nor could they be sued. However, they were
sworn as witnesses and testified in criminal cases. Freedmen could not
vote, nor did many try for fear of offending the Chickasaws. However,
there were exceptions. A family named Newberry apparently voted. They
were the sons of Caldonia Newberry, who was alleged to be the daughter
of Chickasaw "Ben Love and a mixed breed woman." When the Newberrys
went to the polls at Rock Springs in the Chickasaw election of 1890, their
right to vote was challenged. But Frank Colbert, a relative of Ben Love,
told the election judges that the Newberrys were descendants of Love,
and they were allowed to vote.[42]

After 1866, the Chickasaws assumed that they had judicial jurisdiction
over the freedmen until the two-year period had expired, at which time
the blacks would either become citizens or be removed. Fortunately, at
that time there were few serious crimes. But when one occurred, the complexity of the matter of jurisdiction became apparent. A good example
was the case of Robert H. Love, a Chickasaw who was serving as deputy
U.S. marshal. In February of 1868, Love went to the home of Philip
Kirby (alias Wilson), a Chickasaw freedman who was accused of having
murdered another freedman, Leonard Willis. Kirby ran when Love attempted to arrest him, and the marshal shot him. Assuming they had
jurisdiction, the Chickasaws tried and acquitted Love. But on June 2,
Love was arrested, taken before the U.S. commissioner at Van Buren,
Arkansas, and held for trial in the Crawford County, Arkansas, jail.
He was still in custody in March of 1869, when petitions from a
number of prominent Chickasaws and Arkansans asked for his release.
The Chickasaws recognized the vagueness of the question of jurisdiction. In this particular instance, at least, they considered the freedmen members of the Nation *"according to domicile"* because they
lived in the Chickasaw Nation without permits. Because they had not
been rejected by the Chickasaw Nation, they were not citizens of the
United States; yet because they had not been adopted, they were not
citizens of the Nation but were subject to its laws. Therefore, the Chickasaws argued that their courts had jurisdiction until the status of the
freedmen was settled.[43]

Because the Chickasaws failed to adopt the freedmen within the two
years prescribed by the Treaty of 1866, the Chickasaws thereafter had
no redress under Chickasaw laws against blacks who committed crimes
in the Chickasaw country because they placed the freedmen on the same
footing as noncitizen whites. They never tried them in local courts. When
a freedman committed an offense, he was taken before the federal district court at Fort Smith, Arkansas, no matter how petty the offense.
Many were allegedly arrested on the slightest pretext. Sometimes freedmen were apparently sent to Fort Smith on trumped-up charges and
were relieved of their property. In 1872, it was alleged that as soon as
a freedman got a good horse, charges were made that he had introduced
whiskey into the territory. He was arrested and taken to Fort Smith
and came back afoot. Much of the problem resulted from the fact that
the marshals were not on salary but collected fees according to the number of prisoners they captured and brought in. Armed with open sub-
poenas for witnesses, they traveled through the territory, camping out-
of-doors and keeping their prisoners shackled and under guard.[44]

Before the coming of the railroads, much of the crime in the Chickasaw Nation was related to the whiskey trade. Whiskey dealers from the
Chickasaw and Seminole Nations went to Denison and other northern
Texas towns and followed various trails back through the Chickasaw
country to their home territory. Outlaw gangs stole horses and drove
them to Texas, where they exchanged them for whiskey, which they
consumed or carried back to the Indian Territory to be sold at high
prices. Among the gangs of whiskey runners who operated in the Chickasaw Nation were some black gangs. Calvin James led such a gang in
the mid-1880s. In August of 1885, he, Toney Love, Henry Robey, and
Albert Kemp went from the Washita River to Thompson's Crossing on
the Red River to buy whiskey. They left the Texas whiskey shop with
a load, but Love never reached home. Along the way, James killed him,
took his money and whiskey, hid his body, unsaddled his horse, and
turned it loose. The three then continued to their haunts and began
peddling the whiskey. Love's horse found its way home, and suspicion of
foul play fell on Love's three companions. They were captured near
Cherokee Town by freedmen Wash Taylor and Andrew Colbert, and
they were held under guard at the home of Peter Love, Toney's father.
Kemp and Robey finally confessed, putting the blame on James. The
body was reclaimed and the remains taken to Peter Love, who con-

tinued to feed the prisoners and treat them kindly until they were turned
over to Indian Policeman Jeff Carter, who took them to the U.S. marshal at Caddo. Kemp and Robey turned state's evidence when James
was tried before Judge Isaac Parker in Fort Smith. James was convicted
and was hanged on July 23, 1886.[45]

One of the most notorious outlaw gangs of the 1880s was the Dick
Glass gang, a group of black horse thieves and whiskey runners who had
their center of operations on the Canadian River in the western part of
the Seminole Nation and the eastern part of the Potawatomi lands. This
gang specialized in stealing horses from the Potawatomis and Seminoles
and driving them through the Chickasaw Nation to the Arbuckle Mountains
and from there to Texas, where they were sold. In the spring of 1885,
the Glass gang fell on hard times. Because Glass carried a reward of $500
on his head, he was a special object of attention for lawmen. In February,
Chickasaw policemen killed a black desperado at White Bead Hill, and
reports went out that Glass was dead. But Glass was later seen and reported
to have visited his mother in the Creek Nation. A few weeks later two
Texas lawmen, John A. Culp and Rush Meadows, came upon Glass in the
Arbuckle Mountains. When Culp ordered him to raise his hands, Glass
went for his pistol, and the officers shot him from his horse. Glass was
wearing a breastplate that protected him from the bullets. The officers,
however, assumed that they had killed him, and when they approached
him, he shot them and made his escape. A posse was organized, but pursuit was useless, for Glass knew the country very well and apparently had
friends who gave him assistance. During the next few weeks there were
various reports of the death of Glass, but people who knew the gang said
that Glass's own men started the rumors to deceive lawmen.[46]

Time, however, was running short for Glass. Several of his cohorts had
been killed or captured by Seminole and other authorities during the early
months of 1885. In June, his time came. On June 5, Indian Policeman
Robert Murray of Colbert, Chickasaw Nation, telegraphed Indian police
headquarters at the agency in Muskogee that Glass and three companions
had passed through Colbert on their way to Denison, Texas, with a herd
of ponies to trade for whiskey. Sam Sixkiller, captain of the Indian Police,
went by train to Colbert and there organized a posse consisting of policemen Murray, Frank Gooden, and Charles Leflore and C. M. McClellan,
a well-known cattleman of the Cherokee Nation who was in Colbert buy-
ing cattle for his ranch. The posse rode out to Post Oak Grove that night

and sent out a black spy to locate the camp of the Glass gang. The spy found them about five miles south of Emmet. Before daylight on June 7, the lawmen broke camp and hid in the brush along the trail near the gang's camp. When the gang came into sight, Richmond Carolina was driving a wagon loaded with forty gallons of whiskey, and Jim Johnson, Sam Carolina, and Glass were walking behind the wagon, the load evidently too heavy for the tender-shouldered ponies to pull. Sixkiller and his officers stepped into the trail and demanded that the blacks throw up their hands. Glass pulled his pistol, and Sixkiller gave him a shotgun blast in the head and one in the chest, killing him instantly. Jim Johnson was also shot down. Richmond Carolina whipped up the team, but as he went by Leflore and McClellan, they shot him. He fell back into the wagon, apparently dead. Sam Carolina ran for about half a mile before the officers captured him. When they got back to the scene of the shooting, they found that Richmond Carolina had been only slightly wounded, had unhitched the team, taken Glass's Winchester, and escaped. Leflore chased him about five miles and captured him. Glass and Johnson were buried at Colbert, and the Carolina brothers were taken to Muskogee and then to Fort Smith for trial.[47]

Blacks in the Chickasaw Nation were often the object of the U.S. marshals' attention. Sometimes the marshals found themselves outsmarted and overmatched. In 1880, for example, Marshal Willard Ayers was shot and killed by a black at Cherokee Town. Ayers had gone to arrest him for larceny, and when he presented the warrant, the black said that he would go peacefully if Ayers would let him get dressed. He got a six-shooter instead of his clothes and shot the marshal through the head. In 1889, a marshal named Childers and the black man he was attempting to arrest were killed in a shoot-out at Purcell. And in the early 1890s, Israel Childs had a reputation as a desperado in the Chickasaw Nation who had often stood the marshals off. Black fugitives were often killed by marshals. Most of the time, however, they were brought in alive to stand trial, charged with crimes such as cattle rustling, horse stealing, arson, forgery, counterfeiting, introducing whiskey into the territory, and violent acts. When the federal court was established at Ardmore, U.S. commissioners' courts were established at Pauls Valley and other towns. Some cases were dealt with in these courts; others were remanded to the Ardmore court. Near the end of the century, municipal courts were established in the towns. Blacks made frequent appearances before these courts, charged with carrying weapons, disturbing the peace, assault, malicious mischief, cutting wire fences, introducing whiskey, murder, vagrancy, and drunkenness. Blacks who were brought before the local courts were sometimes defended by local white attorneys. The guilty were sometimes fined, sometimes sentenced to the federal prison at Columbus, Ohio, and sometimes, if convicted of capital crimes, hanged.[48] Those convicted of violating municipal laws were fined or put to work on the streets.

While blacks were often the violators of the law, some served as law-enforcement officers in the Chickasaw Nation. For instance, in 1878 Sam Bucher, who had been acting as a posseman, was found dead near Johnson, Chickasaw Nation, having been shot several times. Frank Russell of Davis served as deputy under the constable there. One of the best known marshals in the Indian Territory was Bass Reeves, a former slave from Arkansas. In the mid-1880s his beat was the Creek, Seminole, and Chickasaw Nations. Reeves was a lawman in the Indian Territory for nearly thirty years, and he built a reputation for "getting his man," black, white, or Indian, dead or alive. In 1901, Jack Walters was a deputy U.S. marshal who worked out of the Ardmore court. According to a local newspaper, he had been "appointed especially to look after the wild negroes on Wild Horse" Creek. He sometimes ran into prejudice in doing his job. In the summer of 1901, Charles and Robert McGee shot and killed Wiley Shelton near Pauls Valley. Walters organized a posse and captured Robert McGee. When the U.S. commissioner at Pauls Valley remanded McGee to the custody of the court at Ardmore, Walters and his prisoner were met at the depot in Pauls Valley by a white heckler, who said that a white man should not be placed in the custody of a black. Walters, who resented the abuse, placed the man under arrest at gunpoint. Some of the leading white citizens of Pauls Valley had a warrant sworn for Walters' arrest on the charge of disturbing the peace. Walters was fined $10 and released. Later, at a town meeting, these same citizens drafted resolutions of protest against the hiring of blacks as marshals and asked that Walters be fired. However, the marshal in charge of the district refused to do so. Jack Walters went on doing his work. Only a few days later he collected a $25 reward for capturing Arch Wheeler, a Texas horse thief; the capture was called by the local press "a clever piece of work."[49]

Black lawmen were a common enough sight in the Chickasaw Nation so that confidence men pretended to be lawmen to do their work. In 1895, for instance, Woodford Lawrence was jailed at Ardmore for impersonating a deputy U.S. marshal. What his object was is uncertain. But that of A. W. White was clear. That same year, White went among the blacks in the Ran

community, claiming to be a detective sent to investigate the recent killing of an Indian by an officer. After he had completed his investigation,
he began to arrange contracts with the blacks regarding the land they held.
Many of the blacks in that community were from Alabama, and he demanded a five-dollar fee from each under the threat of exposing them as
intruders and having them expelled from the Chickasaw Nation. He created
so much excitement that word of his activities reached the authorities,
who arrested him for impersonating an officer.[50]

Blacks in the Chickasaw Nation were the victims and perpetrators of
the kinds of violence that characterized the raw western towns and country-
side. Shootings and knifings were frequent. The violence was sometimes
the result of disputes over gambling at "coon-can" or craps, love triangles,
matrimonial difficulties, and disputes between neighbors. Crimes were
often violent because of the prevalence of deadly weapons in the Indian
Territory. Although it was illegal to carry arms, most men and some wom-
en did. Sometimes they sported their weapons too boldly about town or
at public gatherings and were arrested and fined, and sometimes they
killed themselves when their weapons discharged by accident. Shootings
became more common among blacks with the growth of the railroad
towns. The black sections of towns such as Ardmore and Purcell had their
gambling establishments, billiard rooms, dance halls, bawdy houses, and
saloons. These places were often the scene of fights, knifings, and shootings. Some establishments, such as those of Curly Eubanks in Ardmore,
became well known to law enforcers. Gambling and the sale of whiskey
were illegal, and the local law-enforcement officials regularly raided the
"dives," making arrests and confiscating evidence. Now and then, too, a
fit of morality seized the towns; and bawdy houses, honky-tonks, and
dance halls were raided. Many of the blacks who committed crimes in
the Chickasaw Nation had come to the territory from the states. Black
criminals also hid out in the Chickasaw Nation. Law-enforcement officers
cooperated with those from the United States who came to take fugitives
to their home states for trial.[51]

Much of the violence that characterized the frontier was the result of
ignorance, from which most of the inhabitants suffered. Because the freedmen were not adopted by the Chickasaws, what educational opportunities
they had were at first limited to what they themselves could afford. During Reconstruction, they were anxious to have schools and offered to furnish buildings if by some other means the teachers and books could be

obtained for them. In 1874, Commissioner Edward P. Smith said that
they wanted education: "Their children grow up in ignorance, in sight
of schoolhouses which they may not enter." Their only relief came in
the 1870s and early 1880s when the United States supported missionary
educational efforts among the freedmen. With that exception, said
representatives of the freedmen in 1894, they had "been absolutely with
no greater advantages for their children than if they were living in the very
heart of the 'Dark Continent.' "[52] Because the freedmen realized the importance of education in their attempts to win their place in the Chickasaw
Nation, what little opportunity they had to send their children to school
was highly prized. Their struggle against ignorance is presented in detail
in a subsequent chapter.

In 1894, the Bureau of the Census published the following statement
about the Five Civilized Tribes:

Much of their progress is due to a large negro population in the several
nations. The great portion of these negroes were at one time slaves, and
they are now the laborers of the Five Tribes. They are fairly well advanced
and are steadily increasing in numbers, wealth, and intelligence.

Much of what this report said did not apply to the Chickasaw freedmen.
Four years earlier, Indian Agent Leo E. Bennett had written of them:
"They are poor, deplorably ignorant, and are buffetted around from pillar
to post, abused, degraded, debased and denied. No home, no country, no
schools, it is not possible for them to be lower in the moral scale."[53] His
view was the more accurate one. Despite the racism, the poverty, and the
deprivation of their civil rights, the Chickasaw freedmen always regarded
the Chickasaw Nation as their home and constantly resisted attempts to
effect their removal. In 1894 representatives of the freedmen expressed
their desire to remain in the land of their birth, among the people "whose
language, customs, and habits" they understood and felt familiar with
and whose friendship they desired and esteemed.[54] This statement came
after nearly thirty years of fruitless struggle to secure title to the lands
on which they had built their homes.

NOTES

1. *Daily Ardmoreite,* November 20, 1893.
2. *Ibid.,* June 15, 1894.

3. 42 Cong., 3 Sess., *House Report 98,* 461, 564, hereafter cited as *Report 98;* Memorial of the Chickasaw Freedmen, April 19, 1886, and R. L. Owen to J. D. C. Atkins, November 14, 1887, National Archives Record Group 48 (Records of the Office of the Secretary of the Interior), Indian Territory Division, *Chickasaw Freedmen,* Box 392 (60b): 13488-86, 30634-87; "Report of the Board of Indian Commissioners to the Secretary of the Interior for the President, for the Year 1870," *Chronicles of Oklahoma,* 5 (March, 1927), 91; John Laracy, O. S. B., "Sacred Heart Mission and Abbey," *Chronicles of Oklahoma,* 5 (June, 1927), 237.

4. U.S. Census Office, *The Five Civilized Tribes in Indian Territory: The Cherokee, Chickasaw, Choctaw, Creek, and Seminole Nations* (Washington, D.C.: U.S. Census Printing Office, 1894), 7, hereafter cited as *Five Civilized Tribes;* Annual Report of the Secretary of the Interior, 1870, 41 Cong., 3 Sess., *House Executive Document 1,* 4: 757, hereafter cited as *Annual Report, 1870.*

5. *Report of the Secretary of the Interior* (Washington, D.C.: Government Printing Office, 1869), 3: 849-850, hereafter cited as *Annual Report, 1869; Five Civilized Tribes,* 54.

6. 49 Cong., 1 Sess., *Senate Report 1278,* 2: 277-278, hereafter cited as *Report 1278; Report 98,* 46, 738-739; National Archives Record Group 75 (Records of the Bureau of Indian Affairs), *Rolls of Choctaw Freedmen, 1885;* E. McCain, Jr., to Office of Indian Affairs, May 29, 1879, National Archives Microfilm Publications, *Microcopy M234* (Office of Indian Affairs, Letters Received)-872: M1204-79, hereafter cited as *M234,* followed by the roll number; Hiram Price to Willburne Gaines, August 31, 1882, National Archives Record Group 75, *Letters Sent,* Civilization 164: 533; Leo E. Bennett to Commissioner, February 12, 1890, and H. C. Kemp to Secretary, May 25, 1891, National Archives Record Group 75, *Letters Received,* 4845-90, 20063-91; Love Miller to Secretary, August 1, 1903, National Archives Record Group 48 (Records of the Department of the Interior, Office of the Secretary), Indian Territory Division, *Choctaw and Chickasaw Freedmen,* Box 384: 6793-03; Frank Russell (interview), December 26, 1937, Amanda Kimball (interview), June 26, 1937, and R. L. Nichols (interview), December 22, 1937, *Indian-Pioneer History* (Indian Archives Division, Oklahoma Historical Society), 43: 161, 53: 232, 102: 420; Laracy, 245.

7. Linden Davis, Squire Wolf, Isaac Kemp to Carl Schurz, January 16, 1880, *M234*-873: D80-80; Thomas Greenwood to Commissioner, March 18, 1882, *Letters Received,* 5712-82; S. W. Marston to J. Q. Smith, October 5, 1877, and Marston to A. Bell, December 7, 1877, *M234*-868: U232-77, U312-77.

8. 54 Cong., 1 Sess., *Senate Document 182,* 111.

9. *Constitution, and Laws of the Chickasaw Nation, together with the Treaties of 1832, 1833, 1834, 1837, 1852, 1855 and 1866* (Parsons, Kans.: The Foley Railway Printing Company, 1899), 55-56, hereafter cited as *Constitution and Laws*; G. W. Dallas to Commissioner, January 12, 1880, *M234*-873: D74-80; Hiram Price to E. E. McCain, February 11, 1884, *Letters Sent,* Land 121-122: 68; Owen to Atkins, November 14, 1887, *Chickasaw Freedmen,* Box 392(60b): 30634-87; Bennett to Commissioner, February 12, 1890, *Letters Received,* 4845-90; *Chickasaw Enterprise,* November 18, 1893.

10. *Chickasaw Enterprise,* December 23, 1893, January 11 and February 1, 1894.

11. *Ibid.,* July 26 and August 2, 9, and 30, 1894; *Daily Ardmoreite,* August 28 and September 1, 1894.

12. *Chickasaw Enterprise,* September 27, 1894; *Chickasha Express,* April 4, 1895; Tufts to Commissioner, February 6, 1885, Abram Eastman to Atkins, February 13, 1886, and J. W. Hall to Secretary, March 22, 1885, *Chickasaw Freedmen,* Box 392(60b): 2780-85, 5321-86, 6714-85; William M. Cravens to John W. Noble, July 14, 1891, *Letters Received,* 33676-91; Price to McCain, August 22, 1882, *Letters Sent,* Land 146: 274, 170: 518.

13. Parsons to E. P. Smith, October 15, 1873, *M234*-180: P492-73; *Annual Report, 1869,* 3: 850; John P. Lawton to S. S. Cutting, June 6, 1879, *M234*-871: C609-79; *Chickasaw Enterprise,* October 4, 1894, May 16 and December 12, 1901, February 19, 1903; *Daily Ardmoreite,* June 25, July 5, and November 1, 1894, February 18, May 13, June 30, July 7, September 22, October 23, and December 13, 1895, and June 19, 1896; *Indian Journal,* May 22, 1884; Russell, 43: 161; Neil R. Johnson, *The Chickasaw Rancher* (Stillwater, Okla.: Redlands Press, 1961), 38-40, 49, 52, 53, 57, 65.

14. Letter of Cyrus Harris, January 19, 1868, National Archives Record Group 393 (Records of the United States Army Continental Commands, 1821-1920), *District of Indian Territory, Letters Received, 1867-68,* Bundle E, B90-1868; Johnson, 66-69; Kimball, 53: 238; Owen to Atkins, November 14, 1887, *Chickasaw Freedmen,* Box 392(60b): 30634-87; *Five Civilized Tribes,* 51; A. W. Alexander to Archibald McKennon, March 13, 1899, and J. E. Bailey to Dawes Commission, September 29, 1898, Indian Archives Division, *Dawes Commission–Chickasaw;* Statement of Polly Colbert and Statement of Kiziah Love, *The American Slave: A Composite Autobiography,* ed. George P. Rawick (Westport, Conn.: Greenwood Press, 1972), 7: 36, 193; *Annual Report, 1870,* 4: 755; *Chickasaw Enterprise,* March 1, 1894; *Daily Ardmoreite,* November 20, 1893.

15. *Muskogee Phoenix,* December 10 and 17, 1891; *Daily Ardmoreite,* August 25, September 4, October 14, and November 21, 1895; Indian

Archives Microfilm Publications, *Records of the Chickasaw Nation,* CKN 16 (Minute Book of the District Court: Chickasaw Volume 23), 14, 190-209, hereafter cited as *CKN 16.*

16. Muriel H. Wright, "American Indian Corn Dishes," *Chronicles of Oklahoma,* 36 (Summer, 1958), 159-161; Lawton to Cutting, February 16, 1879, *M234*-871: C189-79; Statement of Polly Colbert and Statement of Kiziah Love, *The American Slave,* 7: 34-35, 194; Angie Debo, *The Rise and Fall of the Choctaw Republic,* new ed. (Norman: University of Oklahoma Press, 1967), 112; Johnson, 49; Kimball, 53: 222, 233, 234; *Chickasaw Enterprise,* November 20, 1902; *Daily Ardmoreite,* August 26, 1895.

17. *Report 98,* 461; Marston to Bell, December 7, 1877, *M234*-868: U312-77.

18. *Cherokee Advocate,* September 9, 1876; *Daily Ardmoreite,* June 20, 1895, and June 19, 22, and 23, 1896.

19. *Indian Journal,* April 4, 1889; *Daily Ardmoreite,* August 25, 1894, and August 5, 1895; *Muskogee Phoenix,* March 10, 1892.

20. *Chickasaw Enterprise,* October 11, 1894; *Daily Ardmoreite,* January 18, 19, and 26, and October 3 and 11, 1894, March 13, 14, 15 and 20, 1895, and March 2 and 3, 1896.

21. *Daily Ardmoreite,* January 8 and 10, 1896.

22. *Ibid.,* August 2, 1894; *Chickasaw Enterprise,* August 28 and October 2, 1902.

23. *Chickasha Express,* December 1, 1893; *Daily Ardmoreite,* April 24, 1894, and October 14, 1895.

24. *Report 98,* 462, 466, 598; Dallas to Marston, February 2, 1877, *M234*-867: *M234*-77; Kemp to Secretary, May 25, 1891, *Letters Received,* 20063-91; Adge Stephenson to Tams Bixby, July 5, 1899, and W. L. Bennett to Dawes Commission, February 15, 1899, *Dawes Commission—Chickasaw;* Cutting to E. A. Hayt, August 2, 1878, *M234*-869: C490-78; Fred Humphries to Secretary of the Interior, May 31, 1886, *Letters Received,* 14871-86.

25. Robert Elliott Flickinger, *The Choctaw Freedmen* (Fonda, Iowa: Journal and Times Press, 1914), 125-130, 115-116, 118.

26. *Daily Ardmoreite,* November 10, 1893, January 3, April 23, and August 30, 1894, March 11, June 16, and July 26, 1895, February 25, 1896.

27. *Ibid.,* May 13, 1895.

28. *Chickasha Express,* April 18 and 25, 1895, August 1, 1895, September 5, 1895.

29. *Muskogee Phoenix,* March 20, 1890; *Daily Ardmoreite,* December 17, 1894; *Alliance Courier,* March 8, 1894.

30. Cutting to Hayt, August 2, 1878, *M234*-869: C490-78; Humphries to Secretary, May 31, 1886, *Letters Received,* 14871-86; Russell, 43: 164; *Constitution and Laws,* 104.

31. 59 Cong., 2 Sess., *Senate Document 257,* 40, 50-51, 72-75, hereafter cited as *Document 257;* 59 Cong., 2 Sess., *Senate Document 298,* 11-12.

32. Memorial of the Freedmen of the Chickasaw Nation, National Archives Record Group 75, *Letters Received Relating to Choctaw and Other Freedmen, 1878-84,* 13113-84; *Report 1278,* 2: 279; *Five Civilized Tribes,* 5; Charles H. Burke to Wilburn Cartwright, April 9, 1928, with enclosures, National Archives Record Group 75, *Central Classified Files,* 95003-1922 Chickasaw 053; 59 Cong., 2 Sess., *Senate Report 5013,* 1: 378, 383, and 2: 1516; Mary Eastman to Dawes Commission, September 19, 1898, and Ed Abram to Bixby, January 9, 1900, *Dawes Commission–Chickasaw.*

33. Petition of Harriet Spears, February 22, 1906, *Letters Received,* 64844-06; 59 Cong., 2 Sess., *Senate Report 5013,* 1: 487, 495; R. H. McDuffie to Dawes Commission, December 21, 1899, J. M. McDonald to Dawes Commission, January 3 and 16, 1900, *Dawes Commission–Chickasaw; Reports of the Department of the Interior for the Fiscal Year Ended June 30, 1907* (Washington, D.C.: Government Printing Office, 1907), 107; *Report 98,* 466.

34. 45 Cong., 2 Sess., *House Report 95,* 4; *Report 98,* 466; Ethan Allen Hitchcock, *A Traveler in Indian Territory: The Journal of Ethan Allen Hitchcock, Late Major-General in the United States Army,* ed. Grant Foreman (Cedar Rapids, Iowa: The Torch Press, 1930), 201-202; Burke to Cartwright, April 9, 1928, with enclosures, *Central Classified Files,* 95003-1922 Chickasaw 053; G. W. Harkins to Major Griffith, June 6, 1871, *M234*-179: G188-71.

35. *Report 98,* 463, 465-466, 564; *Daily Ardmoreite,* December 2, 1893, August 25, and 27, 1895.

36. *Daily Ardmoreite,* February 16, March 26, April 8, 1894, and August 6, 1895; *Alliance Courier,* March 8, 1894; *Muskogee Phoenix,* April 23 and May 28, 1891.

37. *Daily Ardmoreite,* August 2, 1894, August 8 and 16 and November 22, 1895, and May 12 and 18, 1896; *Edmond Sun-Democrat,* April 30, 1897; *El Reno News,* April 30, 1897; *Stillwater Gazette,* June 24, 1897.

38. *Daily Ardmoreite,* March 31, July 20, August 18, and September 3, 1894, May 18, 1896.

39. *Ibid.,* May 17, June 24 and 25, 1894, February 27, March 6, August 9, 12, and 13, 1895, March 31, April 2 and 5, 1896.

40. *Chickasha Express,* January 10, 1895.

41. *Daily Ardmoreite,* December 27 and 29, 1895.

42. Memorial of the Freedmen of the Chickasaw Nation, *Letters Received Relating to Choctaw and Other Freedmen, 1878-84,* 13113-84; *Report 1278,* 2: 277-78; 54 Cong., 1 Sess., *Senate Document 182,* 111; *CKN 16,* 77; *Document 257,* 105.

43. Harris to Luther C. White, July 22, 1868, White to Harris, July 29, 1868, Harris to N. G. Taylor, August 12, 1868, John N. B. Latrobe to Charles E. Mix, August 27, 1868, *M234*-142: frames 581, 590, 580, 686; Petition to Andrew Johnson, December 1, 1868, and Holmes Colbert and Colbert Carter to U.S. Grant, March 31, 1869, *M234*-178: frames 106ff, and 103; W. T. Otto to Commissioner of Indian Affairs, September 1, 1868, National Archives Microfilm Publications, *Microcopy M606* (Office of the Secretary of the Interior, Letters Sent)-9: 187.

44. *Report 98,* 581, 466, 467; *Report 1278,* 2: 279; *Indian Champion,* July 5, 1884.

45. *Indian Journal,* August 27, 1885; Glenn Shirley, *Law West of Fort Smith: Frontier Justice in the Indian Territory, 1834-1896* (New York: Collier Books, 1957), 145.

46. *Indian Journal,* February 9 and April 2, 14, 16, and 23, 1885.

47. *Ibid.,* June 11, 1885.

48. *Ibid.,* August 19, 1880; *Muskogee Phoenix,* June 6, 1889, March 26, 1891, December 15, 1892, and October 5, 1893; *Daily Ardmoreite,* December 1, 14, and 29, 1893, January 3, 12, 22, 24, February 6, 10, 19, 27 May 8, 21, August 20, 23, 27, 28, September 3, 25, October 19, 1894, January 17, February 18, March 16, May 23, August 20, 22, 25, November 7, December 11, 1895, June 9, 22, 29, 1896; *Chickasha Express,* January 12, 1894; *The Vindicator,* October 2, 1875; *Indian Champion,* June 28, August 16 and 30, 1884; *Chickasaw Enterprise,* November 18, 1893, January 11, March 15, August 9, and November 8, 1894, August 22 and September 12, 26, and 19, 1901, October 3, 1901, January 20 and 23, March 6, April 12, and July 31, 1902.

49. *Atoka Independent,* March 29, 1878; Russell, 43: 163-164; *Indian Journal;* October 22, 1885; Daniel F. Littlefield, Jr., and Lonnie E. Underhill, "Negro Marshals in Indian Territory," *Journal of Negro History,* 54 (April, 1971), 77-87; Nudie E. Williams, "Bass Reeves: Lawman in the Western Ozarks," *Negro History Bulletin,* 42 (April-June, 1979), 37-39; *Chickasaw Enterprise,* July 18 and 25, 1901. All of Walters' efforts in capturing Robert McGee were in vain; he was acquitted of the charge of muder in 1902.

50. *Daily Ardmoreite,* June 4 and 19, 1885.

51. *Chickasaw Enterprise,* July 26, August 2, 9, and 30, 1894, September 12 and 19, 1901, February 13, May 15, July 31, September 18,

and December 4, 1902; *Alliance Courier,* March 8, 1894; *Daily Ardmore-ite,* December 2, 1893, January 17, February 16, March 6, June 24 and 25, August 28, September 3, October 12 and 18, and December 28, 1894, February 22, March 6, April 2 and 13, May 13 and 31, June 4, 12, and 20, July 7, August 5, September 10, and October 21 and 24, 1895, and February 6 and June 16, 1896; *Indian Journal,* September 30, 1880, July 14, 1887, April 4, 1889; *Muskogee Phoenix,* December 20, 1880, September 10, 1891, September 14, 1893.

52. 54 Cong., 1 Sess., *Senate Document 182,* 110, 111.

53. *Five Civilized Tribes,* 7; Bennett to Commissioner, February 12, 1890, *Letters Received,* 4845-90.

54. 54 Cong., 1 Sess., *Senate Document 182,* 122.

5

Struggle against Ignorance

Of all the rights of which the Chickasaw freedmen were deprived, access to educational facilities was perhaps the most important. Since the Chickasaws did not recognize the blacks as citizens, they were denied access to the few neighborhood schools provided for Chickasaw children. Government assistance was at best minimal and badly handled, and it was too short-lived to be effective. Except in isolated communities, where missionaries maintained schools on limited budgets, the blacks received no formal schooling, and as the decades passed, their ignorance became more costly to them. They could do little on their own to change their economic or legal status or to acquire education. More importantly, their ignorance and illiteracy made their struggle for rights in the Chickasaw Nation more difficult.

What little education the freedmen obtained came through meager efforts of the United States government undertaken in 1873. In 1871 and 1872, despite their limited means, some Chickasaw freedmen in Pickens County got up two "subscription schools," hiring teachers for one year at their own expense. That such paltry efforts could not meet the educational needs of the hundreds of children in the Nation was recognized in 1873 by Choctaw and Chickasaw Agent Albert Parsons, who inquired in Washington about the possibility of the government's supplying two teachers. When Commissioner of Indian Affairs Edward P. Smith visited the Chickasaw country that summer, he tentatively promised teachers if the freedmen could provide furnished school buildings. The leading freedmen, anxiously desiring schools, promised their labor and what money they could give. There were a few mechanics among them, but they had little money to spare.[1]

Parsons proposed the establishment of a school at Fort Arbuckle, in the central part of the Nation, which had been abandoned by the army

in 1870. The surrounding area was densely enough populated by freedmen to support two teachers. It was a healthy location, the buildings
were good, and the grounds were pleasant. Parsons suggested that the
United States ask Dr. John C. Lowrie of the Presbyterian Board of Foreign
Missions to supply two teachers, preferably a husband and wife. Assuming that the government would adopt his plan, Parsons notified the freedmen and set about raising funds and having the men make seats and
benches. He mistakenly thought the noncitizen whites in some districts
might be persuaded to help in order to have schools for their children.
About two hundred freedmen met and agreed to do all they could to
prepare the buildings. They could not, however, supply funds for teachers
and books. Those living near Fort Arbuckle planned to prepare a boarding school to accommodate 150 scholars. They were anxious and expectant,
for Parsons had encouraged them: "I have told them that in one year many
of them who are now partially educated will have completed their education sufficiently to teach neighborhood schools." That way, freedmen of
all ages could be educated.[2]

Commissioner Smith liked Parsons' suggestions, which he explained to
the War Department and to Dr. Lowrie of the Presbyterian Board, whom
he asked to supply teachers. Parsons was to see if the Chickasaws, who
owned the abandoned buildings, would permit their use and, if so, to
purchase them, at a reasonable price, for the government. Believing that
he could get the "somewhat dilapidated" buildings for about one-tenth
of their cost, Parsons attended the public auction of the property at
Tishomingo in mid-December. He learned that the buildings were in worse
shape than he had thought because in the absence of a caretaker, nearly
all of the windows and doors were gone and some buildings had been removed entirely by whites and Indians. Therefore, Parsons did not bid very
high, thinking it would be better to build anew than to buy the remaining
buildings and repair them. Another bid came from Thomas Grant, a white
man who had married a Chickasaw; he claimed the ground on which the
building sat, and he had opened a store in the old sutler's buildings. A
school at Fort Arbuckle would increase his business. Grant proposed to
Parsons that if the buildings became his, he would allow their use, the
government would repair them and relinquish them and their improvements after five years. Parsons liked the proposal because the Chickasaw
law was indefinite on the subject of the sale and conveyance of the buildings, making it unlikely that the government would get a clear title. On
his return to the agency at Boggy Depot, Parsons learned that Dr. Lowrie

had four teachers ready to go to Arbuckle. While they awaited facilities, the freedmen inquired when the schools would come.[3]

The Presbyterian Board of Foreign Missions would nominate teachers, whose salaries of $800 a year would be paid by the Indian Department. Parsons was to notify the Board when the buildings were ready and how many teachers would be needed. Commissioner Smith wrote to Dr. Lowrie:

These children of the freedmen are in a peculiar relation to the Indian Service and it is very desirable that their schools should be conducted as to excite emulation if possible among the Indians and to awaken new interests in educational matters. From the experience of your Board in furnishing teachers for similar schools in the South you will undoubtedly be able to select a corps of educators who will accomplish this result.

The matter was placed in the hands of the Reverend A. C. McClelland of Pittsburgh, Pennsylvania, secretary of the Freedmen's Committee of the Presbyterian Church. Meanwhile, in early January, 1874, Parsons and a carpenter went to Fort Arbuckle to make repairs, get school furniture, and obtain as long a lease as possible. Parsons found the buildings even more dilapidated than he had thought. The mantels, windows, and doors were missing, and the floors were partly carried away. Nevertheless, he leased from Grant—for five years, or longer if necessary—several of the buildings, the square with its wells, a nearby spring, and a small plot of land south of the grounds. Grant was to have the buildings and improvements when the lease expired, and his business, which was primarily with the freedmen, was expected to increase.[4]

Parsons selected the officers' quarters on the south side of the square and the four acres of land that had formerly been gardens. The buildings were fifty by twenty feet, with piazzas on both sides running the length of the buildings. One was converted to living quarters for the teachers and two others to classrooms. The former soldiers' quarters, twenty-five by one-hundred-fifty feet, became a boardinghouse for the children. Because of the extensive repairs and the distance from building materials, the work would take at least two months, and with the little remaining of the $1,000 he had been sent for the repairs, Parsons would put a large cooking stove in the boardinghouse. He also planned to fence the grounds and the garden plot behind the officers' quarters and to put in enough desks for ninety students. "If we have good teachers," he said, "we will do a work here that will tell many years hence."[5]

Parsons' hopes for an early start soon faded. He wanted two women and one man for teachers. Although the Reverend McClelland made inquiries in February, 1874, about such matters as the teachers' transportation expenses to the Chickasaw country and within the country to gather pupils for the school, he received no reply until late July. Meanwhile, the Presbyterian Board and the freedmen waited. McClelland wanted to open the school about September 1, and he insisted on husband and wife teachers, who he believed could work "at greater advantage" than a single man and two women. He wanted the school to succeed

not only for its effect on the freedmen but also by way of example and stimulus upon the Indians for improving the management of their educational work. The negroes can be carried along more rapidly than Indians, and it is to be hoped that the school can be made of great use in awakening a new interest in education and procuring new methods in place of the indifference and inefficiency now prevailing.

It was not until early October that McClelland made his nominations: the Reverend Taylor F. Ealy, who was also a physician, his wife Mary E., and Miss Amanda C. Painter. The Ealys would receive a combined salary of $1,700; Miss Painter would receive $800 a year. The three started for Fort Arbuckle without confirmation of their appointments, arriving there about October 20. They found the buildings in good repair, but no arrangements had been made for housekeeping. They set about making preparations, and while they were at work, a number of the freedmen came to see them. They were soon well acquainted, and the school opened on October 28.[6]

The enthusiasm with which the teachers began waned as the months passed. The agent failed to visit them as they had expected. The teachers received no pay, despite their complaints, until mid-March, 1875. By that time they were in financial difficulties because they had expected to be paid quarterly. George W. Ingalls, appointed in 1874 as agent of the consolidated Union Agency for the Five Civilized Tribes, claimed to have received no appointment notices on the teachers.[7]

No sooner had this problem been solved than another developed. Soon after arriving at Fort Arbuckle, Amanda Painter had married a Dr. Caldwell without consulting the Board. The Caldwells had claimed and used half of the teachers' quarters and grounds and "in many ways" made it "very uncomfortable" for the Ealys. Because the Committee for Missions to the Freedmen was responsible for the "character and efficiency" of the school, the Board decided to replace her and nominated Mrs. Lizzie D. Scott. Ingalls was again behind time and found during a visit to Fort Arbuckle that Mrs. Scott never entered service but was replaced by Miss Rebecca E. Forbes.[8]

School opened for the new year on August 30, 1875, with an appropriation of $2,500. Those funds went for teachers' salaries, while the government supplied Webster's elementary spellers, first, second, and third readers, practical arithmetics, geographies, histories, and supplies.[9]

Bureaucratic problems in communication continued to hamper the teachers' efforts. Miss Forbes' appointment papers were lost, the Ealys did not receive all of the pay due them in 1875, and Miss Forbes, who had begun work on September 1, 1875, had received no salary by early March, 1876. Ealy had made her a personal loan, and he and his wife had gone into debt at Grant's store. They were without personal funds and, more important without funds to conduct the school properly. They did not hear from the agent for months. Agent Ingalls had had the money for months, but he was in Boston. When acting Agent J. J. Upham finally sent the Ealys vouchers to sign, he erred in computing their pay, and the error took time to correct. Ingalls was replaced by the Reverend S. W. Marston, who sent the corrected vouchers to Commissioner E. P. Smith in June, 1876, with a note that the teachers had not been paid for the first quarter of the year because there were no funds. The accounts were finally settled at the end of June.[10]

That same month Marston visited the Fort Arbuckle school and delivered the disturbing news that there might not be another appropriation made for it. When word finally came that an appropriation had been made for fiscal year 1877, the exact amount was uncertain. The Ealys and Miss Forbes went east for the summer. In August, still not knowing for certain whether funds were available for the new school year, the Ealys returned to Fort Arbuckle because they had left their belongings there and had purchased return tickets. Miss Forbes refused to return. Secretary McClelland of the Committee for Missions to the Freedmen and the Ealys anxiously awaited word. Finally, in early September, the Indian Office made $1,500 available to the Fort Arbuckle School. If Mr. and Mrs. Ealy were willing to teach for that amount, the job was theirs. If not, the agent was directed to pay $900 for a male teacher and $600 for a female teacher. Marston immediately sent word back to Washington: "The teachers of the Freedmen Schools connected with this Agency are at their posts, faithfully at work and you will receive their monthly reports in due time."[11]

But Marston had spoken prematurely. When he wrote to Ealy in mid-September asking if he and his wife were willing to work at the reduced salary, the Ealys were not at Fort Arbuckle. They had returned to Schellsburgh, Pennsylvania, not knowing that the school had been funded. They were suffering from ague. They had stayed in the territory for a while, trying to recover but, failing that, had returned east. They could not take up their post again before January, 1877, and therefore offered it to anyone willing to take it. Marston now awaited instructions. Should he try to find another teacher? No, the Indian Office would have to seek a nomination, preferably a husband and wife, from the Presbyterian Committee.[12]

Meanwhile, Wayland Seminary had sent one of its young graduates, George W. Dallas, to teach in the Creek Nation. Arrangements had supposedly been made by Ingalls, but when Dallas arrived in the Creek Nation, Ingalls had left office without making them. Dallas was a Baptist, and although the Indian Office had carefully divided the tribes among denominations, Marston wanted to appoint him to the Fort Arbuckle school, which was under Presbyterian control. Commissioner Smith informed McClelland that the Baptist Home Mission Society had made application for the supervision of the school, that Dallas, a black minister, and his wife wanted the job, and that the freedmen wanted the school continued. He awaited word from McClelland. Since the school was so important, McClelland decided to bring before the next meeting of the Committee on Freedmen the question of whether the Presbyterians wished to retain supervision of the Arbuckle school, and late in November they decided to give it up. Ealy had done good work there despite the "peculiar difficulties" with which he had to contend, and the Committee wished their successors better results.[13]

In light of these developments, Commissioner Smith decided to place one teacher at Fort Arbuckle and to open another school elsewhere in the Chickasaw Nation. If the Presbyterians remained firm in their decision to retire, Marston was to appoint G. W. Dallas to the former. While the Indian Office wanted to continue the freedmen school, it was not sure that Congress would appropriate the money for the next fiscal year. Marston, a Baptist, wanted the school to remain under the supervision of the Presbyterians, but if they withdrew, the Baptist Home Mission Society would nominate someone. Dallas had gone to the Ben James neighborhood, where the freedmen had built a new schoolhouse and were looking to the government for aid. He was favorably impressed, and the freed-

men expressed a willingness to contribute $100 per quarter towards a
school's support. Marston wanted to establish a school there, and he asked
the Presbyterian Committee to reappoint Dr. Ealy to Fort Arbuckle
school.[14]

Commissioner Smith authorized $300 from the unspent appropriation
for the Arbuckle school for the Ben James school and offered Dr. Ealy
$600 for the rest of the fiscal year. Marston corresponded with Ealy and
with S. S. Cutting of the Baptist Home Missionary Society, who found
a teacher to replace Ealy if he would not return or if the Presbyterian Committee did not nominate someone in his place. Meanwhile, Dallas went to
the Ben James neighborhood, but he wrote that the people were so poor
that they could not buy books for the children. The same was reported
from the Choctaw freedmen schools at Doaksville and Boggy Depot. So
Marston asked for an appropriation of $100 to help make the schools
more efficient.[15]

Although the Presbyterian Committee absolutely declined to resume
supervision of the school at Fort Arbuckle, Marston continued to negotiate
with Dr. Ealy. Marston promised him a small bonus. His teaching load,
though heavy, would not be equal to that of him, his wife, and Miss Forbes
combined. Since the new school had been organized in the Ben James
neighborhood, he would not draw students from the whole Chickasaw
Nation. Fortunately for the freedman children, Ealy took the position,
arriving in Muskogee on January 25, 1877, and his appointment was approved by the Baptists.[16]

At Ben James (also called Blue Branch), G. W. Dallas was satisfied
at the end of the first month with the interest shown by both parents
and students. He had averaged twenty-four pupils that month, and the
work was hard: "I am laboring harder than I ever did before. I can not
do otherwise." Sunday work was also fatiguing. He taught spelling and
reading to a large Sunday school, gave Bible narrations, and tried to
teach them singing. But, he said,

they are so dull and ignorant, that I have to work with all the enthusiasm
I can muster so by the end of my Sunday school session, I am almost unfit to preach. Will I have to teach in the month of June? and do I work
the 6 months for $400 and board myself? I have talked with people a
great deal about raising me some money; but they have no money, this is
a fact. I am so hungry for money that it seems to me that I can hardly
hold up longer.[17]

Despite the hardships, the school year ended with promise. During the planting season, when boys and girls worked in the corn and cotton fields, attendance continued to be strong. Some parents who had two or more children allowed one to go to school one day and another the next. Despite such problems, Marston looked forward to the next year. Dallas would probably continue at Blue Branch, and the school at Fort Arbuckle would be continued. Marston was besieged by requests from freedmen for other schools in the Chickasaw Nation. There were at least five more areas in the Choctaw and Chickasaw Nations where equally large schools could be established if funds were available.[18]

The Indian Office set aside $3,500 for freedman schools in the Choctaw and Chickasaw Nations during the fiscal year ending June 30, 1878. The funds would be used for teachers' salaries, books, stationery, and so forth. Dr. Ealy reported that the freedmen near Fort Arbuckle wanted him to remain and that they would pay a little extra, but Commissioner Smith wanted reorganization. He admitted that Ealy was a good teacher and was worth $100 a month, but he did not think that freedman schools required "such an expensive order of teaching" and instructed Marston to grade the schools and set salaries accordingly and to see that the schools opened promptly in the fall.[19]

Ealy soon gave up. At the time, the Ealys and Miss Forbes still had outstanding claims for salary as far back as 1874 and 1875. In 1877, Governor Overton of the Chickasaws had twice tried to collect a tax of $25 from Dr. Ealy under a permit law. Ealy wrote to Marston, "If there is anything to come out of my pocket in this matter, write to me at once. I will stop the school & leave the Nation immediately. I get nothing for preaching. They rather owe me $2500 than that I should pay $25 to remain." He added, "It's hard work in this corner."[20] This threat of a tax was the last straw for Ealy. He did not return to Fort Arbuckle in the fall of 1877.

Marston made changes to give more freedman children access to schools. In July, 1877, he sent George W. Dallas throughout the Chickasaw Nation, visiting the freedmen and "trying to inspire them with a missionary & educational zeal." He traveled among the Choctaw freedmen during the next month. He had great hope for his own school at Blue Branch, for many families migrated to the area and were building houses so that their children might attend the school. Dallas had traveled about five hundred miles by horseback, visiting the principal neighborhoods. "I have found ignorance, poverty and destitution prevalent," he reported. Dallas estimated that, of the thousand freedman children of school age in the two nations, not more than two hundred had ever attended public school. In 1875-76 not more than seventy-five had attended daily and in 1876-77 not more than one hundred. To Dallas, the present system was inefficient; the people were too scattered. The establishment of industrial schools, he believed, would double the good results obtained through neighborhood schools and would be less expensive. Dallas wrote the Commissioner: "Will your Honor, as much as it is in your power, give my poor, ignorant and neglected race, schools for the education of the youth? Or give them two Industrial Laboring schools?"[21]

As Marston had expected, freedmen everywhere asked Dallas to help them get schools established in their neighborhoods. Marston wanted to change locations of the schools to serve more students, but no matter how many more schools he decided to create, $3,500 was the total budget for the freedman schools of both nations. Marston closed down a Choctaw freedman school at Fort Coffee; the building was so poor that school could not be conducted during cold weather, and the children had access to another school at Scullyville, twenty-six miles away. He opened a school at Red River, Chickasaw Nation, where there was a much larger population. With the help of their teacher, the people had built "a very commodious & comfortable school house." The Baptist Home Mission Society approved as teacher the Reverend John P. Lawton, a graduate of Shurtleff College, Illinois, and formerly superintendent of public instruction in St. Clair County, Missouri. He arrived in July and spent the vacation months preaching and helping the freedmen build their school. The school at Fort Arbuckle was continued under James R. Banks, and another was opened at Tishomingo under Mary Rounds, a graduate of Weyland Seminary, who came highly recommended by the Baptist Home Mission Society.[22]

The schools faced their perennial problems. During cotton-picking season the demands of child labor caused attendance to drop:

One can hardly estimate the value of children's labor in the cotton field at this particular season of the year, among these Freedmen without seeing the destitute circumstances in which they are placed. As important as schooling is to these Freedmen children it is even more important that they do not neglect to gather their cotton, on which they depend in a large degree for clothing & provisions.[23]

Marston was also faced with the constant problem of making the money stretch. The Interior Department had prepared first readers for use in

Indian schools, and Marston asked for additional copies to be sent to
Mary Rounds and John P. Lawton. The other schools had a supply of
the book. Marston wanted to buy books and other school supplies in the
open market at St. Louis, and although the books were needed immediately,
it was not until November 1 that Secretary of the Interior Carl Schurz
authorized $250. Despite the delay, Marston was encouraged and believed
that schools would increase in interest and numbers when the teachers
received the books.[24]

In the fall, John P. Lawton sent "quite a flattering account of the interest taken by the parents & children" in his new school at Red River.
Things were not so well with Dallas at Blue Branch. He received his books
but did not get his maps or alphabet charts. The freedmen were suffering
because crops had been poor following the summer drought. Cold weather
came early, and Dallas expected attendance to drop off. In early December
some of the children were still barefoot. From Fort Arbuckle, people reported that James R. Banks was doing good work. Marston was proud of
the work. In 1875 the Union Agency had maintained three schools for the
Chickasaw and Choctaw freedmen with an appropriation of $5,000. Now
five equally efficient schools were being run for only $3,500. He said,
"Give me $5,000 another year and I believe I can support ten schools with
good teachers in as many different neighborhoods where schools are equally
needed."[25]

In March of 1878, the Indian Office learned that for three months a Mrs.
Kinyon near Fort Arbuckle had been keeping a school for about sixty Chickasaw freedman children. The freedmen wanted her to stay on for a year. She
wanted to make her school a public school, but the existing funds would
not pay for any more teachers than had already been appointed. Since her
school had been a subscription school, not organized under the authority of
the Indian Office, there was no way she could draw funds. Indeed, far from
increasing funds for freedman schools, the Indian Office was preparing to do
the opposite. Pressing demands for aid to Indian industrial schools made it
appear that no aid would be given to the freedman schools during the next
fiscal year. Marston was instructed to inform the Baptist Home Mission
Society that any books or school supplies paid for by the Baptists would be
returned to them when the schools closed.[26]

S. S. Cutting of the Baptist Home Mission Society asked Commissioner
E. A. Hayt to rescind the order withdrawing the funds. The freedmen of the
Chickasaw and Choctaw Nations were in dire need, exlcuded as they were
from all rights in the nations. The schools had been the only advantages that

the blacks had had. "I am forced to believe," Cutting said, "that there is
no population of the country so unprotected by law, so helpless, as they."
Little could be done about their spiritual needs without schools, and missionary work would be rendered difficult without schools. Petitions came
from the Indian Territory during the summer. Marston lent his support:
"I think when you come to understand the great need of these Freedmen
schools & the good they are doing among the destitute Choctaw & Chickasaw Freedmen you will consider their continuance favorably." The appeals were effective, for on August 2, Secretary Carl Schurz authorized a
contract to be made with the Baptists to conduct the freedman schools
for one year for no more than $3,500.[27]

Part of the success of the appeals may have been due to the efforts of
George W. Dallas, who visited the commissioner of Indian affairs about
the time the decision was made to renew the appropriations. In Dallas's
view, the improvement of the freedmen's condition rested solely on the
education of the young. He contrasted their dismal condition to the condition of the Creek and Seminole freedmen, who not only had schools
but otherwise participated in Creek and Seminole societies. Dallas urged
the closing of some Chickasaw freedman schools, the opening of others
in more advantageous locations, and the hiring of well-educated black
teachers. Dallas also visited S. S. Cutting, whom he had not met before.
Dallas so impressed Cutting with his "soundness of judgment and de-
votion to his work" that Cutting recommended him to oversee the freedman schools.[28]

The Baptist Home Mission Society proposed changes in school locations. The Fort Arbuckle school had already been moved to Mill Creek,
where a larger number of freedmen resided. Blue Branch was moved to
the southeastern part of the Choctaw Nation and renamed Wheelock. It
was suggested that the Tishomingo school be moved to a larger community
at Cherokee Town. Cutting suggested additional schools at West Lake, Wheelock, Stonewall, and Spring Creek. When Mary Rounds investigated, she
decided to open her school at West Lake, Choctaw Nation, rather than at
Cherokee Town, but the school at Tishomingo remained. Cutting thought
that the funds should be stretched to open at least one more school and
that the freedmen should be asked to provide something—perhaps board
or supplies toward the maintenance of all schools. Dallas had reported
forty to fifty children at Mill Creek, one hundred at Wheelock, thirty-
five at Red River, thirty at West Lake, forty-five at Stonewall, and sixty

at Spring Creek. All of the Baptist schools in the Indian Territory were to
be put under the general supervision of its "general missionary" Daniel
Rogers, who resided at Tahlequah, Cherokee Nation.[29]

The fall of 1878 opened with good reports, but by early 1879, problems
had developed. John P. Lawton at the Red River school took Cutting
seriously and asked the freedmen to provide $200 to supplement the
salary he received from the Baptist Home Mission Society. Freedman
Simon Love asked the secretary of the interior if the request was authorized
because the freedmen had thought it was a free school. The Indian Office
denied having any authority over the matter but encouraged the freedmen
to support their schools if they could. The Chickasaws once more tried, as
they had in earlier years, to enforce their permit laws regarding the teachers, and once more the Indian Office intervened. And there were the usual
bureaucratic problems. The government's methods of transferring money
to the Society's accounts resulted in delays in payment of salaries, and in
one case the Indian Office refused to pay because it was reported that the
schools had been kept only a few days in the month. The offender was apparently Banks, who had closed down his school now and then to do religious work. Cutting was outraged. The contract had said that the Baptists
were to run the schools and that the money was to be placed at their disposal as needed. Cutting wrote, "It is an error if it is supposed that a favor
was done to this society by committing to us the care of these schools."
The Indian Office also refused to pay for books as Cutting felt it had agreed
to do, reports were late because the teachers did not receive report forms
on time, and the forms were biased against the reporting of full-time service.
In March, 1879, Cutting was left no choice but to bring the matter before
the Board, for the Society had received no funds. Meanwhile, the commissioner's office continued to carp about incorrect teachers' reports, the reporting of Sabbath-school teaching, and other religious work, and it returned
reports from as early as the previous July for correction before payment
could be made. Then Cutting discovered that the contracts the Society had
signed called for payment for only the time remaining in the fiscal year
from the date of the contracts, thus depriving the Society of one quarter's
funds.[30]

These matters had no sooner been settled than John P. Lawton's attempt
to collect $200 in contributions from the freedmen caused a furor in the
Red River community. Upon Simon Love's second complaint Indian Bureau officials denied that they had authorized the assessment, which Love

insisted he was willing to pay if it was just. But he was afraid of being "swindled." Cutting, too, denied having authorized anything but voluntary contributions, but Lawton, afraid—and justly so—that he was not going to get his full salary because of the Board's problems with the accounts, had tried to get the freedmen to make up the difference. When he learned that he would get his full salary, he had already collected some funds. The people were upset. He called a meeting, released the people from their pledges, and read the correspondence from Cutting and Washington officials to Simon Love. The freedmen could not understand the great discrepancy between what the Society said and what the Indian Office said. Lawton tried to explain to the freedmen that the more they contributed the better their schools would be. He was convinced that they should contribute something, but he felt that all should do so. Part of the concern of the Red River community apparently resulted from their knowledge that the freedmen elsewhere were not paying. When Lawton left for his home in Missouri for the summer, Simon Love became concerned that the teacher had fallen out with the community and wanted to break up the school and move it to Caddo Creek. That would put the school out of the reach of the children of his community, which had gone to the trouble and expense of building a schoolhouse. It needed some repairs, which they were willing to make. Most important to Love, however, was that the people were getting much better at sending their children to school. Although Lawton was a good teacher, said Love, he was "very old and feeble" and could not "do his duty." Although he was still convinced that Lawton was trying to swindle the freedmen, Love was willing to have him back, saying that the freedmen would have gladly paid Lawton's additional assessment if the Indian Office had directed them to do so.[31]

Lawton had apparently done good work. At the year's end, the students demonstrated their achievements at a public examination. E. L. Allen, the assistant postmaster at Sivell's Bend, Texas, had attended the examination at the end of the 1878-79 school year. He was amazed at the results Lawton had obtained. When he had started, only two children knew the alphabet, and only a few could count. Allen watched them do addition and division and heard them read, spell, and sing. Surprised at such progress, he regretted that Lawton had "got offended" by the freedmen. Love, too, was pleased at the children's progress and asked the secretary of the interior to send Lawton back—if not Lawton, then someone else—because, he said, "we don't want the school to go down."[32]

H. L. Morehouse succeeded S. S. Cutting as corresponding secretary of
the Baptist Home Mission Society in the summer of 1879 and, despite the
financial problems of the preceding year, negotiated another contract to
operate the Choctaw and Chickasaw freedman schools in 1879-80. The
freedmen of the Red River community wrote letters urging continuation
of their school and asking if it was worth their effort to build a new church,
which would serve as a schoolhouse. The community and the school were
growing, but if the freedmen did not get citizenship in the Chickasaw Nation and were forced to remove from the Nation, they wanted to be spared
the expense of a new building. When the secretary of the interior encouraged
them to build a new house, they asked, through their spokesman Simon
Love, for help from the government. If the government would buy the lum-
ber, the freedmen could do the rest, he said. Lawton returned to his teaching station at Red River, but he apparently harbored a grudge against Love
and others for their actions against him in the spring. When he learned that
they had asked for aid in building a new school, he discouraged it. The
present one, though too small, had served for two years. It was a well-
covered log house, about fourteen by twenty-six feet, "with better desks and
seats than one half of the school houses in the state of Missouri." Average
attendance during the previous year had been thirty-one. Besides seven
students who were boarded at the school, there were only about forty
children, including five Texans, near the school. Lawton argued that there
were several much larger freedman settlements in the Chickasaw Nation
that had no aid from the government and "no schools of importance." On
Caddo Creek, for instance, about twenty-five miles north of the Red River
school, there was a settlement of freedmen with seventy-two children.
In Lawton's opinion, the school should be moved to assist such groups
elsewhere, for money spent at Red River would be misspent.[33]

Lawton was right about the interest in education elsewhere. Early in
1880, for instance, Linden Davis, Squire Wolf, and Isaac Kemp appealed
to Secretary of the Interior Carl Schurz concerning the Blue Station subscription school near Tishomingo. They had just built a new house for
their school of forty-seven students. Their teacher, Annie E. Allston, could
remain with them only if she could find support. They had been supporting
it as well as they could, but because of drought and crop failure during the
previous two years, they were more destitute than usual. Daniel Rogers,
head of the Baptist missionary force in the Indian Territory, could not
offer them any help from the Baptist Home Mission Society. They then

appealed to Secretary Schurz for assistance. At the bottom of their letter, Annie E. Allston wrote, "These men are just learning to write."[34]

As the 1879-80 school year drew to a close, the Indian Office proposed a contract for the next year with the stipulation that the teachers' salaries be paid through the office of Agent John Q. Tufts at the Union Agency in Muskogee. Instead of six schools of ten months in the Choctaw and Chickasaw Nations, H. L. Morehouse suggested the establishment of twelve schools of five months each in order to reach a larger number of freedmen. The six teachers appointed as usual could spend their time equally between two schools. The Indian Office approved the idea of shorter sessions but suggested that in the most populous freedman communities the Board support three ten-month schools and maintain six five-month schools elsewhere. Morehouse failed to get approval of his request for an industrial boarding school for the Choctaw and Chickasaw freedmen so that "instruction of a higher grade or somewhat different character could be given." The teachers had all urged the importance of such a school, and Daniel Rogers believed that it "would do more than anything else to elevate these people." The people wanted the school and had started a fund for its support. The Baptists were willing to conduct it if an appropriation could be obtained. Just a little more than the current appropriation would permit some work beyond the elementary level, and Morehouse hoped that the more intelligent and advanced students from the elementary grade schools could be trained to teach and could be sent out to the smaller communities that had no schools.[35]

When the contracts were signed for the 1880-81 school year, they were for six months, renewable at that time. Morehouse insisted on a clause that would allow the teachers to collect funds from the Chickasaw and Choctaw freedmen to assist in supporting the schools. The clause was designed to prevent such misunderstandings as those that had developed in the Red River community in 1879. The government refused. It was a good idea, but the government denied jurisdiction in the matter.[36]

When the school opened in the fall of 1880, there were only two in the Chickasaw Nation: Sulphur Springs, taught by John Lawton, and Washita, taught by James R. Banks. Lawton had left the Red River school on Walnut Bayou because he had conducted the school there while other larger communities had had none. The Red River school, in his estimation, would "rank above an average of the free schools, white or black, west of the Mississippi." Lawton's former students were conducting a "creditable" Sabbath School each Sunday, using *Our Children's Picture Lessons.* He believed that in a year or two, there would be freedmen and freedwomen who would have enough training to teach there. Lawton, who was white, had friends across the river at Sevill's Bend, Texas, where there was a post office. At his Sulphur Springs school on Caddo Creek, there were only three white families anywhere near, and he was seventeen miles from a doctor and sixteen from a post office. He felt that the sacrifice he had made to go there was worth it because there were seventy-five children, most of whom had had no schooling at all. The people at Red River were distressed because Lawton had left them, and as if his loss was not enough, their schoolhouse burned that summer. Through Simon Love they asked the government to send them another teacher. They were ready to rebuild the school as soon as they heard that a teacher had been approved.[37]

That winter, Daniel Rogers visited most of the schools and the large freedman settlements that had no schools. His report was "most encouraging" regarding "the elevating effects of these schools among the freedmen." Under Rogers' direction, schools were moved to new locations on February 1, 1881, in order to give five months' schooling to those who had not had any.[38]

The Red River community failed to get one of the schools, so they sought the intervention of Chickasaw Governor Benjamin F. Overton, who urged the government to send a teacher. Overton described the freedmen of the Walnut Bayou settlement, many of whom he knew personally, as "a good, quiet and industrious people." Education was most important to them—indeed, to the Chickasaw Nation as a whole: "Our moral worth depends entirely upon a proper Education among the common minds of the Nation at large." Overton forwarded a petition from the freedmen, stating that they were willing to rebuild their schoolhouse and charging that Lawton had left them because they would not pay him $200 above his government salary. In response, the commissioner's office suggested that one of the schools be located there, but it was too late. Morehouse defended Lawton and his move to Sulphur Springs. In the spring of 1881, the Indian Office received more complaints from other freedmen. Henry Cole and other Chickasaw freedmen complained about the teacher furnished them by the Baptist Home Mission Society, apparently because he was trying to collect support funds from the freedmen. Complaints also came from Anderson Jolly and others regarding the Baptist schools. The Indian Office directed Agent Tufts to investigate and report.[39]

It is interesting that these complaints coincided with attempts by the African Methodist Episcopal Church to secure part of the funds given to the Baptists. In the fall of 1880, J. Allen Ball of Stringtown, Choctaw Nation, and A. J. Miller of Atoka sought to persuade Henry M. Turner, Bishop of the Eighth Episcopal District, to secure funds for schools as the Baptists had done. Some AME preachers had conducted "pay schools," and they charged that they had been denied positions in the government schools. In fact, Miller accused the Baptist teachers of telling parents that they must send their children to the Baptist Sabbath school. Bishop Turner, in turn, charged the government with subsidizing not only the education of freedmen but also the church interests of the Baptists and the dissemination of "their peculiar religious creeds and dogmas." He asked Secretary Carl Schurz "that no invidious distinctions" be made between the two denominations "and that no special favors be extended" to the Baptists. Turner asked that those AME preachers who were then conducting schools in the territory be made recipients of government funds and asked for half of the funds given to the Baptists to run the same number of schools. Turner was granted funds for the establishment of one school for the freedmen in the spring of 1881, and the Indian Office authorized Agent Tufts to report on that school as well as the Baptist schools. In June, Commissioner Hiram Price pressed Tufts for the reports on both groups, apparently trying to decide to which he wanted to offer a contract.[40]

Both Morehouse and Turner requested funds to conduct schools for the Chickasaw and Choctaw freedmen during the 1881-82 school year. From reports of his teachers, Morehouse became convinced that the general missionary work was likely to be "seriously impaired" by the establishment of schools by the African Methodists. If they were allowed to open schools in the same area as the Baptists, division and dissatisfaction would result. If the Methodists were to receive funds, Morehouse asked that they open schools in other areas. Morehouse once more presented his plan to open several five-month schools to Hiram Price, who had become commissioner of Indian affairs since the last contract had been made. Tufts had found it impossible to visit all of the schools, but he believed that part of the dissatisfaction among some of the freedmen was caused by a belief among them that if the schools were taken out of the Society the money would be sent

directly to them to spend as they wished. Tufts had warned them that if
they continued to complain and quarrel among themselves, the schools
would be moved to other locations. As for Bishop Turner's school, he had
heard no complaint except that the teacher "lent too much to sprinkling
when he should go in for immersion." Tufts recommended that the Baptists
have their contracts renewed and that they reopen the school at Red River.[41]

That fall, the Baptists opened schools at fourteen locations, including
Sulphur Springs, Red River, Washita, Cherokee Town, Red Field (about
two miles north of Cherokee Town), and Stonewall in the Chickasaw Nation. When Bishop Turner named the places at which he proposed to open
schools, Morehouse was concerned. He could not locate "Double Springs"
but feared that it might be near one of his schools. He was also concerned
that the proximity of other of Bishop's proposed schools would destroy
the rapport his teachers had developed with the freedman communities.
The more ambitious and advanced students were taken by their parents
from one five-month school to another so that they could receive ten
months of schooling. Morehouse had also decided that the large freedman settlement on Wild Horse Creek about a mile west of Fort Arbuckle
needed a school and planned to open one there the following February
if necessary.[42]

The government refused to continue funds for Turner's schools beyond
the third quarter of 1881. In the fall Turner toured the Indian Territory
and later told the commissioner that he was the only one in the territory
doing anything for the blacks "worth a snap of your finger." Turner
vowed to take the matter to Congress and asked Commissioner Price to
draft a petition for him to take to the body. He said, "You need not
hesitate for I have influential friends in Congress." The petition was adopted
by the Arkansas Conference of the AME Church on March 8, 1882. It reviewed the church's activities in the territory. In 1878 the Arkansas Conference had organized the Indian Territory Mission Conference and had
built several buildings for school and church. The missionaries had found
that thousands of children without provision for education were becoming
"greater slaves to vice and ignorance." The people were eager to be educated; the Methodists claimed that they had seen parents travel fifty to
seventy-five miles, camp under trees in rain and snow, and sleep outside
for weeks and months to have their children taught. Missionaries had
traveled two hundred miles at a time without seeing a sign of a school.
In his petition, Turner asked for a $10,000 appropriation. During the

next few weeks, petitions of support came from various communities
in the Choctaw Nation as well as from citizens of Texas, calling for appropriations for the Chickasaw and Choctaw freedmen.[43]

Congress passed an appropriations bill, approved on May 17, 1882.
It provided that $10,000 of the $300,000 held in trust under the Treaty
of 1866 was to be used for education of the Chickasaw and Choctaw
freedmen. The Choctaws and Chickasaws were to receive three-fourths
and one-fourth respectively. The tribes were given permission to adopt
the freedmen and make them citizens; in that case, the money provided
by the act would be paid over to the tribe.[44] The law meant simply
that the government was now spending tribal funds instead of its own
for the education of the freedmen. By doing that, the government hoped
to persuade the tribes to adopt the blacks.

In the summer of 1882, concern was expressed from all quarters regarding the schools for 1882-83. King Blue, one of the leading representatives
of the Chickasaw freedmen, highly praised James R. Banks and his school
in Blue's Washita community. Of course, Commissioner Price could not
guarantee the continuance of the school. Morehouse asked for a renewal
of his contracts, still warning against granting aid to schools through more
than one denomination. Teachers had reported "disturbances and divisions"
among the freedmen since the opening of government schools by the AME
Church. The people wanted their schools conducted by their own denominations and began to oppose others, destroying the unity of the neighborhoods. Moorehouse instructed his teachers to take no part in such contro-
versies but to conduct their schools as government schools for the equal
good of all. Meanwhile, Hiram Price delayed his decision regarding contracts until he found out whether either tribe would take serious steps
to adopt their freedmen. The AME Church met in general conference on
July 8 and selected Tishomingo and Colbert Station in the Chickasaw Nation and Nail Station in the Choctaw Nation as sites for new schools. The
people were called together and told to prepare for school in the fall, and
the church solicited petitions from the residents of various communities,
urging the government to support their schools.[45]

The Indian Office finally issued contracts. It made a contract with the
Baptist Home Mission Society for nine schools at $500 each. Morehouse
planned three for ten months and six for five months in twelve different
neighborhoods. That would allow some school to be held in fifteen black
communities. One of the ten-month schools was at Sulphur Springs, and
Morehouse felt it important to get a school under way at Stonewall. By

spreading the services around the country, he hoped to advance the freedmen as quickly as possible and hoped, in time, to have a normal department for training teachers. The African Methodists also received contracts.
They wanted support for new schools at Tishomingo and Colbert Station
(Chickasaw) and at Nail Station, Long Creek, and Allen Bayou (Choctaw)
and wanted to revive the school discontinued by the Baptists at Blue Branch.
When Commissioner Price approved the contract, he told the Methodists
to open schools elsewhere than Nail and Blue Branch because they were
too close to each other and to other schools, and he warned them to find
competent teachers.[46]

J. Allen Ball, in charge of the African Methodist schools in the territory,
was determined to succeed where Bishop Turner had failed. He believed
that Turner's contract had not been renewed because of incompetent teachers. Thus Ball set down rules for teachers, parents, and school boards. The
parents would board and furnish support to teachers, have every child from
five to twenty-one attend school every day, take complaints to the school
board and not create disturbances or disorder in the schoolroom, give control of the children to the teacher during school time, send children promptly to school, and discourage the carrying of tales from school. The school
boards, consisting of thirteen men, would see that a suitable house was
built and maintained, see that teachers were supported, encourage prompt
and regular attendance, aid the teachers in enforcing strict discipline on the
school grounds, and hear and investigate all charges against teachers. The
teachers would teach twenty days of six hours each during each month of
the term, enforce discipline in the classroom (obscene language and "improper acts" were strictly forbidden), attend to no personal matters during school time, remain impartial in family or neighborhood quarrels, be
free of any vice or immoral habit injurious to students (intoxicants were
permitted if prescribed by a physician), and report accurately on school
activities each month.[47]

The Blue Branch school, though in the Choctaw Nation, was attended
by Chickasaw freedmen. Georgianna Reeves, the teacher, had fifteen boys
and nine girls attending in the fall of 1882. Nine of the former and four
of the latter could read and write English when work began. The students
worked in Webster's spellers, McGuffey's readers, Ray's arithmetics, Har-
vey's grammars, Monteith's geographies, and Spencerian copy books. At
Colbert Station, Ruth F. Young had seven boys and five girls attending,
of whom one and three, respectively, could read and write English.[48]

There were the usual problems that made education of the freedmen more difficult. In November, at the height of the cotton-picking season, economic necessity forced parents to keep their children out of school. Enrollment surged again in December. In January, 1883, there were suspicions that the African Methodist teachers were submitting falsified monthly reports. Bishop Turner had personally called the teachers together in December and stressed adherence to the guidelines Ball had set down, and he promised to dismiss any teacher found guilty of a breach of the rules. Then there were reports that some of the schoolhouses were open or without windows and therefore unfit for holding classes. Although J. A. Ball had assured Bishop W. B. Miles that the houses were ready, Miles ordered them repaired, and Commissioner Price directed Agent John Q. Tufts to oversee the schools. From the Indian Territory, A. J. Miller denied charges that some schools had not been conducted the full twenty days. Some of the false charges were laid to the Baptists, who had constantly complained since the Methodists had opened schools in some areas and who, Miller said, had caused rifts in communities by telling parents not to send their children to the Methodists because a Baptist school would be opening soon. Miller maintained that the Methodists had opened schools at places where they were most needed, sometimes over the objections of "one or two crazy men" and despite the "agitation of this Baptist distinction." He admitted that some houses were in a sad state because the teachers had been directed to repair them from money received for their own support. The contracts were too short to give much inducement to repair the houses. There was apparently some basis for the complaints about teachers, for Miller dismissed two. Just when Miller thought that he had satisfactorily answered the complaints, a group of Chickasaw freedmen near the Cross Road school at Blue Station complained that the school operated by the African Methodists did not "meet the demand" of the community. The teacher was incompetent and rather young to teach young men and women. He was not a member of the church and was incompetent to teach Christianity, and enrollment had dropped to seven or eight students. The petitioners—Isaac Kemp, J. S. Green, Largy Colbert, Hence Cheadle, Wilson Shico, and Rufus Glasby—asked for a change.[49]

The rumors, complaints, petitions, incompetency, and interdenominational bickering weakened the arguments for continuation of the freedman schools and encouraged intervention by the Choctaw and Chickasaw Nations. On March 2, 1883, on the eve of the passage of the annual Indian appropriations bill, the Choctaw delegates to Washington asked that Commissioner Price defer any decision on future contracts. However, Price informed them and the Chickasaw delegates that the money had been appropriated out of tribal funds under the act of May 17, 1882, and that whether the money continued to come from those funds depended on whether or not the tribes adopted their freedmen. The Chickasaw delegates claimed that theretofore they had been unaware of the appropriation. They asked that any further actions be suspended until the Nation had an opportunity to consider the act. Called into question, now, was whether the opportunity to act had been lost by the two nations.[50]

In the summer of 1883, the mission societies inquired about funding for the next school year. There were so many poor people in the South that the AME mission board would not be able to do as much during the coming year as it had done the last. And there was the perennial problem of finding good teachers at a "reasonable price." Morehouse, too, inquired for the Baptists. Price apparently waited to hear from Agent Tufts to decide whether the African Methodists or the Baptists or both should continue their schools. Tufts supplied a list of ten schools proposed by the Methodists, of which three were in the Chickasaw country—Red River, Burneyville, and Blue River settlement. But by late August he had no report from the Baptists. Price reprimanded the agent for not having made himself familiar enough with the schools during the preceding year to supply the data Price needed to make his decision. Under the circumstances Price had little choice but to continue the Baptist schools, although he disliked making the decision without the needed information. The Baptists opened eight schools that fall, and both they and the Methodists were late getting under way because of the delays in the Indian Office.[51]

Early in 1884 Commissioner Price recommended to Congress that if the Indians refused to adopt the freedmen, the United States should assist in educating them. In May of 1883, the Choctaws had passed a bill adopting their freedmen and providing for their enrollment as citizens. That act was the doom of freedman schools in the Chickasaw Nation. Despite appeals from freedmen in the Choctaw Nation and from Morehouse, federal appropriations ceased on June 30, 1884. And in February, 1885, the $2,500 that had been assessed as a penalty for the Chickasaws' failure to adopt their freedmen under the law of May 27, 1882, was paid to the United States to replace money expended on freedman education.[52]

During the next several years the Chickasaw freedmen appealed in vain for further educational assistance. In 1885, 1886, and 1887, those of the

Burneyville-Red River region appealed for help. In 1886 and 1890, there were pleas from Colbert Station. In 1886, freedman Fred Humphries appealed for a school for the one hundred children in his community so that "we may not be kept in darkness all our lives." Too, since the teachers had gone, they had had no one to preach the gospel to them. In 1887, there were appeals for schools at Tishomingo. In 1889 there were appeals from George A. L. Dykes of the AME Church and from Chickasaw freedmen near Boggy Depot. By that time, the situation was more distressing because the adopted Choctaw freedmen were having schools regularly conducted for them by the Choctaw Nation. In 1886, Union Agent Robert L. Owen petitioned Chickasaw Governor Jonas Wolf on behalf of the Chickasaw freedmen, but the Chickasaws would have no part of them. Owen met with the freedmen in convention at Tishomingo in the fall of 1887, but to no avail. To all pleas, the answer was the same: no money had been appropriated for Chickasaw freedman education. Chickasaw failure to adopt the freedmen stood in the way of reestablishing the schools.[53]

Thus when the appropriations for freedman education ended in 1884, the Chickasaw freedmen had enjoyed, at best, a decade of scattered attempts at education—attempts debilitated to a large degree by bureaucratic blunders, incompetence, poor management, and denominational struggles. The half-hearted support and lack of attention by government officials was typical of the posture they had assumed regarding the freedmen since the government's failure to remove the blacks when the Chickasaws failed to adopt them under terms of the Treaty of 1866. The government's insistence on administratively hanging the freedmen's future on Choctaw as well as Chickasaw policy resulted once more in exclusion of the Chickasaw freedmen. When the schools closed in 1884, they had enjoyed the benefits of educational efforts among them for the last time in nearly two decades.

NOTES

1. *Chickasaw Volume 53* (Indian Archives Division, Oklahoma Historical Society), 337; A. Parsons to Commissioner of Indian Affairs, May 17, 1873, and Parsons to Edward P. Smith, October 15, 1873, National Archives Microfilm Publications, *Microcopy M234* (Office of Indian Affairs, Letters Received)-180: P112-73, P492-73, hereafter cited as *M234*, followed by the roll number.

2. Parsons to Smith, October 15, 1873, and October 27, 1873, *M234*-180: P429-73, P452-73.

3. Parsons to Smith, December 2 and 18, 1873, *M234*-180: P515-73, P575-73; Smith to Columbus Delano, October 22 and 27, 1873, National Archives Microfilm Publications, *Microcopy M348* (Office of Indian Affairs, Report Books)-23: 300, 311, hereafter cited as *M348*, followed by the roll number; Smith to Parsons, October 27, November 20, and December 13, 1873, National Archives Microfilm Publications, *Microcopy M21* (Office of Indian Affairs, Letters Sent)-114: 354, 457, 528, hereafter cited as *M21*, followed by the roll number.

4. Smith to John C. Lowrie, December 30, 1873, *M21*-116: 28; Lowrie to Smith, January 2, 1874, and Parsons to Smith, January 7 and 9, 1874, *M234*-181: L7-74, P18-74, P47-74.

5. Parsons to Smith, January 9, 1874, *M234*-181: P47-74.

6. Lowrie to A. C. McClelland, February 23, 1874, McClelland to Smith, February 25, 1874, July 29, 1874, September 24, 1874, and October 2, 1874, Parsons to Smith, October 12, 1874, G. W. Ingalls to Smith, November 9, 1874, and Taylor F. Ealy, et al. to Commissioner, October 27, 1874, *M234*-181: M199-74, M890-74, M136-74, M1169-74, P621-74, I1276-74, E141-74; Smith to McClelland, July 31, 1874, *M21*-118: 533.

7. McClelland to Ingalls, February 20, 1875, Ingalls to Smith, February 23 and March 19, 1874, and McClelland to Smith, March 12, 1875, *M234*-182: I204-75, I327-75, M241-75; Smith to McClelland, March 22, 1875, *M21*-123: 486.

8. Elliot E. Swift to John Q. Smith, April 10, 1875, and McClelland to Smith, June 29, 1875, *M234*-182: S550-75, M577-75; Smith to Swift, April 12, April 13, and June 30, 1875, *M21*-124: 145, 152, 528; Ingalls to Smith, July 9, 1875, *M234*-865: I872-75; McClelland to Smith, April 4, 1876, *M234*-866: M267-76; Smith to J. J. Upham, April 13, 1876, *M21*-130: 104.

9. Ingalls to J. Q. Smith, September 30, 1875, *M234*-865: I1260-75; Frank Howard to Ingalls, October 30, 1875, *M234*-182: I1452-75.

10. John Q. Smith to Upham, February 19, 1875, *M21*-128: 467; McClelland to Smith, April 4, 1876, Ealy to Smith, May 5, 1876, S. W. Marston to Smith, June 22, 1876, *M234*-866: E64-76, M267-76, M491-76; Smith to Ealy, April 13, 1876, Smith to McClelland, April 13, 1876, and Smith to Upham, May 22, 1876, *M21*-130: 102, 103, 260.

11. McClelland to Smith, June 30, August 8 and 29, 1876, Marston to Smith, September 11, 1876, and McClelland to S. A. Galpin, September 13, 1876, *M234*-866: M512-76, M667-76, M669-76, M766-76, M824-76, M826-76; Smith to McClelland, July 6, 1876, *M21*-133: 401; Galpin to McClelland, September 11, 1876, and Galpin to Marston, September 11, 1876, *M21*-132: 45, 35.

12. Ealy to Marston, October 6, 1876, with enclosures, Marston to J. Q. Smith, November 15 and October 12, 1876, *M234*-866: M1008-76,

M1156-76; Galpin to Marston, October 19, 1876, and Galpin to McClelland, October 19, 1876, *M21*-132: 144, 145.

13. G. M. P. King to Commissioner, November 13, 1876, and McClelland to J. Q. Smith, November 16 and 28, 1876, *M234*-866: M1136-76, K285-76, M1189-76; Smith to McClelland, November 14, 1876, and Smith to Marston, November 22, 1876, *M21*-132: 189, 206.

14. J. Q. Smith to Marston, December 19, 1876, *M21*-132: 286; Marston to Smith, December 25, 1876, *M234*-866: M1300.

15. J. Q. Smith to Marston, January 3, 1877, and Smith to McClelland, January 4, 1877, *M21*-132: 318, 323; Ealy to Marston, January 4, 1877, and Marston to Smith, July 5, 1877, *M234*-867: M84-77, M52-77.

16. McClelland to J. Q. Smith, January 9, 1877, Marston to Ealy, January 12, 1877, S. S. Cutting to Smith, January 19 and February 20, 1877, Marston to Smith, January 25, 1877, *M234*-867: M68-77, M84-77, C53-77, C148-77, M144-77; Smith to Marston, January 16, 1877, *M21*-132: 363.

17. G. W. Dallas to Marston, February 2, 1877, *M234*-867: M239.

18. Marston to J. Q. Smith, May 7 and June 6, 1877, and William Lewis to Marston, May 31, 1877, *M234*-867: U56-77, U84-77, U92-77.

19. J. Q. Smith to Marston, March 30, 1877, *M21*-136: 27.

20. Upham to Galpin, June 7, 1877, with enclosures, Marston to J. Q. Smith, June 18, and July 4, 1877, *M234*-867: U104½-77, U100-77, U123-77.

21. Marston to J. Q. Smith, August 3, 1877, and Dallas to Commissioner, September 4, 1877, *M234*-868: U150-77, D353-77.

22. Galpin to Marston, June 18, 1877, *M21*-136: 288; Cutting to J. Q. Smith, September 15 and October 10, 1877, Marston to Smith, September 26, 1877, and Marston to E. A. Hayt, October 5, 1877, *M234*-868: C1345-77, C1505-77, U224-77, U233-77.

23. Marston to J. Q. Smith, October 5, 1877, *M234*-868: U232-77.

24. Marston to Hayt, October 6, October 25, and November 10, 1877, *M234*-868: U234-77, U259-77, U277-77; Hayt to Marston, October 17, 1877, *M21*-138: 108; Hayt to Secretary, October 31, 1877, *M348*-29: 388; C. Schurz to Commissioner, November 1, 1877, National Archives Microfilm Publications, *Microcopy M606* (Letters Sent by the Secretary of the Interior)-17: 13, hereafter cited as *M606*, followed by the roll number.

25. Marston to Hayt, November 16, 1877, and Marston to A. Bell, December 7, 1877, with enclosures, *M234*-868: U291-77, U312-77; Marston to Hayt, February 23 and 26, 1878, *M234*-870: M313-78, M356-78.

26. Mrs. Kinyon to Commissioner, March 24, 1878, *M234*-869: K142-78; William M. Leeds to Mrs. Kinyon, April 15, 1878, and Leeds to Marston, May 4, 1878, *M21*-142, 135, 219.

27. Cutting to Hayt, May 24, 1878, and Cutting to Leeds, July 3, 1878,

M234-869: C356-78, C417-78; Marston to Hayt, July 4, 1878, *M234*-870: M1135-78; Schurz to Commissioner, August 2, 1878, *M606*-17: 469.

28. Cutting to Hayt, August 2, 1878, and Schurz to Commissioner, August 6, 1878, *M234*-869: C490-78, I1348-78; Hayt to Cutting, August 6, 1878, *M21*-144: 26-27.

29. Cutting to Hayt, August 30 and October 9, 1878, *M234*-869: C568-78, C688-78.

30. Simon Love to Secretary, January 21 and February 19, 1879, John P. Lawton to Cutting, February 16, 1879, Cutting to Hayt, February 26, 1879, and Cutting to Hayt, February 12, March 15, March 20, March 26, and March 27, 1879, *M234*-871: L112-79, L167-79, C189-79, C142-79, C239-79, C252-79, C277-79, C278-79; Hayt to Love, January 31, 1879, Hayt to Cutting, March 4, March 19, March 26, and March 29, 1879, *M21*-150: 23, 94, 140, 168-169, 156; E. J. Brooks to Cutting, March 7, 1799, *M21*-160: 582-583.

31. Brooks to Love, May 1, 1879, and Brooks to Cutting, June 7, 1879, *M21*-150: 243, 330; Love to Secretary, May 22, June 19, and June 30, 1879, *M234*-872: L494-79, L573-79, frame 32; Lawton to Cutting, June 6, 1879, and Cutting to Brooks, June 10, 1879, *M234*-871: C609-79, C561-79.

32. E. L. Allen to Secretary, June 30, 1879, and Love to Secretary, June 30, 1879, *M234*-872: L596-79, frame 32.

33. Cutting to Hayt, July 21, 1879, *M234*-871: C710-79; Hayt to Cutting, August 2, 1879, *M21*-150: 443; Love to Secretary, August 8, 1879, September 2 and October 2, 1879, and Lawton to Brooks, November 15, 1879, *M234*-872: L727-79, L775-79, L853-79, L1010-79.

34. Linden Davis, Squire Wolf, and Isaac Kemp to Carl Schurz, January 16, 1880, *M234*-873: D80-80.

35. R. E. Trowbridge to H. L. Morehouse, May 28, 1880, *M21*-155: 635; Brooks to Morehouse, July 23, 1880, *M21*-157: 188; Morehouse to Trowbridge, June 24 and July 30, 1880, *M234*-875: M1367-80, M1613-80.

36. Morehouse to Trowbridge, August 11, 1880, *M234*-875: M1701-80; E. N. Marble to Morehouse, August 20, 1880, *M21*-157: 369.

37. Morehouse to Commissioner, September 27, 1880, and Love to Secretary, August 11, 1880, *M234*-875: M2013-80, L1150-80.

38. Morehouse to Trowbridge, December 4, 1880, *M234*-875: M2366-80; Morehouse to Hiram Price, June 20, 1881, National Archives Record Group 75, Records of the Bureau of Indian Affairs, *Letters Received*, 10670-81.

39. John Q. Tufts to Commissioner, February 5, 1881, *Letters Received*, 3325-81 (the petition was signed by Simon and Mink Love; Phil, Mack,

Huston, Alex, Enoch, Dave, Wilbourn, Willis, Frank, Josh, and Hence Gaines; Edmond Mintfield; Isham Overton; Allen and Tom Brown; Tom, Bal, and Scott Willis; Ervin McCane, Sr.; and Ervin McCane, Jr.); Thomas M. Nichols to Morehouse, February 19, 1881, and Marble to Tufts, April 1 and 6, 1881, National Archives Record Group 75, *Letters Sent,* Accounts 165: 72, 310, 340; Morehouse to Nichols, February 22, 1881, *Letters Received,* 3325-81.

40. J. A. Ball to H. M. Turner, November 20, 1880, A. J. Miller to Turner, November 22, 1880, and Turner to Carl Schurz, November 27, 1880, *M234*-877: T1579-80; Marble to Tufts, April 1, 1881, *Letters Sent,* Accounts 165: 310; Price to Tufts, June 16, 1881; *Letters Sent,* Accounts 168: 51.

41. Morehouse to Price, July 12, 1881, Turner to Commissioner, July 30, 1881, and Tufts to Price, July 26, 1881, *Letters Received,* 12064-81, 13442-81, 13194-81.

42. Morehouse to Price, August 16, September 19, and October 19, 1881, *Letters Received,* 14526-81, 16776-81, 18405-81.

43. Turner to Commissioner, December 28, 1881, Turner to Price, January 21, March 2, and March 17, 1882, and P. B. Plumb to Secretary of the Interior, April 14, 1882, *Letters Received,* 112-82, 1721-82, 5395-82, 5775-82, 8966-82; *Congressional Record,* 47 Cong., 1 Sess. (February 17, 1882), 1240.

44. 50 Cong., 1 Sess., *Senate Executive Document 166,* 4, 6; E. L. Stephens to Morehouse, May 9, 1882, *Letters Sent,* Civilization 164: 309.

45. Price to King Blue, July 6, 1882, and Price to Tufts, August 14, 1882, *Letters Sent,* Civilization 164: 428, 503; Morehouse to Price, July 18, 1882, and Ball to Commissioner, July 20, 1882, with enclosures, *Letters Received,* 13067-82, 13485-82.

46. Morehouse to Price, August 18, 1882, Ball to Commissioner, August 17, 1882, and Turner to Commissioner, September 19, 1882, *Letters Received,* 15053-82, 15496-82, 17160-82; Price to W. H. Miles, September 20, 1882, *Letters Sent,* Civilization 164: 565.

47. Ball to Commissioner, October 3 and 23, 1882, and Miles to Price, October 4, 1882, *Letters Received,* 18176-82, 19390-82, 18244-82.

48. Monthly School Reports, November 1882, *Letters Received,* 21854-82, 22294-82.

49. Monthly School Reports, November 1882, Turner to Price, January 8 and 27, 1883, and Miles to Commissioner, February 8, 1883, *Letters Received,* 22294-82, 634-83, 2158-83, 1074-83.

50. Price to Campbell Leflore and Joseph R. Folsom, March 3, 1883, *Letters Sent,* Land 180: 527; John E. Anderson and Jocelyn Brown to

Price, March 6, 1883, O. Ferriss to Commissioner, May 22, 1883, *Letters Received,* 4420-83, 9471-83.

51. Miles to Price, July 23, 1883, Morehouse to Price, August 6, September 5, and October 30, 1883, Tufts to Price, August 27, 1883, Miles to Commissioner, September 10, 1883, and Dallas to Price, September 13, 1883, *Letters Received,* 13566-83, 14312-83, 15616-83, 19914-83, 16003-83, 16818-83, 17373-83; Price to Tufts, September 5, 1883, *Letters Sent,* Civilization 173: 661.

52. Price to A. S. Willis, January 30, 1884, *Letters Sent,* Civilization 181: 317; Dallas to Commissioner, July 16, 1884, and Morehouse to Price, July 29, 1884, *Letters Received,* 13888-84, 13996-84; J. D. C. Atkins to G. W. Harkins and H. F. Murray, March 24, 1886, *Letters Sent,* Finance 121: 318A.

53. Abram Eastman to Atkins, February 13, 1886, and R. L. Owen to Atkins, July 29, 1887, National Archives Record Group 47 (Office of the Secretary of the Interior), Indian Territory Division, *Chickasaw Freedmen,* Box 392 (60b), 5321-86, 20116-87; E. McCain to Secretary, March 29, 1885, March 2, 1886, and January 27, 1887, Love to Secretary, May 4, 1885, Bennett to Commissioner, March 27, 1890, Fred Humphries to Secretary, May 31, 1886, Owen to Atkins, July 29, 1887, W. N. Jackson to Owen, November 21, 1887, George A. L. Dykes to John H. Oberly, May 6, 1889, Soloman Abrams and Henry Kemp to Secretary, August 6, 1889, and Owen to Commissioner, April 12, 1886, *Letters Received,* 7108-85, 7177-86, 3094-87, 10857-85, 9577-90, 14871-86, 20116-87, 31449-87, 15119-89, 22553-89, 10260-86; Atkins to Love, July 8, 1885, and Atkins to Owens, August 23, 1887, *Letters Sent,* Civilization 52: 69B and Land 163: 394.

6

Struggle for Rights

For different reasons, the Choctaw adoption of their freedmen in the 1880s boded ill for both the Chickasaws and their freedmen. For the Chickasaws, it represented a breach in the solid front theretofore presented by the two tribes in insisting that the United States fulfill its treaty obligations and remove the freedmen from the nations. For the freedmen, it meant the reduction of their numbers and, as a result, of the strength of their appeal for rights. They also knew that great changes were about to take place in the Indian Territory and that, unlike their Choctaw freedmen counterparts, they were likely to be left out of any share in the Chickasaw domain. Thus soon after the act of adoption by the Choctaw council, the Chickasaw freedmen began a more active struggle for rights while the Chickasaws more actively sought to effect their removal.

The Chickasaw delegates to Washington protested against congressional ratification of the Choctaw act without conferring with the Chickasaws or obtaining their consent. The Chickasaw freedmen met in convention at Stonewall and chose King Blue to visit Washington and push their case for citizenship. They sent with him a petition signed by one hundred Chickasaws, asking for citizenship for the freedmen and naming John Atkins as their delegate to Washington.[1]

In Washington, King Blue and Isaac Alexander presented a memorial to Congress, reaffirming the freedmen's desire to remain in the Chickasaw Nation. It said, "There they have families, wives and children, and property; in fact everything that is dear to them is there; and they would consider it a great hardship to be forced to leave their firesides and to seek new homes." It argued that the language of Article 3 of the Treaty of 1866 indicated that the government intended the complete enfranchisement

of the Chickasaw and Choctaw freedmen; however, the Chickasaws
had steadfastly refused to adopt the blacks and refused to allow them to
vote. The freedmen charged that the Chickasaws were willing to sell the
freedmen's rights for the Chickasaws' share of the $300,000 set aside
by the treaty. The freedmen did not elect to remove from the Chickasaw
country for a number of reasons:

As natives, we are attached to the people amongst whom we have been
born and bred; we like the Chickasaws, as friends; and we know, by the
experience of the past, that we can live with them in the future in the
close union of sincere fraternity and brotherly love.

They wished to be free men in reality, but without the vote, the word
freeman was a sham. Action was up to the federal government, for the
freedmen could not become citizens through adoption by the Chickasaw
legislature or through intermarriage with Chickasaws. Although they
would not complain that they had been treated badly by the Chickasaws,
the laws did not operate equally upon Indians and blacks. They wanted
no special favors; they asked that they be put on the same footing as
other adopted citizens of the Nation under the seventh section of the
Chickasaw constitution, which granted all the privileges of native-born
citizens except eligibility to hold the office of governor. The freedmen's
memorial, endorsed by the Chickasaws Fletcher Frazier and John Dyer,
favorably impressed Commissioner Hiram Price, who believed the freedmen had been brought to the Chickasaw country against their will. Now
that they had valuable improvements on the land, they deserved protection. Their only hope rested in the United States government, which
was not bound to carry out the treaty faithfully. Price therefore recommended congressional action to establish the freedmen's citizenship in
the Chickasaw Nation.[2]
    On April 14, 1884, a bill to make the freedmen citizens of the Chick-
asaw Nation was introduced in the U.S. House, and a similar bill was
introduced in the Senate by Henry L. Dawes. Chairman of the House
subcommittee studying the bill was R. S. Stevens, general manager of
the MK&T Railroad at the time it was built through the Indian Territory. Railroad interests would have much to gain by forcing adoption
of the blacks, thus subverting Chickasaw autonomy in the matter. Halpert
E. Paine, attorney for the Chickasaw Nation, protested against the House

bill, arguing that the Treaty of 1866 had left the decision concerning adoption of the freedmen to the Chickasaws and denying the right of Congress to force adoption upon the tribe. Paine had not conferred with the Chickasaws concerning their refusal to adopt the freedmen, but the Choctaw delegates told him that the freedmen constituted a large part of the population of the Chickasaw Nation, and their numbers increased quickly. The Chickasaws were afraid that, once enfranchised, the blacks would take possession of the government. Paine asked for time to confer with the Chickasaws. On the home front, local newspapers charged the freedmen with "ingratitude for the hospitalities of the Chickasaws these eighteen years," for the bill was "very likely to engender unpleasant relations between the Chickasaws and themselves."[3]

The Chickasaw delegation was absent from Washington at the time, probably because of the political situation at home. On February 8 had occurred the death of Governor Benjamin F. Overton, who had been the Nation's most steadfast opponent of the freedmen. Overton was replaced by Ah-chuck-ah-nubbe, President of the Senate. But he, too, died, and Jonas Wolf was chosen to replace him in April. Wolf called a special session of the legislature on May 8 to consider the freedman matter in light of the bill pending in Congress. He warned the lawmakers that the law, if passed, would result in "great injury" to the Chickasaws, and he urged them to take action for the best interests of the Nation. At the time, there were an estimated four thousand freedmen in the Chickasaw Nation, including the black intruders from nearby states. It was feared that their adoption would result in political control of the Nation by the "adopted element," both black and white, for the number of Chickasaw voters was estimated at only five hundred.[4]

That summer, Chickasaw Humphrey Colbert of Stonewall inquired concerning the bill. He told Commissioner Price that there were at least one hundred full bloods who favored it and expressed the opinion that the Chickasaws would preserve their nationality much longer by adopting the freedmen if it could be guaranteed that the concept of land tenure remained the same—held in common. That, too, would eliminate any need to guarantee the freedmen forty acres of land as well as any discussion of "sectionizing" or dividing the lands. By the time of Colbert's inquiry, however, it was apparent that the bill was dead.[5] There the matter rested for nearly three years.

During that period, Chickasaw imposition upon the freedmen became more frequent. As the number of inhabitants, mostly intruders, increased in the Chickasaw Nation, land became more scarce. Throughout the years, freedmen had asked the Indian Office about the amount of land they could improve and whether, once improved, the land could be taken from them. Some freedmen now pressed for deeds to their farms, but until the freedmen were adopted and until the Chickasaws decided to take allotments of land in severalty, no such patents were possible. The Chickasaws kept the freedmen from improving their condition by placing obstacles in the way of their economic growth. Some tried to open up larger farms and to hire laborers from the United States to work for them. But the Chickasaws would not allow the blacks to hire laborers, and since the Choctaws had adopted their blacks, the Chickasaw freedmen had been without educational privileges.[6]

The Chickasaws not only opposed the hiring of United States citizens as laborers, but they discouraged intermarriage between them and the Chickasaw freedmen. In early 1885 they began to enforce laws requiring the intermarried blacks to pay for permits to remain in the Nation. The Chickasaws had always required permits to be purchased for laborers imported from the states. In the late 1880s, there was a conservative turn in Chickasaw politics, and the Chickasaw legislature began to react against the great number of intruders, especially the white cattlemen in Pickens County. Early in 1886, after permits had been purchased, an agent of the Chickasaw government traveled through the country and retrieved some of them, much to the alarm of the freedmen. But the Indian Office reassured them that if the permits had been paid for, they were good for the specified time unless forfeited for some violation of the law.[7] But other actions of the Chickasaws were also cause for alarm.

On October 22, 1885, the legislature had passed an act rejecting the adoption of the freedmen and outlining, "in justice to their [Chickasaw] posterity," the reasons for doing so. First, the Chickasaws could see no reason why they should be required to do so. Second, they believed that the freedmen had already cost them too much. Following the example of the whites, they had paid enormous prices for the blacks as slaves and had been forced to liberate them as a result of the war. Therefore, they refused to adopt the freedmen on any terms. Governor Jonas Wolf was empowered to appoint two delegates to go to Washington during the

next session of Congress to ask the government to remove the freedmen "to the country known as Ok-la-ho-ma . . . or to make some suitable
disposition of the Freedmen question, so that they be not forced upon us
as equal citizens." In early March of 1886, the Chickasaw delegation presented their memorial to the President.[8]

The freedmen countered with a memorial of their own. They met at
Stonewall on April 19, with Andy Black as chairman and D. N. Grayson
as secretary, and drafted a document in which they maintained that they
had remained among the Chickasaws when given the choice to remove shortly after the war because they had "lived with the Indians all the days of
our life and do not know the rules of no body else but the Indians." They
claimed all the rights of the Chickasaws, including suffrage, and they placed
the responsibility for obtaining those rights on Congress.[9]

In January, 1887, Chickasaw delegates G. W. Harkins and H. F. Murray
once more made plain to the President the reasons for Chickasaw opposition to adoption: they were afraid of the freedmen's numbers. Almost two
years earlier, Harkins had testified before congressional investigators that
the Chickasaws were not like the Choctaws because the freedmen and "the
dissatisfied class of full-bloods" were in a majority. If the Chickasaws
adopted the freedmen, he had said, they would have no government; the
freedmen and the full bloods would control the country. "The half-breeds
and intelligent full-bloods are afraid to give them that power," he had concluded.[10] The Chickasaw memorial of 1887 demonstrated that the Chickasaws were more concerned about these matters than ever.

At the time of removal from Mississippi the Chickasaws had numbered
almost five thousand and their slaves about twelve hundred. Since that
time, however, the freedmen's numbers had greatly increased, according
to the Chickasaws, for several reasons. First, their natural increase had
been much greater than that of the Chickasaws. Second, regiments of
black United States troops had been stationed in the Nation after the Civil
War, and around them had gathered great numbers of the former slaves
of both the Chickasaws and Choctaws. When these soldiers were mustered
out of the service, many married and settled in the Nation. Third, many
freedmen whom the Chickasaws had sold as slaves before the war returned
after the war and claimed the same privileges as those emancipated by the
Treaty of 1866. By 1887, in two of the four counties of the Nation, Pickens
and Pontotoc, freedmen outnumbered the Indians, the Chickasaws claimed,

and would have constituted nearly half of the voting population of Tisho-mingo County.[11]

To the Chickasaws, these people were illegally residing in the Chicka-saw Nation because of stipulations of the Treaty of 1866 and the act of the Chickasaw legislature of November 9, 1866, which had asked for re-moval of the freedmen. Since then, said the Chickasaws, the freedmen had

enjoyed the free use of all the land they have seen fit to cultivate, and all the rights which the Chickasaws themselves have enjoyed, except the right to vote and the right to share in the annuities, moneys, and public domain of the nation.

The presence of large numbers of freedmen from the United States and from the Choctaw Nation complicated the problem. The Chickasaws found it impossible to separate one class from another because of intermarriage, and they felt that a rigorous enforcement of their right to exclude all except their own freedmen would work a hardship on the latter. Therefore, the Chickasaws claimed to have made no distinction between their descendants and those who had no interest in the treaty and to have furnished "both classes with all the land they have seen fit to cultivate, and have treated both classes alike with uniform kindness and justice." Although the freed-men resided in the Nation and had mingled with the Indians, they had not been subject to the civil or criminal jurisdiction of the Nation since the Treaty of 1866.[12]

The matter was further complicated by the immigration of numbers of the Choctaw freedmen to the Chickasaw Nation. The Choctaw freedmen did not constitute a high percentage of the Choctaw Nation's population; thus their recent adoption had not been attended by any fears. Their im-migration so swelled the ranks of the freedmen already in the Chickasaw Nation that the Chickasaws feared that if they were given the vote they would significantly assist the Chickasaw blacks in taking over the govern-ment "and ultimately . . . deprive the Chickasaw people of their govern-ment and country." Thus, the Chickasaws refused to adopt the freedmen under any circumstances and believed that the friendly relations between the Indians and the freedmen could not last much longer. The Chickasaws insisted on their right to determine the question for themselves, a right

which they felt was not conditional upon approval by the United States
of their basis for decision. They asked the government to fulfill its treaty
obligations and remove the freedmen to the Leased District, to the Oklahoma lands, or to any other lands the freedmen might choose.[13]

Commissioner J. D. C. Atkins was convinced that in 1887 there was no
longer any authority to remove the freedmen from the Chickasaw Nation,
either with or without their consent. However, he recommended that if
any congressional legislation authorized their removal, the Chickasaws
should be required to refund the $55,000 that had been advanced to them
from the $300,000 provided for in the treaty and the amount should be
appropriated for the benefit of the freedmen.[14]

That spring and summer, the blacks once more sought assistance from
the Indian Office. One group claimed that the Chickasaws had built fences
within fifty yards of their houses in violation of Chickasaw laws. They had
appealed to the governor of the Nation, who said that they had no rights.
Another group from Tishomingo County sent W. B. Jackson to Muskogee
to appeal to Union Agent Robert L. Owen for educational assistance. Owen
wanted to help and planned a meeting in Tishomingo in September, when
he hoped to meet with freedmen from all of the black communities in the
Chickasaw Nation as well as with the Chickasaw governor and legislators.
Commissioner Atkins, however, dampened Owen's hopes by stressing that
there were no funds available for educating the freedmen. However, he instructed Owen to make his visit to Tishomingo and urge the Chickasaws
to take such action as was right and just. He pointed out to Owen that the
Chickasaws had been overpaid $55,000 on account of the blacks and sug-
gested that if, for political reasons, they were unwilling to adopt the blacks,
they should at least provide for the education of the black children.[15]

On September 14, as planned, Owen met the following committee representing the freedmen of the Chickasaw Nation: W. N. Jackson, Wash Taylor,
and Sam Cheadle of Tishomingo County; Phillip Stephenson, Mack Stephenson, and Dick Roberts of Pickens County; Isham Love, Caleb Love, and
Abram Eastman of Panola County; Jack Alexander, Wilson Chico (or
Sheco), and Lee Kemp of Pontotoc County; Henry Kemp of the Stringtown settlement of Chickasaw freedmen in the Choctaw Nation; and T. J.
Humphries of the Caddo settlement in the Choctaw Nation. Representing
some two or three thousand freedmen, they reported that their people were
doing "tolerably well" with their farming and stock raising, that the Chickasaws treated them well, that they were without schools, that they would

like to be adopted by the Chickasaws, and that although they were willing
to remove in 1866, since then they had grown attached to the land they
farmed and wished to remain unless the government thought it best that
they go.[16]

Owen told them that he would report their resolutions and offered his
services to them. After private consultation, the committee handed Owen
their decision, written as follows: "The hole Number of men has A Greed
to be left in the hand of the united State if the Chickasaw do Not take us."
Before leaving, they gave Owen the names and post offices of their leading
men: Isham Love (Colbert), W. N. Jackson (Washita Settlement), Isham
Flint (Mill Creek), Cap H. Harper (Cherokee Town), Isham Alexander
(Johnsonville), King Blue (Stonewall), Wilson Chico and Lee Kemp (Tisho-
mingo), Jim Williams (Fort Arbuckle), Mack Stephenson (Woodward),
Si Love (Burneyville), Charles Cohee (Dresden), Henry Kemp (Stringtown,
Choctaw Nation), and T. J. Humphries (Caddo, Choctaw Nation).[17]

Owen then met with eight members of the Chickasaw legislature, urging
them to take action to improve the freedmen's condition. But he got no-
where. They said that the government could recover the $55,000 from
money that the United States held for the Chickasaws. They insisted that
they had no unfriendly feelings for the freedmen but that they would
never, under any circumstances, adopt them because of their numbers and
because of the difficulty of establishing citizenship rolls. They insisted
that the United States must fulfill its obligation to remove the freedmen
under Article 3 of the treaty. Because of this stiff resistance, Owen asked
that Congress pass legislation for removal of the freedmen to the land
acquired from the Creeks adjacent to the Chickasaw Nation.[18]

Owen then asked the leading freedmen of the communities to supply
him with information regarding their condition and numbers. They
generally reported that they got along well with the Chickasaws and
wished to stay in the Nation, where they had their homes. They generally
complained, however, of their poverty and the lack of educational opportunities for their children, and some complained that the Chickasaws
ignored their property lines. Thus some asked that they be allowed to
establish a colony on other lands. Cap Harper reported that near Wynnewood there were 157 freedmen exclusive of intermarried freedmen and
freedmen adopted by other Indian nations. On Spring Creek were 311.
Charles Cohee of Berwyn reported 306 on the Lower Washita. Wilson
Chico reported 123 at Cross Roads. Isham Love reported 109 at Colbert

Station. At the Arbuckle settlement were 395. Eighteen were reported at Caddo in the Chocktaw Nation, and at Blue Station were reported 116. Just across the line from there in the Choctaw Nation were sixty-two or more.[19]

Besides the complaints channeled through Owen, many went directly from the freedmen to Commissioner J. D. C. Atkins during the spring of 1888. The freedmen were concerned with the lack of schools, the rights of blacks who married Chickasaw freedmen, and Chickasaw permit laws, but most of the complaints concerned the treatment of freedmen by whites who had married Chickasaws. According to the freedmen, these "squaw men," as they called them, disregarded the Chickasaw laws concerning the public domain and fenced up to and sometimes across the small five-, ten-, or fifteen-acre plots of the freedmen. Unlike the intermarried freedmen, the "squaw men" could improve as much land as they wished and could hire laborers from the United States. Atkins referred many of these complaints to Owen for investigation.[20]

Such complaints simply added evidence to a conclusion that Owen had put forth in his annual report in the fall of 1887: the government must do something for the freedmen. Since many freedmen had made improvements on land that had been occupied but not owned by their fathers, he felt it only just, if the freedmen were forced to remove, to pay them full value for the improvements in addition to the $100 per capita promised in the Treaty of 1866. There remained $17,375 of the original $300,000. Atkins believed that amount should be appropriated and the $55,125 that had already been paid to the Chickasaws should be recovered to assist the freedmen in removing. He believed that the Chickasaws were so anxious to be rid of their freedmen that they would not object to legislation asking them to return the funds, provided that the same legislation asked for the removal of the freedmen.[21]

The Chickasaws had earlier expressed their willingness to return the money. In the fall of 1887, their legislature again passed a memorial and resolution in which they reviewed their relationship with the freedmen. They saw their offer of land to the west and $100 per capita as a "boon" to the freedmen, one enjoyed by no other freedmen anywhere. Whereas the other Indians had offered the freedmen a franchise and home among them, the Chickasaws had provided them a place where they could build "their own government, schools, and churches, under the fostering care of the United States Government." The Chickasaws claimed that they had steadily refused to adopt the freedmen and that they had accepted $55,000 under the impression that it was an advance made under the forty-sixth article of the Treaty of 1866, for the admission of the Kansas Indians to their western lands and not for the freedmen. Insisting that they had a "kindly and friendly feeling towards the freedmen," the Chickasaw legislature gave the freedmen two years from the passage of the act to sell their improvements "to the best advantage" and provided for the refund to the United States of the $55,000 to be used in removal of the blacks. Finally, they provided for copies of the memorial and resolution to be placed in the hands of every member of the U.S. Senate and House of Representatives.[22]

In May, 1888, Commissioner Atkins drafted and submitted a bill that provided for the removal of all freedmen who consented to the Oklahoma lands. They were to be enrolled and their improvements appraised. They would not be required to remove until they had sold their improvements, but if the Chickasaw Nation should pay the freedman the assessed value, he had sixty days within which to remove. Once a freedman had disposed of his improvements, he and every member of his family would receive $100. Those refusing to remove would be put on "the same footing as other citizens of the United States, resident in said nation." The freedmen who removed would receive allotments in severalty in Oklahoma under the provisions of the General Allotment Act. Finally, $77,375 would be appropriated to make the per-capita payment. Atkins doubted that the amount would be sufficient, since there were an estimated three to four thousand freedmen in the Chickasaw Nation, but it was enough to "test the practicability of this effort for their relief." He believed that the proposed legislation was acceptable to both the Chickasaws and the freedmen "although the latter would doubtless prefer to remain, if they could be accorded the rights of citizenship and school facilities."[23] As with many such bills, Congress took no action, for by the time Atkins submitted the bill, Oklahoma was no longer being seriously considered as a potential area for colonizing the freedmen. In early 1889 the government reached agreement with the Creeks and Seminoles, and on April 22, the lands were opened to public settlement. Congress did not pass legislation relating to the Chickasaw freedmen until 1893.

Meanwhile the freedmen remained in a forlorn condition. The problems that beset them from 1888 to 1893 were much the same as those that had plagued them since the war. Foremost was the uncertainty of their status among the Chickasaws, who steadfastly refused to grant them any relief. The platform of the Chickasaw National Party in the election of 1888 read, in part, that the group opposed "the adoption of the negro in any way, shape, or form." The National Party was on the ascendancy in the Nation, a fact that boded ill for the freedmen in the years ahead. In the summer of 1889, James Williams, of Hennepin, Chickasaw Nation, communicated through the new agent, Leo E. Bennett, the desires of some of the freedmen to become citizens of the Nation. Secretary T. J. Morgan, knowing that the Chickasaws were not likely to adopt the blacks, instructed Bennett to render them every assistance in securing a hearing before the Chickasaw authorities and in ameliorating their condition. Bennett was to stress that since the Oklahoma lands were no longer available for the freedmen's settlement, their removal was no longer practical.[24]

In the fall of 1889, the freedmen took more active steps to secure rights as Chickasaw citizens. Some of them sought legal counsel. As a group, they petitioned the Chickasaw legislature. They met in convention at Stonewall on September 1, drafted a bill for their adoption, and selected two delegates from each of seven freedman communities to present the bill to the legislature. The bill was read by Governor William Byrd before a joint session of both houses, dominated by the conservative National Party members, but the speaker of the house told the freedmen that the agenda was so full that they should probably go home and come back when the legislature reconvened on October 14. The freedmen did so, but their bill was ignored when the legislature met. Jacob Mitchell, one of the fourteen freedman delegates, sought advice from Washington. According to Mitchell the freedmen believed that they were in "imminent danger" of losing the rights to which they felt entitled. The other four Civilized Tribes had adopted their freedmen, and the Chickasaw freedmen were afraid that if they did not secure their rights immediately they would be left out altogether. As Mitchell put it, "The probabilities of great changes in this country seem most likely and we must see to our rights at once or we will forever lose them."[25]

"Great changes" were indeed in the offing. The Oklahoma lands had been opened to non-Indian settlement in April, thus removing the possibility of a freedman colony there. There had been constant talk of "sectionizing" Chickasaw lands and allotting them in severalty. With passage of the General Allotment Act in 1887, the possibility seemed nearer, although the Chickasaws, among other tribes, had been excepted from the provisions of the bill.

The freedmen went to Tishomingo again the early days of 1890, only to hear their plea for adoption turned down by the Chickasaws, who re-

affirmed their determination never to adopt the blacks. The blacks elected
Mobile Richardson and Marcus Hamilton as corresponding secretaries and
asked Agent Bennett to follow his instructions from the Indian Office
and give them assistance. They were impatient; they had been free for
twenty-four years but had never voted. Now they asked that the government compel the Chickasaws to act. On February 7, the freedmen met
in general convention at Emmet, with L. J. Kemp as president and Jackson Alexander as secretary. They drafted a statement expressing their
dissatisfaction with their condition and their displeasure that nothing had
been done in their behalf. They now wondered if anything could be done
without bloodshed and threatened that unless they got an answer soon,
there would "be considerable trouble" between them and the Chickasaws.[26]

To Bennett, blame for the freedmen's condition rested on the United
States government:

The close of twenty-five years of 'freedom' (?) finds the Chickasaw
Freedmen the most wretched people in this Western Country. They are
poor, deplorably ignorant, and are buffetted around from pillar to post,
abused, degraded, debased and denied. No home, no country, no government, no schools; it is not possible for them to be lower in the moral scale.

Since it was not practical for the government to remove the freedmen
from the Chickasaw country, he said, the "desire to deal honestly with
these poor, benighted human beings ought to prompt some equitable
settlement of their status." To Bennett the freedmen were the most
"mistreated and most shamefully abused people on earth."[27] In September, 1890, Acting Commissioner R. V. Belt recommended that the
freedmen's complaints be forwarded to the House Committee on Indian
Affairs.[28] Once more, as in so many previous instances, no legislation
was forthcoming.

In 1891 and 1892 the freedmen met frequently to push for their rights.
At Stonewall on April 2, 1891, with Edmond Brown as chairman, they
drafted another appeal to the governor. In the next month, freedmen in
Pontotoc, Tishomingo, Panola, and Pickens counties met and elected
E. D. Colbert and H. C. Kemp as corresponding secretaries, who asked
the secretary of the interior to secure for them the treatment received
by freedmen of the other Civilized Tribes. Secretary Morgan's answer
was simply a statement of the treaty stipulations upon which the freedmen's claims to rights were based.[29]

Of particular concern to the freedmen in the spring of 1891 was an act of the Chickasaw legislature that excluded the freedmen from the per-capita payments that resulted from the sale of national lands. In 1889 the Choctaws and Chickasaws had claimed additional compensation for certain parts of the Leased District. They contended that the lands were to be used only for the settlement of other Indians and freedmen and that they were due more money because the land had been used differently. When the claim was sent to Congress, it was recommended that any settlement should safeguard the interests of the freedmen. When Congress was debating the opening of the surplus lands in the Cheyenne and Arapaho reservation to non-Indian settlement, it decided to grant an award of $2,991,450 to the Choctaws and Chickasaws, but no provision was made for the freedmen. President Benjamin Harrison, convinced that no additional money was due the tribes, sent the matter back to Congress for reconsideration. In his special message to Congress, Harrison expressed concern that the tribal legislatures were preparing to distribute the funds per capita but were excluding from the payment the freedmen and adopted whites. Since the treaty stipulations had not been complied with regarding the freedmen, especially among the Chickasaws, the United States should have made some provision for them. The President thought that it was time for "the protective intervention of Congress." However, Congress simply passed a resolution reaffirming the original act.[30]

On March 3, 1891, Congress appropriated nearly three million dollars for the 2,393,170 acres of surplus lands, one-fourth of which, the Chickasaws' share, was $474,862.50. On April 1, the Chickasaw legislature authorized receipt of the funds and the signing of a deed of conveyance to the land. One-quarter of the funds went for attorney's fees; the rest was distributed per capita on the basis of a census of Chickasaws by blood authorized by the legislature on March 30, 1891.[31]

Spurred to action by these events, a group of freedmen, with Ervin McCain as secretary, inquired late in 1891 concerning the advantages of sending a delegation to Washington to represent the freedmen of the different counties before the next Congress. In January, 1892, they met in convention at Wynnewood and elected two delegates to go to Washington to seek redress concerning tenure of land, schools, voice in the management of the government, and vote in the counties in which they resided. In early February, Charles Cohee and Marcus Hamilton went to Washington with appropriate letters of introduction from Agent Bennett.[32]

At about the time the freedman delegates arrived in Washington, Senator Henry L. Dawes introduced a bill for the relief of the Chickasaw freedmen. First, it authorized the secretary of the interior to remove all persons of African descent who were residents of the Chickasaw Nation on September 13, 1865, and who had not been adopted as citizens. Second, the secretary was to obtain from the Chickasaws a cession of as much land adjoining Oklahoma Territory as necessary to give allotments of eighty acres to each freedman. Third, the secretary was to designate a special agent to determine which freedmen would consent to remove and to appraise the value of their improvements. Fourth, freedmen were to be given time to dispose of their improvements and to harvest crops. Fifth, each person removing would be paid $100 upon disposal of his property. Sixth, $77,570 would be appropriated to make the per-capita payments, provided that the Chickasaw Nation would refund to the United States the $55,000 it had received. Finally, all blacks who refused to leave the Chickasaw Nation would be placed on the same footing as other United States citizens residing there and subject to the same rules as other citizens.[33]

On February 17, 1892, the President addressed Congress concerning an Indian appropriations bill, assuming in his speech that the money to be paid the Chickasaws and Choctaws under Section 15 of the bill was for land ceded in fact by Article 3 of the Treaty of 1866. He also assumed that "an absolute, unqualified title was conveyed to the United States." Chickasaw delegates B. C. Burney and Overton Love argued on February 26 that the title was conveyed in trust only. They reminded the Congress that the $300,000 was held in trust for the freedmen if the tribes did not adopt them and if they refused to leave the nations. If within two years the freedmen were adopted or should refuse to leave the nations, then and only then did the money go to the Indians. The sum was to cover the costs of removing the freedmen, not to pay for the land. In fact, the Chickasaws claimed, the sum was arrived at by multiplying $100 times the three thousand freedmen then among the Indians. They maintained that they were confronted with difficulties that the Choctaws had not faced. Among the freedmen in their nation were Choctaw freedmen, black soldiers from the states mustered out at Fort Sill, and blacks from the United States "who had been attracted to this African stronghold in the Chickasaw Nation." The Chickasaws refused to confer citizenship upon their freedmen and therefore received no part of the money.[34]

On April 21, 1892, Congress passed a joint resolution authorizing the

President to appoint a commission to negotiate with Chickasaw commissioners an agreement providing for the removal of all persons of African descent who had been slaves on September 13, 1865, and had not
been admitted to Choctaw citizenship and for their location on lands
west of the Chickasaw Nation.[35] However, the negotiations never took
place.

Between 1888 and 1893, while the freedmen were active in attempting to secure their citizenship in the Nation, they were beset by other
problems. In his annual report for 1888, Agent Robert L. Owen had
said that his office was kept busy in "adjusting trespasses on them or
by them."[36] One such case had arisen in June of that year. Thomas
Randolph of Purcell claimed that he had taken up residence at his
place in 1887. Although at that time no one had a claim to the place,
in the spring of 1888 a man named Hayle claimed to have purchased
a right to it from one Lee, who had camped about three weeks on the
site in 1886 with a herd of horses. Lee had made no improvements.
Hayle lived about twenty or twenty-five miles away and apparently did
not have the means to improve the place but gave it to a man named
Blackwell for his use in return for Blackwell's fencing it. Blackwell,
who ran a livery stable in Purcell, had fenced it and was using it for
pasture. When he took over, Randolph had already plowed some ground
in preparation for planting, but the Chickasaws had ordered him not
to plant or to make any more improvements. Thus in 1888, Randolph
had made no crops, not even a garden. He had appealed to Owen, who
had referred him to the Chickasaw courts. Said Randolph, "Now colored
people stands a dredfull poor show of having any justice done them in or
by the courts of the Chickasaws." There was no recourse for them unless
they could "go to a higher justice." In Randolph's opinion, the "squaw
men" controlled affairs in the Chickasaw Nation.[37]

In 1889 Simon Love complained that the Chickasaws were trying to
make the freedmen leave the places they had been the first to settle on
and had worked hard to improve. In February 1890, Mobile Richardson
of Fort Arbuckle complained that he was intruded upon by a white man
and did not know "how or what to do." The man, who claimed that
Richardson had no right on the place, was cutting timber near Richardson's house and at the time of the complaint was cutting between the
house and a field not four hundred yards from Richardson's door. The
following May, a group of freedmen met at Colbert and drew up a formal

complaint through their spokesman G. W. Hall: the Chickasaws did not want the blacks to fence enough land to make a good living, insisted that the blacks could improve only forty acres, but did all they could to prevent them from fencing that much.[38]

Such complaints caused Agent Bennett to write of the freedmen in 1890:

How can they obtain land and hold it once enclosed and cultivated? Are they to straddle their fence with a gun in hand and shoot down the man who trespasses on them? Under the present laws and under the present customs this seems to be the only way they can hold their little patches. They have no redress or protection in Chickasaw courts . . . because they seemingly have no redress, they are trampled upon and pushed aside by the Chickasaw Indian or his leaser (another name for "boomer").

It was the duty of the United States, said Bennett, to protect the freedmen from both the Chickasaws and the boomers, who were "flocking in large numbers into the Chickasaw country."[39]

"Boomers" was a pejorative term for people who squatted illegally on land in an attempt to force the opening of the lands to settlement. However, many of the boomers were United States citizens who rented lands from the Chickasaws, who through the renters were able to increase their incomes. The Chickasaws had steadfastly denied the freedmen the right to hire citizens of the United States, but they had allowed the blacks to rent land to noncitizens. With the ascendancy of the National Party in Chickasaw politics, there were more attempts to enforce the permit laws. In 1889 and 1891 Simon Love complained that the Indians would not issue permits to noncitizens hired by the freedmen, and the noncitizens were afraid to work for the blacks for fear that the blacks would be put out of the Nation. In 1891, the Chickasaws refused to issue permits to the blacks. They arrested as intruders two men on Love's farm. The men had given Love the money with which to purchase their permits as the law required, but Agent Bennett had refused to issue them. Without laborers, Love had a "nice cotton crop" left untended. He complained that Bennett did not "recognize" the permitted blacks, as former agent Owen had done.[40]

While most of the cases of trespass coming before the agents resulted from white or Chickasaw infringement upon the freedmen, some resulted from blacks who trespassed upon Indians or other blacks. There was the

case of John Flounder, for instance, a former slave who had been owned
by a Chickasaw woman married to a white man named McDonna. She
had died about 1849 and McDonna had returned to Texas, taking Flounder
with him. Flounder was freed in Texas and was not in the Chickasaw Nation at the time of the treaty. He had later returned to the Nation and
had claimed to be a Chickasaw freedman, renting a small improvement
from a full-blood Chickasaw, Daniel Speaker, and was to have received
a part of the crop as his pay for work done on the place. Speaker died,
and in 1889 Flounder claimed to have purchased the improvements
and refused to turn them over to Speaker's widow.[41]

Another case in point was that of Pauline Bruner, the daughter of
Charity, a Chickasaw, and Big Jack, a half-Creek, half-black slave of
Creek Watt Grayson. Big Jack died, and Charity then married Manuel
Williams. When Pauline was about sixteen, the family moved to the
south bank of the Canadian River, about five miles south of Sacred
Heart Mission, where they built several houses and improved forty acres.
About 1888 Charity and Williams died. Pauline Bruner went to claim
the improvements, but John Tibbs, a black from the states, took them
over, claiming to be guardian of Williams' nephew, to whom Williams
had allegedly willed the improvements. Mrs. Bruner said that it was her
place; she had "worked it," and one of her "girls was burned to death
working it," she said. When she went to Tibbs "to reason with him,"
he knocked her down and beat her "rudely."[42]

Another matter of prime concern to the freedmen between 1888 and
1893 was the lack of educational facilities for their children. They had
had no schools, except a few run by missionaries, since 1884. The Chickasaw freedmen later complained that with the exception of the few
years of government funding of freedman education in the 1870s and
early 1880s, their children had had no opportunities for advancement
through education. In his report for 1889, Owen said that the children
were not only growing up in ignorance but also in "consequent misery
and crime," and he called the freedmen's condition "the most deplorable
of any people in the United States."[43] Despite their sympathy, Owen and
other government officials had to turn a deaf ear to the pleas that had
come in throughout 1889. In March and June, inquiries had come from
Simon Love of Pauls Valley. In April Ervin McCain of Marietta reported
that the freedmen of his community had a schoolhouse ready for their
twenty-five children and asked the United States to supply a teacher. In

May, George A. L. Dykes, superintendent of schools and buildings for
the Indian Missions Conference of the African Methodist Episcopal Church,
asked for a thousand dollars to hire teachers, proposing to use the freedman churches for schoolhouses. In August, Soloman Abrams and Henry
Kemp of Boggy Depot asked for at least three free schools because the
freedmen were not financially able to support them. The answer was
always the same: educational matters among the Five Civilized Tribes
were tribal concerns, and the government could not appropriate funds.[44]

In 1890, McCain inquired once more, arguing that if the freedmen did
not belong to the Chickasaws, then they must belong to the United States,
whose government was obligated to educate them. He said that it looked
as if "some nation ought to claim us." In March, the Reverend Nelson
Johnson informed Agent Bennett that there were forty-five children of
school age in the settlement near Colbert. They had had no school in four
or five years, but had built a schoolhouse twenty-four by thirty feet. Now
they asked for federal funds to operate the school. In June a group met
at Colbert, with G. W. Hall as spokesman, and formally requested instructions on how to get a school for their children. The request was
signed by Hall, K. A. Love, U. C. Jameson, Frank Thompson, I. Love,
C. C. Jameson, F. A. Kemp, and Abram Eastman, who estimated that
there were between eight hundred and a thousand freedman children
without schools in the Nation. In August an appeal came from Bell Randolph of Wynnewood, who said that the freedman children were "ignorant,
almost savages; we are not really sivilized [sic]." She asked for teachers.
In her opinion, the United States had as much right "to give us schools as
they do to furnish penetenturies [sic] for our misdemeners [sic]." And the
following month, a group of freedmen met in convention at Emmet to
draft a petition. Signed by Wilson Chico, Isaac Kemp, Henry Nail, Alex
Nail, Eli Eastman, Richard Eastman, Dave McCoy, Lee Kemp, and Smith
Kemp, the petition asked for an investigation of why the Chickasaw
freedmen were not receiving educational privileges like the Choctaw freedmen and requested information concerning what funds due the Chickasaws might be diverted to the Chickasaw freedmen.[45]

In 1891 T. J. White attempted to start a "college" at Emmet and asked
for federal assistance, but Secretary Thomas J. Morgan suggested that White
incorporate his project under the laws of a nearby state or of the Territory
of Oklahoma or to seek passage of an act of incorporation during the next
session of Congress. To Fred Humphrey of Wynnewood and to Ervin McCain

of Marietta, Morgan reaffirmed the department's usual answer: educational matters of the Five Civilized Tribes were tribal affairs and out of the department's hands. And to Humphrey, Morgan suggested that the freedmen lay their problem before "some religious societies who were already supporting schools there." Late in 1892, some of the freedmen's appeals apparently reached the United States commissioner of education. Morgan verified the dismal condition of the Chickasaw freedmen and suggested that the commissioner get further facts from Agent Leo E. Bennett and Miss Alice Robertson, who had spent most of her life among the Creeks and had established a mission school among them.[46] Appeals such as these were fruitless. Educational privileges were at least another decade away for the freedmen.

Thus the freedmen appeared to have lost in their early struggle for rights because they were caught between the opposing desires of the Chickasaws and the United States. To the former, particularly the mixed-blood elite, the blacks represented a potential political bloc if they allied themselves with the Chickasaw full bloods. The Chickasaws therefore rejected the idea of adopting the freedmen, but the United States opposed their desires to have the blacks removed. At first, officials were apparently not willing to recognize the failure of the United States to fulfill its obligations under the Treaty of 1866. Later, official support for removing the freedmen from the Chickasaw Nation quickly eroded when the potential resettlement areas attracted the attention of land-hungry Americans, whose desires for land were of more concern to the United States than were the obligations to the Chickasaw freedmen. But in the early 1890s, the freedmen's sense of imminent change in the Indian Territory was justified. During the succeeding years, they would continue their struggle for rights in the Chickasaw Nation. In this one, however, unlike their earlier struggle, they would have a powerful ally in the United States Congress, which began to take more drastic steps to dissolve the common title to lands in the Indian nations and to allot lands in severalty to the tribal members. The question was whether the freedmen would share in the tribal lands.

NOTES

1. 55 Cong., 1 Sess., *Senate Document 157,* 13; Resolution of the Chickasaw Freedmen, February 8, 1884, National Archives Record Group

75, *Letters Received Relating to Choctaw and Other Freedmen, 1878-84,* 6947-84.

2. Memorial of the Freedmen of the Chickasaw Nation, *Letters Received Relating to Choctaw and Other Freedmen, 1878-84,* 13113-84; Hiram Price to Secretary of the Interior, April 12, 1884, National Archives Record Group 75, *Letters Sent,* Report 48: 129.

3. Halpert E. Paine to Committee on Indian Affairs, April 22, 1884, 50 Cong., 1 Sess., *Senate Executive Document 166,* 17-18, hereafter cited as *Document 166; Indian Champion,* April 26 and May 3, 1884.

4. John Bartlett Meserve, "Governor Jonas Wolf and Governor Palmer Simeon Mosely," *Chronicles of Oklahoma,* 18 (September 1940), 241, 244; *Indian Journal,* May 15, 1884; *Indian Champion,* May 10 and 24, 1884.

5. Humphrey Colbert to Price, June 14, 1884, National Archives Record Group 48 (Office of the Secretary of the Interior), Indian Territory Division, *Chickasaw Freedmen,* Box 392(60b), 11925-84 (subsequent references to this file are from Box 392); Price to Colbert, June 27, 1884, *Letters Sent,* Land 127: 98.

6. Price to Willburne Gaines, August 31, 1883, *Letters Sent,* Civilization 164: 533; Price to E. E. McClain [McCain], August 22, 1882, and February 11, 1884, *Letters Sent,* Land 170: 518, and Land Letter Books 121-122: 68; Price to James Love, September 6, 1884, *Letters Sent,* Land Letter Books 129-130: 340; McCain to J. Q. Tufts, January 26, 1885, Tufts to Commissioner, February 6, 1885, Abram Eastman to J. D. C. Atkins, February 13, 1883, and McCain to Secretary, March 2, 1886, *Chickasaw Freedmen,* 2780-85, 5321-86, 7177-86.

7. J. W. Hall to Secretary, March 22, 1885, *Chickasaw Freedmen,* 6714-85; 54 Cong., 1 Sess., *Senate Document 182,* 109; A. B. Upshaw to Simon Love, April 2, 1886, *Letters Sent,* Land Letter Book 146: 274.

8. *Constitution, and Laws of the Chickasaw Nation together with the Treaties of 1832, 1833, 1834, 1837, 1852, 1855 and 1866* (Parsons, Kans.: The Foley Railway Printing Company, 1899), 171-173, hereafter cited as *Constitution and Laws;* 55 Cong., 1 Sess., *Senate Document 157,* 3, 28-39; Memorial of the Chickasaw Nation, received March 16, 1886, *Chickasaw Freedmen,* 7773-86.

9. Memorial of the Chickasaw Freedmen, April 19, 1886, *Chickasaw Freedmen,* 13488-86.

10. 49 Cong., 1 Sess., *Senate Report 1278,* 2: 277.

11. Memorial of the Chickasaw Nation, January 15, 1887, National Archives Record Group 75, *Letters Received,* 1471-87; *Document 166,* 4, 11-12; see also, *Annual Report of the Commissioner of Indian Affairs to the Secretary of the Interior for the Year 1887* (Washington, D.C.:

Government Printing Office, 1887), LXIII, hereafter cited as *Annual Report, 1887.*

12. Memorial of the Chickasaw Nation, January 15, 1887, *Letters Received,* 1471-87.

13. *Ibid.*

14. Atkins to Secretary, January 25, 1887, *Letters Sent,* Land Letter Book 155: 321.

15. Samuel Jones, Charles Cohee, and Brister Williams to Secretary, May 14, 1887, and R. L. Owen to Atkins, July 29, 1887, *Chickasaw Freedmen,* 13378-87, 20116-87.

16. Owen to Atkins, September 17, 1887, *Chickasaw Freedmen,* 25002-87; *Document 166,* 8.

17. *Document 166,* 8.

18. *Ibid.,* 8-9.

19. Owen to Atkins, November 14, 1887, with enclosures, *Chickasaw Freedmen.*

20. W. N. Jackson to Owen, November 21, 1887, and Thomas Randolph to Secretary, May 7, 1888, *Chickasaw Freedmen;* Atkins to Owen, March 16, 1888, and Atkins to James C. Jamison, April 23, 1888, *Letters Sent,* Land Letter Book 171-172: 318, 428.

21. *Annual Report, 1887,* LXII-LXIV.

22. *Document 166,* 9-10; 54 Cong., 1 Sess., *Senate Document 182,* 109; 55 Cong., 1 Sess., *Senate Document 157,* 29-30.

23. William F. Vilas to Speaker of the House, May 9, 1888, *Document 166,* 1, 5-7; *Annual Report of the Commissioner of Indian Affairs to the Secretary of the Interior for the Year 1888* (Washington, D.C.: Government Printing Office, 1888), LX-LXI, hereafter cited as *Annual Report, 1888; Indian Chieftain,* June 7, 1888.

24. *Annual Report, 1888,* 116; Leo E. Bennett to Commissioner, July 23, 1889, *Letters Received,* 20572-89; T. J. Morgan to Bennett, August 9, 1889, *Letters Sent,* Land Letter Book 188: 126.

25. J. Fletcher Sharp to Commissioner, October 25, 1889, and Jacob Mitchell to Commissioner, October 29, 1889, *Letters Received,* 30933-89, 31236-89.

26. Mobile Richardson and Marcus Hamilton to Leo Bennett, January 16, 1890, and L. J. Kemp to Whom It May Concern, February 7, 1890, *Letters Received,* 4845-90, 4212-90.

27. Bennett to Commissioner, February 12, 1890, *Letters Received,* 4845-90.

28. R. V. Belt to Secretary, September 26, 1890, *Letters Sent,* Land Letter Book 204: 427.

29. Petition of Chickasaw Freedmen, April 2, 1891, and H. C. Kemp to Secretary, May 25, 1891, *Letters Received,* 14496-91, 20063-91; Morgan to Kemp and E. D. Colbert, June 11, 1891, *Letters Sent,* Land Letter Book 218: 242.

30. *Constitution and Laws,* 236-237, 253-254, 271-272; 54 Cong., 1 Sess., *Senate Document 182,* 118-119.

31. *Constitution and Laws,* 279-285.

32. Arvin [Ervin] McCain, et al. to John W. Noble, December 8, 1891, *Letters Received,* 44541-91. The inquiry was signed as well by Scott Wright, Aaron Wright, Richard Johnson, Jack Davis, Frank Wilson, and Jonas Cherry. The convention chairman and secretary were Bart Franklin and A. C. Mayes, and the convention committee consisted of Zack Allen, Simon Love, Charlie Williams, James Williams, Dixie Smith, George Stevenson, Jacob Mitchell, Noah Smith, William Alexander, Newton Burney, Bill Fisher, and Richard Prince. Bennett to Commissioner, February 5, 1892, *Letters Received,* 5037-92, with enclosure.

33. Senate Bill 2033, February 9, 1892, *Letters Received,* 5579-92; *Congressional Record,* 52 Cong., 1 Sess. (February 3, 1892), 789.

34. 52 Cong., 1 Sess., *Senate Miscellaneous Document 82,* 1-2.

35. Joint Resolution, April 21, 1892, *Letters Received,* 14826-92.

36. *Annual Report, 1888,* 132.

37. Randolph to Commissioner, received June 22, 1888, *Chickasaw Freedmen,* 15841-88.

38. Love to Secretary, June 4, 1889, Richardson to Bennett, February 7, 1890, and G. W. Hall to Bennett, May 19, 1890, *Letters Received,* 15600-89, 4844-90, 17568-90.

39. Bennett to Commissioner, February 12, 1890, *Letters Received,* 4845-90.

40. Love to Secretary, received March 18, 1889, and Love to William M. Cravens, July 11, 1891, *Letters Received,* 7057-89, 33676-91.

41. Bennett to Commissioner, September 3, 1889, with enclosures, *Letters Received,* 25016-89.

42. Bennett to Commissioner, February 12, 1890, with enclosures, *Letters Received,* 4844-90.

43. *Annual Report of the Commissioner of Indian Affairs to the Secretary of the Interior for the Year 1889* (Washington, D.C.: Government Printing Office, 1889), 206; 54 Cong., 1 Sess., *Senate Document 182,* 110.

44. Love to Secretary, March 18 and June 4, 1889, McCain to Department of Indian Affairs, April 15, 1889, George A. L. Dykes to John H. Oberly, May 6, 1889, and Soloman Abrams and Henry Kemp to Secre-

tary, August 6, 1889, *Letters Received,* 7057-89, 15600-89, 10317-89, 15119-89, 22553-89; Belt to J. W. Roberts, May 2, 1889, Belt to Dykes, June 11, 1889, and Belt to Abrams and Kemp, August 28, 1889, *Letters Sent,* Education 17: 211A and 50B, and 18: 167B.

45. McCain to Secretary, January 24, 1890, Bennett to Commissioner, March 27, 1890, June 5, 1890, with enclosure, and August 16, 1890, and Isaac Kemp, et al. to Commissioner, September 13, 1890, *Letters Received,* 2805-90, 9577-90, 17568-90, 25459-90, 18842-90.

46. Morgan to T. J. White, April 20, 1891, *Letters Sent,* Land Letter Book 215: 155; Morgan to Fred Humphrey, April 24, 1891, Belt to Mc-Cain, August 22, 1891, and Morgan to William T. Harris, November 2, 1892, *Letters Sent,* Education 165: 8, and 170: 368, and 193: 454; McCain to Morgan, August 9, 1891, *Letters Received,* 29718-91.

7

The Dawes Commission and Enrollment

In every Congress after 1870, there had been efforts to establish a territorial government in the Indian Territory, to dissolve the Indian nations, and to open their surplus lands to non-Indian settlement. The opening of the unassigned lands in 1889 and the subsequent formation of the Oklahoma Territory had momentarily satisfied the American demand for more free land. However, economic development of the West made it necessary to solve the "Indian problem." For twenty years following the Civil War, there had been a great interest on the part of reformers and others in assimilating the Indians into American society. The General Allotment Act of 1887, also known as the Dawes Act, had been an attempt at assimilation. It gave the President discretionary powers to make the reservation Indians give up their common title to the land and take allotments of land in severalty. After each Indian had received his allotment, the government, with tribal consent, could sell the surplus lands to non-Indian settlers. However, because of the nature of their land title, the Chickasaws, Choctaws, Cherokees, Creeks, Seminoles, Osages, Kaws, Quapaws, and Confederated Peorias of the Indian Territory had been excepted. Now Congress turned its attention toward those tribes and in early 1893 took a step that drastically changed the course of events for the Chickasaws and the other Civilized Tribes and their freedmen. An Indian appropriations bill of March 3 provided for a commission to treat with the tribes to secure allotment of land in severalty, dissolution of tribal government, and territorial status for the Indian Territory. After persuading the Indians to relinquish the titles to their lands, the commissioners were to determine the size of allotments and to prepare tribal rolls. All of this was preparatory to the formation of one or more states embracing the lands of the Indian Territory. Creation of the Dawes Commission, originally consisting of Henry L. Dawes, Meredith H. Kidd, and Archibald S. McKennon,[1] was the first step toward the dissolution of the Chickasaw and other Indian Nations. The work of the Commission therefore profoundly affected the lives of the Chickasaw freedmen.

As soon as the commissioners received their instructions, they set up headquarters first at Muskogee, Creek Nation, and then at South McAlester, Choctaw Nation. They informed the chiefs or governors of the tribes of their purpose and asked for an early conference, at which the commissioners explained their desire to negotiate with the tribes. At first the tribes appeared to favor negotiation, but when they learned in Washington that there would be no change in their tribal status unless they desired it, they became less disposed to negotiate. The commissioners later charged that tribal officials, who were large landholders, were resisting change in order to continue filling their pockets at tribal expense. The Dawes Commission met with a large number of Chickasaws at Tishomingo on February 6, 1894, and then traveled through the Nation explaining their mission. They submitted for Chickasaw consideration a proposition to dissolve the Chickasaw Nation, allot its land in severalty, and divide the tribal funds per capita. They also explained that among the official charges were specific instructions regarding the Chickasaw freedmen. Since they had no tribal rights, the Commission was instructed by the Indian Office to try to obtain Chickasaw consent to give the freedmen allotments of land. However, the national council met in regular session and took no action on the proposal.[2]

In their first three annual reports and in their public statements, the Dawes Commission members presented what they purported to be a realistic picture of affairs in the Indian Territory but which, in fact, reflected the arguments of land-hungry white citizens and politicians. They denounced the alleged exploitation of full-blood Indians by the mixed bloods, who held political power in the nations. They told how white intruders suffered inconveniences, stressed the great number of violent crimes in the territory, and emphasized the lack of development of its natural resources. In their first report in 1894 they called attention to the Chickasaw treatment of the freedmen:

They now treat the whole class as aliens without any legal right to abide among them, or to claim any protection under their laws. They are shut out of the schools of the tribe, and from their courts, and are granted no privileges of occupancy of any part of the land for a home, and are helplessly exposed to the hostilities of the citizen Indian and the personal animosity of the former master. Peaceable, law-abiding, and hard working, they have sought in vain to be regarded as a part of the people to whose wealth their industry is daily contributing a very essential portion.[3]

Such reports resulted in some congressional action. In early 1894, a House bill was introduced to ameliorate the condition of the Chickasaw freedmen by establishing a commission to investigate the matter and to make a roll of all freedmen who were entitled to benefits under the Treaty of 1866 and proposing an appropriation for the freedmen's benefit. Commissioner of Indian Affairs D. M. Browning thought the legislation unnecessary, since the Dawes Commission had been instructed already to try to secure provision for the blacks in their negotiations with the Chickasaws. Because the United States had failed to remove the freedmen according to the treaty stipulations, Browning believed that they could not now be settled in the Chickasaw Nation without the consent of the Choctaw and Chickasaw Nations. As long as the Dawes Commission was empowered to negotiate with the tribes, he would not recommend any action by Congress. Under a Senate resolution of March 29, 1894, the Senate Committee on Indian Affairs, with H. M. Teller as chairman, visited the Indian Territory to inquire into the condition of the Five Civilized Tribes and the thousands of whites who were living in the Indian nations. Although the committee members were not empowered to look into the condition of the freedmen, they did note that the Chickasaws were the only tribe that failed to maintain freedman schools and that denied freedman suffrage. Even though the freedman population was somewhat larger than the Chickasaw population, the children grew up in ignorance except in a few cases where schools had been maintained by individual means. Teller's committee recommended in its preliminary report that the problem of the freedmen was so complex that proposed solutions be delayed and that a more complete investigation be made.[4]

Knowing that their status would be affected by any change in status of the Chickasaws, the Chickasaw freedmen established the Chickasaw Freedmen's Association to coordinate efforts to protect their status, rights, and interests in negotiations with the Dawes Commission. They decided that they needed legal counsel to present their claims before Congress, the President, the Dawes Commission, and the courts; thus they met in convention in 1894 and chose Joseph P. Mullen of Ardmore and Robert V. Belt of Washington as their attorneys.[5]

The freedmen made some advances in their claims on August 15, 1894, when in an Indian appropriations act Congress approved the twenty-one-year-old Chickasaw "Act to Adopt the negroes of the Chickasaw Nation," approved by the Chickasaw governor on January 10, 1873. Congressmen ignored the fact that the Chickasaws had passed an act in 1885 in opposition to adoption and argued that the 1873 act was binding, not having been repealed by subsequent acts of the Chickasaw legislature. The freedmen were encouraged by this congressional action, despite its making more confused an already confusing situation. It indicated that Congress was determined to fulfill its treaty stipulations regarding them. However, there was always the possibility that a final settlement might not be in the freedmen's favor or might protract the delay in settling the matter.[6]

On October 15 the freedmen met in convention and entered formal contracts with Mullen and Belt, who were to seek provisions for allotments for the freedmen or, failing that, to secure land for them elsewhere. They were also to seek legislation for the payment of damages sustained by the freedmen as a result of the long delay in carrying out the treaty stipulations and of the denial of educational privileges and titles to their land. The attorneys presented to the secretary of the interior an appeal that set forth the freedmen's claims and status. At the secretary's suggestion the Committee of the Chickasaw Freedmen's Association—Charles Cohee, Isaac C. Kemp, George W. Hall, and Mack Stevenson—presented a statement of their grievances through Belt and Mullen to the Dawes Commission. After reviewing the Treaty of 1866 and the failure by both the Chickasaws and the government to fulfill its stipulations, the freedmen pointed out that they had no role in negotiating the treaty and insisted, therefore, that the United States was duty bound to look after their interests. The committee also noted their attempts to obtain justice and congressional failure to act. They wrote:

The Chickasaw freedmen have waited many long and weary years for the settlement of their status, and the adjustment of their rights, privileges, immunities, claims, etc., so that they might have some security in the enjoyment of the fruits of their labors, educate their children, and surround themselves and their homes with some of the comforts of civilization.

Year after year, the agents and the commissioner of Indian affairs had reported their "wretched and deplorable condition." In contrast to their condition, the freedmen noted that of the freedmen of the other Civilized Tribes. Those who represented a large part of Seminole and Creek population, they said, stood as evidence to counter the fears of the Chickasaws that the freedman vote would "be detrimental to the welfare and interests of the Chickasaw Nation."[7]

The committee blamed the United States for not acting in their behalf. Had they suffered such injustice in a foreign land, they said, the people of the United States would have acted:

We are prone to believe that had our cries of distress come from some distant island of the sea, instead of from the midst of an Indian tribe right here in the United States, the power and influence of the Government of the United States would have been exerted to extricate us from our bondage and barbarism.

Nothing now could correct the effects of years of suffering, injustice, and ignorance, but relief could be given to the present generation. The freedmen blamed their condition on the diplomacy of the Choctaws and Chickasaws, who had secured treaty language that made adoption optional while the other tribes had been required to adopt their freedmen outright. Since 1866, the tribes had kept delegates in Washington, which the freedmen could not afford, to block legislation that might benefit the freedmen. Why had the government allowed the Choctaws and Chickasaws to succeed? Had the other nations "been more disloyal to the United States than the Choctaws and Chickasaws? Or were the former slaves of the latter less deserving than those of the other nations?" the committee asked.[8]

To the freedmen, a Chickasaw claim then pending for additional compensation for the Leased District might possibly be the last opportunity for the government to remedy the wrongs they had suffered. They had received none of the money paid the Chickasaws for surplus lands in the Cheyenne and Arapaho reservation, part of which had been in the Leased District and had been opened to public settlement on April 19, 1892. In 1894, the Choctaws and Chickasaws claimed extra compensation for surplus lands in the Kiowa, Comanche, and Wichita lands, also in the Leased District. The freedmen believed that the tribes would win this claim for about three and one-half million dollars, since the government had recognized the earlier claim. Would the Chickasaws be allowed to distribute their share per capita to only Chickasaws by blood, as had been the case with the first appropriation? Of that appropriation the freedmen wrote:

But of that immense sum of money not a schoolhouse was built for the education of the children of the freedmen, now and heretofore growing up in ignorance in the Chickasaw country, and not a cent of it was in any way used to ameliorate and improve the condition or to advance the welfare and interests of the Chickasaw freedmen.[9]

The Committee of the Chickasaw Freedmen's Association presented the following claims to the Dawes Commission. First, they asked for rights, privileges, and immunities equal to those of Chickasaw citizens, including suffrage, equal educational privileges, equal protection under the law, and equal shares in the moneys and public domain of the Nation. Second, they claimed indemnification for damage, loss, and injury sustained since 1866 as a result of being denied their rights as citizens. Third, they asked that, once their rights were secured, the Chickasaw lands be surveyed and allotted in severalty, at least to the freedmen. The freedmen hoped to settle their claims by an agreement between the United States and the Chickasaws, but if that failed and it became necessary for the freedmen to remove from the Nation, they asked for a sufficient amount of the surplus lands in the Kiowa, Comanche, and Wichita country to be set aside for them and for removal expenses, $100 per capita, indemnification for damages suffered since 1866, and allotment of land in severalty, with restrictions placed on the freedmen's ability to dispose of it. The freedmen's committee also appealed to the Dawes Commission to draft some measure for their behalf to be placed before Congress.[10]

In early 1895 there was more action in Congress. Bills for the Chickasaw freedmen were introduced in both houses, but no laws emerged.[11] Congress did, however, authorize a survey of the lands of the Five Civilized Tribes and expand the size of the Dawes Commission. Frank C. Armstrong replaced Kidd, and Thomas B. Cabaniss and Alexander B. Montgomery were added. Reorganized, the commission returned to the Indian Territory in the spring of 1895 and again sought to negotiate the dissolution of the nations, trying to convince the tribes that it was in their best interests. The tribal leaders all but ignored them. In the fall, however, the Chickasaws indicated that they were willing to listen to the commission's propositions. When

they appointed a commission to meet with the Dawes Commission, they
failed to meet but, instead, met with their counterparts of the Choctaw
Nation and drafted a rejection of the propositions suggested by the Dawes
Commission.[12]

While the Chickasaws steadfastly resisted the overtures of the Dawes
Commission, the freedmen sought their rights by other means. In February,
1895, for instance, freedman Edmond Humley sought clarification of the
freedmen's rights under the 1894 congressional act that had approved the
Chickasaw adoption act of 1873. Humley's letter indicated that the freedmen assumed that the act gave them rights as citizens of the Chickasaw
Nation. With that assumption, Humley had advertised for sale some walnut
logs that he had cut on his improvement. According to Chickasaw law,
only citizens could sell timber, and the sale was regulated by timber agents
of the Nation. The Chickasaws, of course, did not recognize the freedmen
as citizens. The Chickasaws seized the logs, and Humley appealed for help.
Browning suggested to Belt that perhaps the freedmen should test their
rights under law by suit in the courts of the Chickasaw Nation. If they
were afraid of prejudice in the courts, they should go to the United States
courts that had been established in the Indian Territory in 1889 and 1890.
That fall, Judge C. B. Kilgore, in hearing a case of larceny in the United
States court at Ardmore, decided that Section 18 of the congressional act
of 1894 had admitted all of the Chickasaw freedmen to citizenship in the
Chickasaw Nation and that an offense committed by one Chickasaw freedman against another was within the jurisdiction of the Chickasaw Nation
and not the jurisdiction of his court. In protesting the decision, the Chickasaws argued that the Nation had repealed the act in 1885, that the freedmen were without law, and that their presence in the Chickasaw Nation
was "a menace to themselves and to society in general." A few weeks later
Judge Kilgore reversed himself and sentenced a Chickasaw freedman to the
penetentiary for stealing cattle from another freedman.[13]

There were attempts elsewhere to clarify the status of the freedmen. On
January 20, 1896, a bill for their benefit was introduced in the House of
Representatives. And in February, King Blue and Joe Blue met with Chickasaw Governor Palmer S. Mosely, who denied that any congressional act
had granted the freedmen citizenship and refused to do anything for them.
The Blues then asked the Department of the Interior for clarification of
their status as citizens of the Chickasaw Nation. Commissioner Browning
replied that the Indian Office had no authority to force the Chickasaw

Nation to adopt the freedmen under existing laws, since the Chickasaws claimed to have repealed the adoption act of 1873. The force of the congressional act of 1894 had to be determined by the courts. Browning suggested that the only way that the matter could be determined was to bring a test case before the courts of the United States in the Indian Territory.[14]

In the summer of 1896, Congress made an effective inroad upon tribal resistance to its desires. On June 10, it authorized the Dawes Commission to hear and determine the applications for all persons, including freedmen, who might apply for citizenship in the Indian nations and to enroll the citizens. The existing rolls of the several tribes were confirmed, and the commission was charged with correcting the rolls by adding any names that had been omitted by fraud or wrong. The commission's roll was to be considered correct, and any tribe or person who did not agree with the decision of the tribal authorities or the Dawes Commission had sixty days to appeal to the U.S. district court. Finally, the act declared it the duty of the United States to establish a government in the Indian Territory to "rectify the many inequalities and discriminations now existing in said Territory, and afford needful protection to the lives and property of all citizens and residents thereof."[15]

That fall, under legislative authority, Chickasaw governor R. M. Harris appointed four commissioners as attorneys to confer with the Dawes Commission in all cases of citizenship and other business. The attorneys were also empowered to represent the Chickasaws before the United States district court and other tribunals regarding any question relating to Chickasaw citizenship. The governor was also authorized to hire two American attorneys to assist the Chickasaw attorneys in prosecuting their cases.[16]

The Chickasaw commission was not present at Muskogee on December 8, when the Dawes Commission negotiated with the Choctaws, but apparently in the name of both the Choctaws and Chickasaws, an agreement was made by which the tribes transferred title to their land in trust to the United States for the purpose of allotment in severalty. They agreed to allot an equal share in value to the citizens of the tribes except the freedmen, as provided for in the Treaty of 1866. Minerals were not to pass to the allottee but would remain in trust for the sole use of the Choctaws and Chickasaws, exclusive of the freedmen. It was also agreed that if it should be decided that the Chickasaw freedmen were not entitled to the forty acres of land provided for in the Treaty of 1866 and that the Choctaw freedmen were, then the lands allotted to the latter were to be deducted from the portion allotted to the Choctaw citizens and were not to affect the value of the allotments of the Chickasaw citizens. The freedmen who might be entitled to an allotment of forty acres were entitled to land equal in value to forty acres of the average-quality land of the two nations.[17]

The Chickasaws, of course, protested. In January, 1897, they created a commission to protest against congressional ratification of the agreement. The Chickasaws had been included in the agreement stipulations but had not been present at the negotiations. They considered themselves independent of the Choctaws. Should they desire to negotiate the cessation of their tribal government, they had the right to do so, but they could not allow the Choctaws to usurp their authority in determining the disposition of their pro-rata share of the Choctaw lands and minerals. The Chickasaw commissioners were empowered to negotiate with the Dawes Commission for a change from the present manner of holding land in common to holding it in severalty by the Chickasaw people, provided that the government would pay over to the people all the moneys due them. They were also empowered to negotiate for an inalienable status for allotments and fair rental per annum on town sites. Two Chickasaw commissioners were authorized to work with the United States commissioners in classifying the lands to be allotted. However, any agreement between the Chickasaw commissioners and the United States had to be ratified by the Chickasaw legislature and then approved by a vote of the Chickasaw people. In their protest to the secretary of the interior, the Chickasaw delegates charged that since the Chickasaws were not represented in the making of the agreement, they had had no opportunity to protect their rights or interests. They asserted that they had not adopted their freedmen and regarded them as citizens of the United States, who were not entitled to a share in the common domain, moneys, or other property of the tribe. The commissioners insisted on the freedmen's removal under Article 3 of the Treaty of 1866.[18]

Meanwhile, attorney R. V. Belt had conferred with the secretary of the interior and the Dawes Commission regarding the agreement of December 8, 1896. He had formally protested against the agreement, arguing that Congress could force compliance with a treaty by an Indian tribe and that its approval in 1894 of the Chickasaw act of adoption of 1873 had "the effect of clothing the Chickasaw freedmen with the treaty rights." He protested against the negotiation, approval, or ratification of any agreement that did not provide for allotments of forty acres for the freed-men. The secretary, however, made no mention of this protest when he sent the agreement to Congress for consideration.[19]

The Chickasaws were by then apparently convinced that they must negotiate in order to protect their interests. On March 1, 1897, they created a commission to negotiate with the Dawes Commission concerning the equal division of their lands, their coal and mineral interests, the perpetuation of their present form of government for as long as possible, their right to decide their own citizenship cases, the settlement of claims growing out of treaties with the United States, and the preservation of their patent inviolate. Any agreements were to be submitted for a vote of approval by the Chickasaw legislature and by a vote of the people.[20]

At Atoka on April 23, 1897, the Dawes Commission reached an agreement with the Chickasaw and Choctaw commissioners. First, the tribes agreed to give allotments of equal value to members of the tribes, except the Choctaw freedmen. Town sites, lands around public buildings, and school sites were set aside for use of tribal members, except the freedmen. The lands were to be appraised and those allotted to the Choctaw freedmen were to be deducted from the Choctaws' portion of the lands and would not diminish the value of the Chickasaw lands. The Choctaw freedmen were to receive allotments equal in value to forty acres of the average land of the two nations. Tribal members, except the Choctaw freedmen, would be permitted to select allotments on the improvements that belonged to them. Allotments, including those of the Choctaw freedmen, were to be nontaxable and inalienable for twenty-one years. Among other things, the agreement provided for the use of the money derived from the sale of lots for the benefit of the Choctaw and Chickasaw tribes, the Chickasaw freedmen excepted. Coal and asphalt remained the common property of tribal members of the tribes, the freedmen excepted. Royalties derived from these resources would be used for the equal benefit of tribal members in paying taxes and supporting schools, except for the freedmen. The tribes agreed to submit subsequent legislation passed by their legislatures for approval by the President of the United States. When the tribal governments ceased, the Choctaws and Chickasaws would become citizens of the United States. Indian-affairs officials were encouraged by the Atoka Agreement, and the acting commissioner called it "the most important proposition relating to Indian affairs" that the government had had to deal with in years.[21]

It was the first major step toward dissolving the Indian nations. Learning that they had been left out of the Atoka Agreement, the Chickasaw freedmen met in convention at Dawes Academy, near Berwyn, on May 29, 1897, to draft a protest against its approval. The agreement had provided allotments for the Choctaw freedmen, and the freedmen of the Cherokee, Creek, and Seminole Nations would apparently be provided for. The freedmen were afraid that only they, of all the freedmen of the territory, would be left without legal status, considered intruders without any rights or privileges, and divested of the homes and improvements they had "made under many privations and with great toil during the past thirty years." To them, it was

contrary to every principle of justice, right, and humanity for the Chickasaw freedmen to be thus descriminated against by the United States, or that they should be finally left homeless and robbed of the earnings of years of toil accumulated in the midst of sorrows, disappointments, and delays, under embarrassment which they were and have been helpless to relieve by any action of their own, but to which they have quietly and peaceably submitted, waiting the strong arm of the Government to rescue them in accordance with the spirit and intent of the treaty of 1866.[22]

The freedmen asked the President and Congress to incorporate into the Atoka Agreement, before it was ratified, provisions for allotments for them and provisions for securing their rights and privileges. Otherwise, they asked the President and the Congress to reject the agreement. If ratification occurred, then they wanted it conditional upon concurrent legislation that would provide for appraisal of the freedmen's improvements; payment for their value, less a fee for their attorneys, Robert V. Belt and Joseph P. Mullen; allotments in the Kiowa and Comanche Reservation in the old Leased District; payment of the expense of removing the freedmen to their allotments; $100 per capita, less attorneys' fees; and indemnification for the economic and educational damage they had suffered during the years of exclusion from rights in the Chickasaw Nation.[23] Belt placed this protest before Congress and sent copies to the Dawes Commission.

On June 8, 1897, Belt filed a brief with the Interior Department, maintaining that the Chickasaw freedmen were citizens of the Chickasaw Nation by virtue of the Adoption Act of 1873, which said that it "shall be in full force and effect from and after its approval by the proper authority of the United States." Belt argued that no time was set on its approval,

that no direct or specific repeal of it had since been passed, and that the
act of 1873 had become binding by virtue of the congressional act of 1894,
when the freedmen had become citizens, entitled to all rights, privileges,
and immunities and to forty acres each. If the Chickasaws maintained that
subsequent acts repealed it, then Belt asked if it had not become law by
reason of its approval by Congress, which he maintained "amounts to a
completed enactment of law by Congress." He cited legal precedents for
the settlement, through congressional acts, of disputes arising out of a
treaty. For the Chickasaw freedmen, Belt claimed that approval constituted
"a fixing and settlement of their status legally" and determined their
rights to all the benefits due them under the treaty.[24]

Belt protested against the Atoka Agreement because it ignored the freedmen's rights altogether. In his view, the Treaty of 1866 constituted "a
clear contract" that said that the freedmen would be provided for by the
Chickasaw Nation or removed and provided for elsewhere by the United
States. It was now necessary for the government to see that one alternative
or the other was carried out. The Chickasaws had always maintained that
they had ceded the Leased District for the location of other Indians and
freedmen. Congress, too, had recognized the purpose of that cession when,
in 1891, it had made the appropriation of nearly three million dollars to
pay the Choctaws and Chickasaws additional compensation for that part
of the Leased District not allotted to the Cheyennes and Arapahoes. There
was a bill pending in the summer of 1897 for a similar appropriation for
about two and one-half million acres in the Leased District occupied by
the Kiowas and Comanches. Belt also cited the decision of Judge Isaac
Parker in UNITED STATES v. D. L. PAYNE (1881), emphasizing that
every branch of the government recognized the validity of the freedmen's
claim to a home. To Belt, there could be no fair conclusion but that the
Chickasaw freedmen were entitled to "Chickasaw citizenship, with the
rights, privileges, and immunities said treaty specified, and with 40 acres
of land each" in the Chickasaw country, or they should be removed to
other lands, paid $100 each, and reimbursed for the full value of the im-
provements they had made in the Chickasaw Nation during the past thirty
years. According to the resolutions the freedmen had adopted at Dawes
Academy on May 29, it was their desire to remain in the Chickasaw country
and to be removed only as a last resort.[25]

On June 21, 1897, Halpert E. Paine, attorney for the Chickasaw Nation,
responded to Belt, asserting that no acts of the Choctaws regarding the

freedmen were binding on the Chickasaws. The Choctaws, he argued, could
not grant to the Choctaw freedmen a share in the land equal to those of
Choctaw and Chickasaw citizens without the concurrence of the Chickasaws, under the Treaty of 1855. If any act of the Choctaw council purported
to do so, it could make those freedmen equal owners in only the Choctaw
three-quarters share of the aggregate lands. Since the Choctaws alone could
not make their freedmen equal sharers in the land with the Chickasaws,
neither could they grant to each black forty acres of land, whether they
intended the grant to come from the land held in common by the tribes
or from the Choctaws' undivided three-fourths share. Either act would
diminish the Chickasaw share, and Congress did not have the power to
validate or authorize the transfer of Chickasaw property to the Choctaw
freedmen without Chickasaw consent. To the Chickasaws the Treaty of
1866 was clear. The Chickasaws owed the blacks nothing. The freedmen
had not been adopted within the time prescribed by the treaty. The congressional act of August 15, 1894, had no validity, for since the act of
adoption of 1873, the Chickasaws had passed four acts that in effect repealed the earlier act.[26]

A few days later, Belt reviewed the provisions of the 1866 treaty regarding the freedmen for the Dawes Commission and asked the Commission to submit some fair plan regarding the rights and claims of the freedmen. He also made a formal protest to the new secretary of the interior,
Cornelius N. Bliss, who had sent the Atoka Agreement to Congress with
the report that it was "satisfactory to those persons having interests in
the Choctaw and Chickasaw Nations, or who may be affected by the
agreement." On June 29, Belt reminded the secretary of his strong protest on behalf of the Chickasaw freedmen before the former secretary
in early 1897. How could the department ignore as "persons having interests" the thousands of freedmen who had been waiting since 1866
to receive their rights? The proposed agreement would leave them "naked
intruders, divested and despoiled of the fruits of their toil" during the
past thirty years. Once more, Belt asked that no agreement be approved
unless it provided for the freedmen or unless contemporaneous legislation
was passed to ensure their rights.[27] Secretary Bliss placed the portests before the Senate Committee on Indian Affairs.

Apparently pleased with Belt's activities on their behalf, on August 13,
1897, the freedmen made a new contract with Belt and Mullen. By an
agreement in 1894, the freedmen had agreed to pay them a monthly

salary of $200 while Congress was in session, but the freedmen had been unable to pay it. Under the new contract, they agreed to pay a contingent fee of 25 percent of all moneys, lands, and other valuable considerations procured for them by the attorneys.[28]

By this time, Congress had made other significant inroads on the Indians' resolve. On June 7, 1897, it had given the United States courts exclusive jurisdiction over all civil and criminal cases arising in the Indian Territory after January 1, 1898, if the tribes did not make agreements with the Dawes Commission. The laws of Arkansas and of the United States were extended to all residents in the territory, irrespective of race. The act also clarified the act of June 10, 1896, by construing "rolls of citizenship" to mean the last authenticated rolls approved by the councils of the tribes, the descendants of those on the rolls, and those later added by the councils, the courts, or the Dawes Commission under the act of 1896. All other names were open to investigation by the commission. Anyone whose name was stricken by the commission had the right to appeal to the United States courts. Finally, no acts passed by the national councils of the tribes were valid unless approved by the President of the United States.[29]

In response to this act, on July 31, 1897, the Chickasaws authorized the governor to furnish the Dawes Commission with a correct roll of the Chickasaws by blood and citizens by intermarriage. The roll made prior to June 10, 1896, was to be amended to account for births and marriages since that date. The act also apparently prompted the Chickasaw legislature to act on the Atoka Agreement. In November, the Chickasaws empowered Governor R. M. Harris to announce a special election to ratify or reject the agreement made between the United States and the Choctaw and Chickasaw commissioners. Only Chickasaws by blood who were then recognized as qualified voters could vote on the treaty.[30] Although the legislature had approved the agreement, the voters rejected it.

Realizing that the freedman question was a major obstacle in the Dawes Commission's way, the Interior Department looked to Congress for a solution. On January 24, 1898, the secretary sent to Congress a statement concerning the status of the Choctaw and Chickasaw freedmen. Of the latter, he said that their status depended upon the question of whether the Chickasaw law of 1873, approved by the congressional act of 1894, had been repealed before its approval; the question was for judicial determination. If the law had been repealed, the freedmen were not citizens, Congress could not pass any act making them citizens without the consent of the Chickasaws, and any relief given them must be at the expense of the government if such relief exceeded the Chickasaw share of the $300,000. If they were citizens by virtue of the act of 1894, then Congress had the power to enact legislation to enforce their rights as such.[31]

Congress took final control of affairs in the Indian Territory on June 28, 1898, with "An Act for the Protection of the People of the Indian Territory, and Other Purposes," commonly known as the Curtis Act, which effectively terminated the tribal title to lands of the Five Civilized Tribes without their consent. It placed questions regarding citizenship, property, and rights under the jurisdiction of the federal courts. The making of tribal rolls and survey of lands had already been authorized. The Curtis Act provided for the equal allotment of lands in severalty to members of the tribes but reserved title to oil, coal, asphalt, and mineral deposits, as well as town sites and other lands, such as those surrounding schools, churches, public buildings, and cemeteries. Provisions were made for leasing tribal mineral deposits, incorporating towns, and establishing municipal governments. The laws of Arkansas were extended over the Indian Territory, and jurisdiction for their enforcement was placed in the federal courts. The Curtis Act prohibited the payment of tribal funds to tribal governments and placed disbursement of such funds under the supervision of the secretary of the interior.

In making tribal rolls, the Dawes Commission was directed to make a roll as well of the Chickasaw freedmen entitled to rights under the Treaty of 1866 and their descendants and to allot each freedman forty acres of land, including their improvements, to be used by them until their rights under the treaty were finally determined by Congress. The tribes were given the option of making agreements to determine the rights of persons who claimed citizenship in two or more tribes, as was the case of the Choctaw and Chickasaw freedmen, but if no agreement was made and selection of a tribe was not made in due time, the person would be enrolled in the tribe with whom he resided. The rolls made by the Dawes Commission were to be final.

Upon passage of the Curtis Act, the laws of the Indian tribes were no longer enforced by the United States courts in the Indian Territory. On July 1, 1898, the tribal courts of the Cherokees and Seminoles were abolished, and all pending civil and criminal cases were transferred to the United States courts. The courts of the Chickasaws, Choctaws, and Creeks were extended until October 1. The Atoka Agreement, somewhat amended, was ratified by Congress and was included in the Curtis Act, and the Chickasaws and Choctaws were given until December 1 to ratify it. In that event, the provisions of the Curtis Act applied to these tribes only where they did not conflict with the provisions of the Atoka Agreement, except for Article 14, which provided for the incorporation of towns.[32] The Curtis Act provided for allotment to Chickasaw freedmen, but the Atoka Agreement excluded them. Thus adoption of the agreement was critical.

The freedmen moved quickly to plan strategy concerning their enrollment and allotment of lands under the Curtis Act. At the call of Charles Cohee, president of the Chickasaw Freedmen's Association, the Chickasaw freedmen and the Choctaw freedmen living in the Chickasaw Nation met in convention at Dawes Academy, near Berwyn, on August 4 and 5, 1898. Cohee served as president and Henry Stevenson and William James as secretary and assistant secretary of the convention, which passed several resolutions.

The freedmen had high praise for Robert V. Belt and Joseph P. Mullen for their role in securing the freedmen's benefits under the Curtis Act. Under former contracts, the freedmen had agreed to pay the attorneys a fee equal to 25 percent of the value of lands allotted to the freedmen. A convention committee of twelve—Joseph Murray, Richmond Prince, William Pickens, Lee Newberry, Robert Anderson, William Alexander, Newton Burney, Nelson Eastman, Henry Clay, George Stevenson, Ben Williams, and William McKinney—devised a means by which the fees could be paid. They fixed an average value of the land to be allotted them at $2.50 per acre and fixed the amount due from each freedman at $25. At the time of enrollment, the freedmen would make four promissory notes for $6.25 each, payable to Belt and Mullen, the first due on December 1, 1898, and the others due on November 1 of the three succeeding years, all notes bearing 10 percent annual interest until paid. Notes for minors were made by parents, and those for orphans, the insane, prisoners, and idiots were to be made by guardians, next friends, or legal representatives. If payment was not made, Belt and Mullen were to receive the possession and free use of ten acres of the defaulter's allotment for five years or until the note and interest were paid. The freedmen's convention approved the plan and formally adopted it.[33]

The freedmen also agreed to retain Belt and Mullen to represent minors and orphans without guardians or administrators, freedmen who were debilitated by insanity or imprisonment, and the ignorant who knew "little or

nothing of their pedigree, genealogy, or history" and would have difficulty
giving satisfactory proofs to the Dawes Commission. Belt and Mullen would
appear on their behalf before the commission and present the freedmen's
claims for damages at the next session of Congress. The freedmen blamed
both the Chickasaws and the United States for inaction on their case between 1866 and 1898 and for causing them to suffer "great distress and
inconvenience" because of their unsettled condition and ignorance. While
it was impossible to place dollar values on their loss, the freedmen believed
that they were due compensation by which they could educate their
children and improve their homes and farms.[34]

The Dawes Commission had asked the freedmen to select a committee
of reliable men to assist in identifying freedmen eligible for enrollment.
The freedmen's convention elected Cohee, Mack Stevenson, Henry Gaines,
Soloman McGilbry, and Samuel Jones to attend the Dawes Commission
during the enrollment of the Chickasaw freedmen and to assist the freedmen and the attorneys in placing the eligible freedmen's names on the official roll. To defray expenses, the committee of freedmen was to receive
fifty cents from each head of family who appeared before the commission.
Cohee, Lee Newberry, and Nelson Eastman were charged with obtaining
tents and camping outfits necessary for setting up mobile enrolling stations.
And the convention directed the chairman of each subordinate association
of the Chickasaw Freedmen's Association to obtain the names of orphan
freedmen and those freedmen in prison and to secure legal guardians for
orphans, idiots, and the insane.[35]

On August 24, 1898, the amended Atoka Agreement as contained in
Section 29 of the Curtis Act was submitted for ratification to the Chickasaw and Choctaw voters. Whether the Chickasaw freedmen could vote
became an issue. U.S. Assistant Attorney General Willis Van Deventer
ruled that, unlike the Choctaw freedmen, they could not vote because
they had never been adopted and made citizens of the Chickasaw Nation.
When Choctaw Governor Green McCurtain issued a proclamation to that
effect, he disfranchised about seven hundred freedmen, apparently Chickasaw freedmen, who lived in the Choctaw Nation and had evidently voted
in earlier Choctaw elections. They promised to force the election judges to
take their votes; as the election approached, tension grew, and some believed that a detachment of troops would be necessary to keep the
peace.[36] Voters of the two nations ratified the agreement by a narrow
margin.

The freedmen had committed themselves to payment of a staggering fee to Belt and Mullen. When Henry L. Dawes read the proceedings of the August convention, he was outraged. To him, it appeared that Belt and Mullen were trying to fleece the freedmen; he asked the Interior Department to investigate. The freedmen had apparently set the high fee because they believed that some of their people could not pay in 1898 and that some would or could never pay; by collecting from those that could pay, they apparently hoped to obtain reasonable compensation for the attorneys' work during the preceding five years. Belt and Mullen apparently realized that if all the freedmen paid, the per-capita fee would indeed be too high and oppressive. Thus, on September 1, 1898, they signed a waiver of one-half of the fee.[37]

As the Dawes Commission prepared to go to the Chickasaw Nation, inquiries came from attorneys in the Chickasaw country who had been retained by freedmen to represent them. They wanted to know what kind of proof would be required in the freedman cases; whether testimony by other blacks would be accepted; whether, because of the expense of travel, affidavits would be accepted; and whether blood lines would have to be proved through the mother. In response to such inquiries and to those of the freedmen themselves, the Dawes Commission decided that those who could not appear before them in person must present an application upon the commission's return to Muskogee. Those Chickasaw freedmen living in the Choctaw Nation were afraid that they might be left off the Chickasaw rolls. Near Brazil and Talihina communities, word spread that the freedmen would have to go to the Chickasaw Nation to enroll. Some had spouses who had been owned by Choctaws and were now adopted Choctaw citizens. All were poor and could not afford the long, costly trip. Thus, the Dawes Commission decided to enroll those Chickasaw freedmen at the time the Choctaw freedmen were enrolled. Other special cases arose. For instance, Mary Eastman, who had been reared on Wild Horse Creek in the western part of the Nation, had gone to Muskogee in 1896 to teach school. Mary's father was an Indian, but her mother was black, so Mary declared herself a black and asked if she could appear before the commission at Muskogee. In another instance, Bill Fisher's physician informed the commission that Fisher was "totally disabled" by an attack of dysentery.[38]

Enrollment began in the early fall of 1898. The Dawes Commission published notices that enrollment parties would take the Chickasaw

census at Stonewall, Pauls Valley, Ardmore, Tishomingo, Lebanon, and
Colbert, between September 1 and October 14, 1898. Persons claiming
rights as Chickasaw freedmen would be examined orally, under oath, by
the commissioners. If any additional information was necessary, witnesses
would be called.[39] The Dawes Commission set up its tents at Stonewall
on September 1, 1898. The freedmen's committee established their camps
and set up an office tent nearby. Commissioner Archibald McKennon,
who was in charge of the freedmen enrollment, objected to the assessment of a fifty-cent fee for each adult freedman enrolled but withdrew
his objection when he learned from Joseph P. Mullen, who was there to
advise the freedmen, that it was to defray the expenses of the freedman
committee.[40]

During the enrollment at Stonewall, however, Mullen collected no
attorneys' fees because of strife in the freedmen's ranks. In 1896 the
Stonewall and Wynnewood communities had withdrawn from the Chickasaw Freedmen's Association and had since then opposed it, its attorneys,
and their fees. Mullen and the freedmen's committee worked to see that
every bona-fide freedman was enrolled, realizing all the while that the Stonewall freedmen would resist paying the fee to which the freedmen had agreed
in convention. Believing that the Dawes Commission would back them,
Charles Cohee and the other black committeemen asked McKennon whether they should try to execute the promissory notes as they had planned.
His reply was that they did not need a lawyer then, that they never
needed one, and that the fee was too high. McKennon's attitude and the
hostility of the Stonewall freedmen caused the committee and Mullen to
refrain from asking the freedmen to sign notes. After the enrollment
closed at Stonewall, Cohee and Mullen again discussed the fee with Mc-
Kennon, who still insisted that 25 percent was too much. Thus the matter
stood. The freedmen who were inclined to pay believed that the others
would acquiesce when they finally realized that they would in reality be
the owners of forty acres per capital of the average lands of the two nations.[41]

From Stonewall, the Dawes Commission moved to Pauls Valley,
where matters went differently. The freedmen's committee set up
their office tent next to McKennon's enrolling tent, and Mullen advised
the freedmen as before. Most of the freedmen who enrolled made no
objections to executing the notes, with the waivers attached, to pay
attorneys' fees. Some of those with large families agreed to wait until
the commission arrived at Ardmore, when they could more comfortably

Dawes Commission in the Field, Chickasaw Nation, 1898.

execute the notes in Mullen's office. After the enrollment was completed, Mullen went on to Ardmore while the Dawes Commission remained an extra day in Pauls Valley.[42]

The reason for remaining there may have been charges that Mullen was perpetrating fraud upon the freedmen. It had been rumored, for instance, that Mullen had represented himself as an agent of the secretary of the interior. A deputy U.S. marshal and a local lawyer had apparently told Tams Bixby, chairman of the Dawes Commission, that Mullen had said that he was authorized by the secretary to superintend the commission's taking of the freedman census. Bixby wired an inquiry to the secretary, who replied, "Mullen not appointed by Secretary to make enrollment of Freedmen, or otherwise." It was also reported that persons in the tent of the freedmen's committee had collected money from the freedmen, who were led to believe that the money was to defray the expenses of the Dawes Commission. Thus the Dawes Commission left Pauls Valley with a great deal of suspicion regarding Mullen, and Tams Bixby allegedly publicly called him a fraud.[43]

When the Dawes Commission established its enrollment camp in Ardmore on September 19, it set boundaries around the camp and forbade Mullen and other attorneys or claim agents to pitch their tents inside them. The commissioners wanted both the Chickasaw and the freedman committees to camp near the enrollment tent for convenience, but the freedmen did not because Tams Bixby, over their protests that Mullen was not a fraud, refused to allow them to set up their office tent, in which they made out the notes for attorneys' fees. During the enrollment, the commission learned that one freedman committeeman had taken a widowed freedwoman with two children into one of the commission's tents and told her that in order to get her name on its roll she must pay him a dollar for her and each of her children. When he was confronted by the Dawes Commission, he returned the money, claiming that he had known the woman since childhood and had only wanted to take care of her money for her. The commission dismissed him from service. The commissioners also learned that claim agents and attorneys were charging Indians and freedmen whose enrollment was in doubt large fees to get them on the rolls. With these incidents and rumors of similar ones, the commission tried to put the freedmen on guard. They publicly told the freedmen that no one had the right to collect money to ensure their enrollment, that no funds were due the commission, its

expenses being paid by the government, and that no attorney was necessary, since it was the Dawes Commission's duty to see that all who had
legal claims were enrolled. The commissioners also warned the freedmen and Indians about Mullen's alleged fraud at Stonewall and directed
the freedmen's committee to allow no one in or about its offices or
tents to demand money from anyone. Instead, the commission would
recommend that the Chickasaw legislature appropriate funds to pay the
freedmen committeemen for their work.[44]

The Dawes Commission thus sabotaged Mullen's chances of collecting his fees under the plan devised by the freedmen at the convention
in August. To him, the contracts he and Belt had made with the freedmen were valid, and he believed that Bixby had wronged him greatly by
blocking his chances of recovering his fees and by labeling him a fraud.
Mullen blamed much of the opposition to him on the bitter prejudice
against the blacks. At Stonewall and Pauls Valley, he said, he had been
approached frequently by Indians and whites who asked why he was
counseling and advising the freedmen and who often used "rough and
profane language against the negroes and indirectly against" him. At
Pauls Valley, he had been forced to move from one boarding place
to another to avoid trouble. People warned him to "go slow" in his
work. He tried to explain the rights of the freedmen, and sometimes
a person would say that he could understand why a "yankee" and a
"radical" would be in league with the blacks but not "a southern man"
like Mullen. These same people, Mullen charged, misquoted him or took
his comments out of context. Some were critical because of his role as
adviser to the freedmen, and it was easy to make some people believe
that he was guilty of fraud.[45]

At Ardmore, when Mullen heard about the charges of fraud leveled
at him by Tams Bixby, he addressed a reply to the charges on September
21, 1898. Mullen reviewed his and Belt's relationship with the freedmen
since 1894, stressing the complexity of their persistent efforts on behalf
of the freedmen and the amount of time, effort, and personal funds they
had expended, "often to the neglect of other important and remunerative
businesses" and of their families. Much of the credit belonged to them
for legislation securing the freedmen's rights. The contracts for fees had
been made aboveboard. In both instances, 1894 and 1897, the freedmen
had set their own fees, and copies of the contracts had been sent at the
time to the appropriate authorities in Washington. Mullen insisted that

he and Belt had always been open in their dealings; to suggest fraud on
their part did them a great injustice.[46]

Belt and Mullen had received practically nothing for their efforts.
From time to time the freedmen had raised money to be used in prosecuting their claims. All of the money had presumably been spent for
that purpose, but Mullen insisted that he and Belt had received no more
than a hundred dollars during the last five years. Some in the Chickasaw
Freedmen's Association, he charged, did not give it their "earnest and faith-
ful support and co-operation." Efforts were "being made, to divert the
Chickasaw freedmen from their purpose, by creating dissensions and confusion in their deliberations and among the members of the association, in
diverse ways." Such efforts were aimed at serving interests other than those
of the freedmen or their attorneys. Mullen insisted that during the enroll-
ments at Stonewall and Pauls Valley he had acted only in the interests
of the freedmen. He had even contemplated leaving Stonewall because he
did not believe that his services were needed but had been prevailed upon
by the freedmen's committee to remain. He had also told one member of
the Dawes Commission that he would leave whenever either group felt
that his presence was not needed. His position as counsel for the freedmen could not be denied. For years, he and Belt had been recognized
as such by the Interior Department, Congress, and even the Dawes
Commission itself. For some reason, there was now an attempt to dis-
credit him. He asked the Dawes Commission to grant him a hearing,
which was granted on September 25.[47]

Bixby confronted Mullen with the allegations and rumors that the
Dawes Commission had heard regarding him. Mullen once more denied
the charges and apparently made his case. The commissioners had previously decided to forbid Mullen to accompany the enrolling party to
any other point in the Nation, but they now invited him to accompany
them further. Mullen declined because he believed that the first person
who disliked what he was doing would cause him further trouble with
the commission. Too, he believed that Charles Cohee and the freedmen's
committee had matters well in hand and that Archibald McKennon had
been giving every freedman who had bona-fide claims a fair and full hearing. After the Dawes Commission completed its sessions at Colbert, it
moved at popular request to Duncan and Chickasha, in the western part
of the Nation, from October 17 through 22. Throughout the remaining
enrollment sessions, Mullen remained in communication with Charles

Cohee, and when the commission's work ended in the Chickasaw Nation on November 28, 1898, the commission had enrolled 4,331 freedmen.[48]

At Tishomingo, the Dawes Commission pressed upon the Chickasaw governor the necessity of an appropriation for the services of the Chickasaw freedmen's committee. At first the Chickasaw legislature refused to make the appropriation before the regular meeting of the Chickasaw Council, but the commissioners persisted, the paperwork was completed, and the legislature later appropriated the funds.[49]

In the wake of events at Ardmore and after conferring with Belt, Mullen and the freedmen's committee had decided not to make any more promissory notes with the freedmen. However, now that the freedmen were enrolled, he continued to work to secure their property and civil rights. In December, 1898, the Chickasaw freedmen planned a convention to adopt measures to obtain educational privileges, to consider the problem of attorney's fees, and to acquaint the freedmen with the regulations regarding tribal lands and with certain sections of the Curtis Act. Mullen would be there to help them. But one thing was clear: Belt and Mullen expected the freedmen to live up to the contract made with them, and they were prepared to submit a claim to the government for the unpaid fees.[50]

In early January, 1899, Mullen and Belt complained to the secretary of the interior that members of the Dawes Commission had encouraged and influenced the freedmen not to arrange payment of their contracted fees. Mullen submitted an extended statement, reviewing the history of their relationship with the freedmen and giving his version of events during the Chickasaw enrollment. His statement was endorsed by Charles Cohee and William M. Yates, National Secretary of the Choctaw Freedmen's Association. The Dawes Commission members replied to the complaints by giving their version of the affairs at the enrollment and saying, "If the Commission, or any member of it, did or said anything more than herein before stated, calculated to prejudice Mr. Mullen in the estimation of his clients, no one of the members now remembers it."[51]

As the enrollment progressed, the Chickasaws had become alarmed at the number of freedmen the Dawes Commission was enrolling. They estimated that when the enrollment was completed there would be more freedmen than Chickasaws. If each freedman received an allotment of forty acres, the Chickasaws would be deprived of 338,000 acres until it was decided whether the blacks were legally entitled to the land under the

Treaty of 1866. As one Chickasaw lady put it, the freedmen had used the
land unmolested for thirty-three years. It seemed unfair to her to give them
Chickasaw land since, she mistakenly believed, most of the slaveholders
had been intermarried whites:

We are a proud people and we protest against draining our bitter cups
to the dregs by dividing our last spot on earth with a Negro. Like the
white race we are willing to divide such a portion of our pottage with
the Negro as we can spare; but not, no never, our birthright!

On October 8, 1898, the Chickasaw legislature passed a memorial to
Congress, asking that the Congress scheduled to convene in December
pass "judicious and imparitial" legislation that would be equitable to
both the Chickasaws and to the freedmen, who the Chickasaws said
were their friends and not their enemies. At this time there were an
estimated 4,500 Chickasaw freedmen and 4,230 Chickasaws.[52]
    Throughout the 1890s Congress and the Dawes Commission had
used the condition of the freedmen as an argument for dissolving the
Indian nations and creating a territorial government in the Indian Territory. However, when it became apparent that the Chickasaws and
Choctaws would finally negotiate an agreement, the Dawes Commissioners
were so interested in obtaining a pact that they did not secure provisions
for the Chickasaw freedmen. Although the freedmen were enrolled as a
preliminary step to dissolving the nation, whether they could legally hold
the allotments they would receive was still in question. When, in the fall
of 1898, the Chickasaws called for "equitable" congressional legislation
for them and the freedmen, they meant denial of allotments to the freedmen, and during the next decade the Chickasaws did not relent in their
refusal of the blacks. Since it had not yet been finally determined whether
the freedmen had a right to share in the public domain of the Chickasaw
Nation, they looked forward with some anxiety to the beginning of the
allotment process and with some apprehension lest the chance to obtain
title to their homes finally slip past them.

NOTES

    1. Lawrence Mills, *Oklahoma Indian Land Laws* (St. Louis, Mo.:
Thomas Law Book Company, 1924), 335-339; Loren N. Brown, "The
Dawes Commission," *Chronicles of Oklahoma*, 9 (March, 1931), 73-76;

United States Commissioner to the Five Civilized Tribes, *Laws, Decisions, and Regulations Affecting the Work of the Commissioner to the Five Civilized Tribes, 1893-1906* (Washington, D.C.: Government Printing Office, 1906), 11-12, hereafter cited as *Laws and Decisions*. A thorough study of efforts toward assimilation following the Civil War is Henry E. Fritz, *The Movement for Indian Assimilation, 1860-1890* (Philadelphia: University of Pennsylvania Press, 1963). Members of the Dawes Commission other than those mentioned included Frank C. Armstrong (1895-1905), Tams Bixby and Thomas B. Needles (1897-1905), Clifton R. Breckenridge (1900-1905), and William E. Stanley (1903-1904).

2. D. M. Browning to Secretary, March 7, 1894, National Archives Record Group 75 (Records of the Bureau of Indian Affairs), *Letters Sent,* Land Letter Book 275: 436; 53 Cong., 3 Sess., *Senate Miscellaneous Document 24,* 1, 3, 4, hereafter cited as *Document 24.*

3. *Document 24,* 7-12; 54 Cong., 1 Sess., *Senate Document 12,* 11-21, hereafter cited as *Document 12;* Angie Debo, *And Still the Waters Run* (Princeton, N.J.: Princeton University Press, 1972), 23-24; Brown, 85-86.

4. Browning to Secretary, March 7, 1894, *Letters Sent,* Land Letter Book 275: 436; 54 Cong., 1 Sess., *Senate Document 182,* 112, hereafter cited as *Document 182.*

5. J. P. Mullen to Henry L. Dawes, Tams Bixby, A. S. McKennon, and Thomas B. Needles, September 21, 1898, Indian Archives Division, Oklahoma Historical Society, *Dawes Commission–Chickasaw.*

6. *Document 182,* 109-110; 55 Cong., 1 Sess., *Senate Document 157,* 4, hereafter cited as *Document 157; Document 182,* 113.

7. Mullen to Dawes, Bixby, McKennon and Needles, September 21, 1898, *Dawes Commission–Chickasaw; Document 182,* 102, 110, 113.

8. *Ibid.,* 112-113, 115, 116-117, 118.

9. *Ibid.,* 119.

10. *Ibid.,* 122-123.

11. *Congressional Record,* 53 Cong., 3 Sess. (February 6 and 9, 1895), 1815, 2009.

12. *Document 12,* 1-11, 21; Browning to R. V. Belt, February 28, 1895, *Letters Sent,* Land Letter Book 299: 211.

13. Thomas P. Smith to Robert H. West, October 29, 1895, and Browning to West, January 11, 1896, *Letters Sent,* Land Letter Book 317: 346; 324: 94.

14. King Blue and Joe Blue to Secretary of the Interior, February 3, 1896, National Archives Record Group 75, *Letters Received,* 6105-96; Browning to King Blue, February 14, 1896, and April 21, 1896, *Letters Sent,* Land Letter Book 325: 154, 330: 453.

15. *Laws and Decisions,* 12-13; Debo, 32; Brown, 88-89.

16. *Constitution, and Laws of the Chickasaw Nation together with the Treaties of 1832, 1833, 1834, 1837, 1852, 1855 and 1866* (Parsons, Kans.: The Foley Railway Printing Company, 1899), 356-357, hereafter cited as *Constitution and Laws.*

17. Agreement between Five Civilized Tribes Commission and Choctaws, February 18, 1896, Indian Archives Division, *Dawes Commission–Choctaw;* 55 Cong., 1 Sess., *Senate Document 183,* 2, hereafter cited as *Document 183.*

18. *Constitution and Laws,* 377-379; Indian Archives Division, *Chickasaw–Federal Relations,* 7085; Protest of the Chickasaw delegates against the Choctaw Agreement, February 1, 1897, *Dawes Commission–Choctaw and Dawes Commission–Chickasaw.* R. M. Harris was chairman of the Chickasaw commission that filed the protest; William L. Byrd, R. L. Boyd, T. C. Walker, William M. Guy, S. B. Kemp, Isaac O. Lewis, Richard McLish, and J. Brown signed the document.

19. *Document 183,* 2-3.

20. *Constitution and Laws,* 381-382.

21. 55 Cong., 1 Sess., *Senate Document 93,* 3-11.

22. *Document 157,* 33-35.

23. *Ibid.,* 35-36.

24. *Ibid.,* 4-5; *See also* Mullen to Dawes, et al., September 21, 1898, *Dawes Commission–Choctaw.*

25. *Document 157,* 6-8.

26. *Ibid.,* 9-13.

27. *Document 183,* 1, 3-6; *Indian Chieftain,* July 29, 1897.

28. Mullen to Dawes, et al., September 21, 1898, *Dawes Commission–Chickasaw.*

29. *Laws and Decisions,* 13-14.

30. *Constitution and Laws,* 383-384, 403-404.

31. *Cherokee Advocate,* January 29, 1898.

32. *Constitution and Laws,* 523-549.

33. Proceedings of the Convention of Chickasaw Freedmen, August 4 and 5, 1898, National Archives Record Group 48 (Records of the Office of the Secretary of the Interior), Indian Territory Division, *Choctaw and Chickasaw Freedmen,* Box 384, 271-98.

34. *Ibid.*

35. *Ibid.;* Mullen to Bixby, August 16, 1898, *Dawes Commission–Chickasaw.*

36. R. M. Harris to Bixby, August 16, 1898, *Dawes Commission–Chickasaw;* Willis Van Deventer to Secretary, August 9, 1898, *Letters Received,*

36672-98; *Muskogee Phoenix,* August 18, 1898; 56 Cong., 1 Sess., *House Document 5,* 2: 9, hereafter cited as *Document 5; Indian Journal,* August 19, 1898.

37. Dawes to Secretary of the Interior, August 24, 1898, *Choctaw and Chickasaw Freedmen,* Box 384, 271-98; Mullen to Dawes, et al., September 21, 1898, *Dawes Commission—Chickasaw.*

38. J. F. Sharp to McKennon, August 3, 1898, *Dawes Commission—Choctaw;* Irvin O. Curtice to McKennon, August 20, 1898, Mattie West to Dawes Commission, October 18, 1898, Bixby to A. L. Aylesworth, September 12, 1898, Burl Hernbeck, et al. to Dawes Commission, September 17, 1898, W. A. Welch to McKennon, September 10, 1898, H. Nail to McKenno September 29, 1898, Mary Eastman to Dawes Commission, September 19, 1898, and J. E. Bailey to Dawes Commission, September 29, 1898, *Dawes Commission—Chickasaw; Indian Chieftain,* September 15, 1898.

39. *Document 5,* 2: 14; *Constitution and Laws,* 445-448; 60 Cong., 1 Sess., *Senate Document 505,* 13-14, hereafter cited as *Document 505.*

40. Statement of Mullen, December 1898, *Choctaw and Chickasaw Freedmen,* Box 384, 271-98.

41. *Ibid.*

42. *Ibid.*

43. *Ibid.;* Dawes Commission to Secretary of the Interior, January 11, 1899, *Choctaw and Chickasaw Freedmen,* Box 384, 271-98.

44. *Ibid.*

45. Statement of Mullen, December 1898, *Choctaw and Chickasaw Freedmen,* Box 384, 271-98.

46. Mullen to Dawes, et al., September 21, 1898, *Dawes Commission—Chickasaw.*

47. *Ibid.*

48. *Document 505,* 14; Statement of Mullen, December 1898, *Choctaw and Chickasaw Freedmen,* Box 384, 271-98.

49. Dawes Commission to Secretary of the Interior, January 11, 1899, *Choctaw and Chickasaw Freedmen,* Box 384, 271-98.

50. Statement of Mullen, December 1898, *Choctaw and Chickasaw Freedmen,* Box 384, 271-98.

51. *Ibid.,* Dawes Commission to Secretary, January 11, 1899, *Choctaw and Chickasaw Freedmen,* Box 384, 271-98.

52. Irene Waite-Kerr to William McKinley, January 10, 1899, *Dawes Commission—Chickasaw; Constitution and Laws,* 420-423; *Annual Report of the Secretary of the Interior for the Fiscal Year Ended June 30, 1898* (Washington, D.C.: Government Printing Office, 1898), 159.

8

Allotment

The Atoka Agreement, amended and included in the Curtis Act, provided for forty-acre allotments for the Chickasaw freedmen to use until their rights under the Treaty of 1866 were determined by congressional action. The Chickasaws maintained that the freedmen were entitled to neither citizenship nor the allotments and that they had ratified the agreement only because it had been amended.[1] Although the freedmen had been enrolled and had been guaranteed the use of the allotments, the titles to their homes were, if anything, less secure than they had ever been, for as time passed, it became more evident that their status must finally be determined. Unlike their counterparts among the other tribes, they did not have thirty five years of tribal status on which to base their arguments, and the final decision could well go against them.

The freedmen were perhaps more unsettled than they had been since the Civil War. They beseiged the secretary of the interior and the Dawes Commission with questions about the clarification of their status. They understood little about the projected allotment. As one lawyer put it, they were "as a rule, very ignorant on such subjects and are at a loss to know what to do." They were unsure if they could select lands and hold them until allotment without further action by Congress, if they were strictly limited to forty acres, if families could select land in a body, if mortgages made on improvements before enrollment were valid, if one would be allowed to make a new selection if he lost his place through foreclosure, if two parties could receive allotments in the same section of land, if a freedman could own a house that was in one section and a field in another, or if they could occupy their present places during 1899 if they wanted to take allotments other than at those places. During enrollment, many freedmen had found that the land they held in excess of

forty acres was grabbed up by white intruders and those who were not
enrolled had their entire lands and improvements taken by whites. Some
white renters found that the lands they occupied changed hands. When
those lands fell into freedmen's hands, they were unsure whether to pay
rents to the blacks or to simply occupy the land and await the final resolution of the freedmen's status. Those freedmen who had not been rejected
but had been labeled "doubtful" during enrollment did not know if they
could hold on to their improvements and therefore did not know whether
to continue to improve their lands. They sometimes found their improvements rented by someone else.[2]

Those who had been enrolled had their problems, too. Gebell Gillespie
had settled his place near Wiley in 1883. At the time there was no improvement within three-quarters of a mile. In 1898, however, a man named
Hill moved in, built two houses near Gillespie's field on the same quarter
section on which Gillespie's house sat, cut logs, built two large cribs, and
tried to force Gillespie off the property. Hill claimed Chickasaw citizenship, but he had been rejected during enrollment.[3]

Some Indians used the unsettled state of affairs to occupy the improvements held by blacks. A black family named Gordon moved to the vicinity
of Center about 1890, allegedly coming from Mexico. One of the young
men of the family married a Chickasaw freedwoman but moved away. In
1899, an Indian had a place on the same section as the Gordons and wanted
to sell his improvements to another Chickasaw citizen, who was unsure if
he could take an allotment on it and get possession. In another instance,
T. S. Strickland of Johnson asked for removal of Jabe James, whose farm
and houses Strickland wanted to take as an allotment. And near Wynnewood, C. F. Stuart, a Chickasaw citizen, moved onto the property of
freedwoman Lucy McKinney, who had put up the original improvements
on the place. Stuart had taken down her fence around a little pasture and
had put up his own and claimed the land.[4]

Black opportunists, too, took advantage of the unsettled state of affairs.
From Center, freedwoman Nettie Stephenson complained that she had
worked hard to have a good farm, but other freedmen had selected allotments and claimed nearly all of it. In the same community Philip Brown
and Nelson Clark made selections of farms improved by noncitizen whites,
some with wells, houses, and cleared land. They demanded rent in order
for the occupants to remain. Brown hired an attorney to give the renters
notice. At Okra, Frances Grayson's brother-in-law Ben Grayson tried to
take the place that she and her husband had settled in 1870. She wrote:

"I am a law biden sitzen and i wants an advice from you for i Dont want to make no move unless i no that I am Right for i want to be on the Rite side of the law." At the same time, freedman B. C. Colbert, who had settled at Okra in 1892, complained that another Chickasaw freedman, Arthur Jackson, had settled forty acres, including part of Colbert's field. In December, 1899, Jackson sold a white man eighty acres of land, including two buildings held by Colbert and his family. The white man was a noncitizen who rented from a citizen, was carrying a gun, and threatened to drive Colbert off his own property. The Dawes Commission instructed those complaining to report the names of any noncitizens who were intruders but stressed that any renters who had made valuable and lasting improvements on prospective allotments after passage of the Curtis Act might be entitled to compensation for the improvements under that act. But freedmen were perfectly within their rights to rent their families' approximate share of Chickasaw lands and could take action for the ejection of noncitizen lessees after January 1, 1900.[5]

Indians and whites alike tried to prevent freedmen from bettering their lot by selecting good lands for allotments. E. D. Love of Mead, for instance, tried to get the Dawes Commission to prohibit a freedman from settling on the same section of land on which Love had his improvements, although Love himself did not claim that particular piece of land. The Dawes Commission informed him that he had no right to hold land outside his own improvements. In the Wheeler community, a controversy arose when the family of Jesse McGee chose the land they wished to take as allotments. McGee was a Chickasaw who was married to a freedwoman, the daughter of Rhoda Jackson, a former slave of Tennessee Bynum. Because McGee was blind, he apparently hired an agent to make selections for him, his wife, and their six children in the amount that would be due Chickasaws by blood, not freedmen. It was generally held that they claimed 551 acres each. His agent served notice on the occupants of the land claimed, all white renters, to vacate. When these whites complained, they charged that the McGees were holding too much land and tried to question McGee's rights because he lived with a black, but the Dawes Commission said that living with blacks did not affect McGee's rights and that the Dawes Commission could not settle disputes until a land office was established in the Chickasaw country.[6]

For the freedmen, there was no such thing as an allotment at that time: they simply held the land to use. Citizens or those claiming citizenship were allowed to make selections of land preliminary to allotment. In the

Chickasaw Nation, most simply selected the land on which their present improvements stood and did not encroach upon others, but in some areas, such as the Ardmore Block, where population was dense, every section had to be subdivided and conflicts such as those above often arose. Allotment could come only after appraisal of the lands, which work was not begun in the Choctaw Nation until July of 1899. Because of sickness among the appraisers, work was slow until the fall, when they were joined by appraisers who had completed work in the Seminole lands. The appraisal parties did not enter the Chickasaw Nation until April 20, 1900, but once there, they completed the work rapidly, appraising nearly one and one-quarter million acres during the next two months. The values of the land were plotted on maps, and when the final citizenship rolls were completed, land offices were to be opened and allotment begun.[7]

While they waited, the freedmen saw little improvement in their lot. In 1899, smallpox invaded the Indian Territory and reached epidemic proportions because of conditions there. The Indians were traditionally fond of visiting the ill and, apparently oblivious to the danger of the disease, contributed to its spread. Some of the more influential men among the Indians opposed vaccination, and quack doctors convinced the populace that vaccination caused the disease to spread. The Chickasaw freedmen did not escape the ravages of the disease. On December 20, a committee of citizens at Colbert petitioned the U.S. Indian inspector for relief. He immediately dispatched a medical team to visit Colbert and other parts of the Chickasaw Nation to bring the disease under control. They found that the first case had appeared in a freedman family named Pitman, who lived about three miles east of Colbert, and that there were currently thirty-six cases, all except five of whom were blacks. Of the nine deaths that had occurred, eight were blacks. The medical team found forty-one uninfected members of the families of those who had been ill. Those were vaccinated immediately and quarantines were established. Other cases were discovered at Kemp, about twelve miles east of Colbert, and at Chickasha. At the latter place, a U.S. Indian policeman was stationed to enforce the quarantine, and strict compliance to it there and elsewhere stopped the disease in the Chickasaw Nation while it ravaged parts of the other tribal nations.[8]

The freedmen received no educational advantages, although the United States had assumed some control of the educational systems in the Indian Territory under the general provisions of the Curtis Act. On November 4, 1898, Secretary Cornelius N. Bliss issued regulations, which were amended

in 1899, establishing the office of Superintendent of Schools for the Indian
Territory, whose duty was to inspect, organize, and reorganize schools and
to make the changes necessary to remedy any defects in the educational
systems in the territory. In each nation there was established an office of
school supervisor, charged with visiting and inspecting the schools and reporting statistics concerning teachers and enrollment. The superintendent
was authorized to open as many day schools as funds permitted. Because
the Atoka Agreement had been ratified as part of the Curtis Act, the freedmen of the Chickasaw and Choctaw Nations had been denied access to the
school funds generated by royalties from coal and asphalt in the two nations. The blacks were poverty-ridden and could not have borne the burden
of a tax even if they had had the legal right to tax themselves. They were
excluded from schools established for noncitizen whites and Indians. In
late 1898, Indian Inspector J. George Wright asked Chickasaw Governor
D. H. Johnston to supply him the number of children, including the Chickasaw freedmen, of school age in the Nation and to inform him of any provision that the Chickasaws were making for the children's education. His
answer was one the freedmen had often heard during the preceding thirty
years: "our authorities have never recognized them as citizens and we not
feeling any obligation in any way as to the education of their offspring,
have never made a census of them." In 1900, John D. Benedict, superintendent of schools in the Indian Territory, asked that something be done
for the freedmen.[9] But by 1902, there were only two schools that enrolled
Chickasaw freedmen.

Enrollment for allotment had created difficulties for some Chickasaw
freedmen living in the Choctaw Nation. The Dawes Commission had enrolled them as Chickasaw freedmen although they had enjoyed the same
rights as Choctaw freedmen since the Choctaw Act of Adoption in 1883.
They had had access to the national courts, they had been selecting allotments as Choctaw freedmen, they had attended Choctaw freedman
schools, and the noncitizen husbands of the freedmen had regularly obtained permits from the Choctaw district judges. After enrollment, however, they were treated as intruders.[10]

As enrollment progressed, the Chickasaws and Choctaws became
concerned with the growing numbers of persons admitted to the rolls,
and that concern remained with them. On September 5, 1899, they had
concluded an agreement with the Dawes Commission whereby no person
born after October 31, 1899, or anyone intermarrying after that date,

could be admitted to the rolls. They agreed to submit the question of the Chickasaw freedmen's and intermarried persons' rights to allotments to the U.S. Court of Claims, provided any suit for such rights was instituted before April 1, 1900. This agreement failed to be ratified. However, early in 1900, there were congressional attempts to settle the freedman question. Bills were introduced in the Senate to allow either the Chickasaws or the freedmen to sue in the federal courts to determine if the freedmen had rights to allotments. Proponents of the bills were determined that the freedmen should retain possession of the land. If the courts decreed in their favor, their title was secure; if not, the government should pay the Chickasaws for the land and give it to the freedmen. Acting Commissioner A. C. Tonner did not favor such a suit at the time and doubted whether title to the land could be taken from the Choctaws and Chickasaws and given to the freedmen without the tribes' consent if the court decree went against the freedmen.[11]

The freedmen and the Chickasaws watched these activities with interest. The freedmen were uneasy. Some were told by the Chickasaws that only those who were formerly held in bondage by the Chickasaws would be given allotments, and the freedmen were concerned that their children might be excluded. The Dawes Commission was besieged by inquiries concerning individuals' status. Some who had appeared for enrollment found that they had not been enrolled. They asked for appointments to meet the commission at various places in the Indian Territory to make their cases. One example was the case of Sam Jones and his family. Jones had been one of the freedmen commissioners who had assisted the Dawes Commission during enrollment in the Chickasaw Nation. His daughter Victoria had married and had had a child after enrollment, and when Jones wrote to the commission to get the child enrolled, he found that his whole family had been excluded. He asked Dawes Commissioner A. S. McKennon for help: "Since we got through enrolling I've told both Black red and white that you tryed to do right and just to all men." Jones also enlisted the aid of Charles Cohee, the well-known freedman leader, who had been with Jones when he enrolled at Stonewall. Others who had failed to appear for various reasons sought enrollment. Some were aged or had been ill. Others were out of the Nation and had not enrolled. Sixty-year-old Cornelius Bacon was living at Nowata, Cherokee Nation, and had failed to appear before the commission. He had been the slave of Harvy Bacon, as had his father and mother, Jim and Lucy. In the spring of 1899 he received a letter from his "young mistress," who told him that he should come to the Chickasaw Nation and prove his rights

and that she would testify for him. A few freedmen were in prison. Hardy
Colbert, about sixty or seventy, had been the slave of Jim Colbert "when
the Indians were indians." He sent word from the federal prison at Leavenworth, Kansas, to select a place for him and to make sure that his family
got places. Another such case was Jack Humday, the son of Ed Humday.
According to Charles Cohee, Jack and his children were enrolled, but
his wife was not. She proved, upon investigation, to be a noncitizen. Other
freedmen who had been enrolled tried to enroll their infants who had been
born since enrollment.[12]

There were those who had been disqualified for various reasons. Some
pleaded ignorance of procedures during enrollment and asked for a rehear-
ing. Some tried to prove that although they had left the Chickasaw Nation
in the 1860s, they had returned by the time prescribed by the treaty. Some
argued that they had been stolen from the Indians and returned to the Nation as soon after the war as possible. Since they had never been paid for,
they argued, they were "territory property" and therefore had a right to
be enrolled. And Edmond Colbert wanted to bring witnesses to prove that
he had not been sold out of the Nation for "a gallon of whiskey and a
poney."[13]

One of the major problems the Dawes Commission faced was the matter
of names. Some enrolled with relatives whose names differed from theirs,
and the families became confused. Others became concerned that they
were known by one name but had signed up under the names of their
former masters rather than their own. In investigating many of the cases,
the Dawes Commission sought the aid of Charles Cohee, who knew most
of the freedmen. They turned as well to the former slave owners and their
descendants for aid in identifying certain families of blacks.[14]

The Chickasaws were anxious to have the question of freedman rights
settled. In his message of September 9, 1900, Governor D. H. Johnston
urged the Chickasaw legislature to send Congress a memorial requesting
that provision be made for the suit before the Court of Claims, with right
to appeal to the Supreme Court. The Chickasaw legislature passed legislation empowering the governor to take whatever steps necessary to protect
Chickasaw interest regarding the freedmen, but when Johnston attempted
to follow the dictates of the act, it was not approved by the President of
the United States.[15]

It was apparently clear to the Chickasaws and Choctaws and to the Dawes
Commission that an agreement supplemental to the Curtis Act was necessary because the Atoka Agreement was obviously not satisfactory for the

final closing of tribal affairs. They realized, too, that the rolls must be closed. Thus, on February 7, 1901, the tribes and the commission reached an agreement, later amended through conferences with all parties involved, and submitted it to Congress for consideration. The agreement proposed to close the rolls of Chickasaw and Choctaw citizens and freedmen on September 1, 1901; no newborns or persons intermarried after that date would be admitted. It provided for a speedy conclusion of the citizenship cases then before the U.S. courts of the Indian Territory and set the date of December 1 as the last date for the Dawes Commission to receive applications for enrollment. The rolls made by the commission would be considered final and would form the basis for allotment and division of tribal property. Heirs were to receive the allotment of any person who died after September 1, 1901, but before allotments were made. The agreement would become law upon its ratification by Congress and by a majority of the eligible voters of the two tribes.[16]

Until Congress provided the means of closing the rolls, the Dawes Commission continued to receive applications. On June 30, 1901, the commissioners had listed for enrollment 1,447 cases of Chickasaw freedmen, involving 5,466 persons. They had listed 94 newborn freedmen during the fiscal year and recorded 8 deaths. They had as well 80 doubtful or contested cases, involving 213 persons, and had rejected 8 cases, involving 9 people. Six applications, involving 20 people, had been heard but remained undecided when the fiscal year ended. Most of the freedmen had been enrolled during the enrollment in the Nation in 1898, and those that now made application were questioned closely concerning their whereabouts at the outbreak of the Civil War and at the time of the ratification of the Treaty of 1866. Because the freedmen had not been adopted by the Chickasaws, there were no official records relating to them, and the commissioners exercised extreme caution in hearing the testimony offered in the applicants' behalf. During the next fiscal year, the commission received only five applications, involving ten persons. They had also recorded the births of 197 infants and recorded 14 deaths. That brought the total of admitted freedmen to 5,667. Enrollment was apparently near its end, and classification of lands had been completed in the Chickasaw Nation on January 15, 1901.[17] All was ready for allotment, but that could not occur until the rolls were officially closed.

Congress failed to ratify the supplemental agreements by which the tribes and the Dawes Commission had tried to close the rolls. On March 21,

1902, however, another agreement was made. Disgruntled Chickasaws and Choctaws met in Tishomingo on May 9 and drafted resolutions opposing the agreement as a "great departure from the intent of the Atoka Agreement" and therefore detrimental to the tribes. One resolution opposed allotment of any land to the Chickasaw freedmen. Nevertheless, the agreement was approved by Congress on July 1, 1902, and ratified by the Choctaw and Chickasaw voters at an election on September 25. The agreement gave the Chickasaws and Choctaws allotments of land equal in value to 320 acres of the average allottable land of the nations and the freedmen of the two nations allotments equal in value to forty acres of the average allottable land. The freedman allotments were inalienable during the lifetime of the allottee up to twenty-one years from the date he received his allotment certificate. Encumbrances of lands allotted to the freedmen by any deed, debt, or other obligation contracted before the time at which the land was alienable were forbidden. After allotment to all, excess lands were to be sold at public auction. If an allotment had not been selected for any Indian or freedman, the Dawes Commission was to select for him, and all tribal members and freedmen were given ninety days from the ratification of the agreement to divest themselves of all land holdings larger than the allotments to which they were entitled. The heirs of those who died between the ratification and the date of allotment were to receive the allotments of the deceased. The Dawes Commission was authorized to select allotments for any who, at the end of one year, had refused to select allotments.

The agreement set the date of its final ratification as the date for closing the rolls. The commission was directed to forward the rolls in segments to the secretary of the interior so as to expedite the process of allotment, which could begin as soon as persons' names were approved on the partial rolls.

The agreement conferred upon the U.S. Court of Claims the right to determine whether the Chickasaw freedmen had a right to share in the lands of the Choctaw and Chickasaw nations under the Treaty of 1866. The attorney general of the United States was directed to file, within sixty days after the ratification of the agreement, a bill of interpleader against the Choctaw and Chickasaw freedmen, the court costs of the freedmen to be borne by the United States. Meanwhile, the Dawes Commission was directed to make a roll of the Chickasaw freedmen and their descendants and to make allotments to them, not as temporary allotments but as final ones.

If it was finally decided that the freedmen were not entitled to allotments, the Court of Claims was to render a decree against the United States for the value of lands allotted to the Chickasaw freedmen.[18]

The agreement had been the brainchild of Tams Bixby, acting chairman of the Dawes Commission. The Commission itself was split in opinion on the stipulations concerning the freedman allotments. To Commissioners Thomas B. Needles and Clifton R. Breckenridge, it did not seem equitable that the United States should have to pay for the lands that might be allotte to the blacks, and they expressed their concerns to the secretary of the interior while the agreement was in the draft stage. They said that it might be argued that as a people without rights the freedmen were "exceptionally fortunate" in being allowed to use the land without paying rent or taxes. They believed, however, that the blacks should not be turned out without payment for the improvements that they had worked hard to make. If the courts decided that the freedmen had no rights as Chickasaw citizens, the Chickasaws should not lose their land. Above all, Needles and Breckenridge did not believe that the freedmen should have free possession of the land. They therefore suggested that the blacks be allowed to buy the land in some "preferred way." Such an arrangement would be equitable to all, they thought.[19]

When it appeared that the matter of the freedmen's rights would finally be settled by the U.S. Courts, attorneys from the Indian Territory sought to be named as attorney for the freedmen, and the freedmen wanted to send delegations to Washington. Robert V. Belt also applied for the position, claiming an intimate knowledge of freedman affairs. The old rift between the freedman factions opened up once more, with the freedmen at Wynnewood insisting that the freedmen wanted neither Belt nor J. P. Mullen as attorney, while Charles Cohee and B. C. Franklin, president and secretary of the Chickasaw Freedmen's Association, insisted that they did. The secretary of the interior avoided all old antagonisms by appointing Charles W. Needham of Washington.[20]

On November 26, 1902, the attorney general filed a bill of interpleader in the Court of Claims as called for in the agreement of July 1. Notice was served upon tribal leaders and the freedmen and was published in the local newspapers. In the early months of 1903, rumors circulated in the freedman communities that freedman representatives were expected to go to Washington in relation to the case. Freedmen reported "a great many plots and plans" in the territory. But the secretary of the interior assured them that their interests were being attended to by Needham.[21]

The Court of Claims handed down its decision on April 27, and it did
not favor the freedmen. It said that the freedmen were on the same footing in the Chickasaw Nation as citizens of the United States and therefore
had no right or interest independently of the agreement of March 21,
1902, in the property held in common by the Nation. Neither were they
entitled to any part of tribal funds under the control of the United States.
In its decree, the court held that the third article of the Treaty of 1866
remained unaffected by any subsequent laws enacted by the Chickasaw
legislature. By electing to remain in the Chickasaw Nation, the freedmen
forfeited all right to their share of the $300,000 appropriated by the
treaty and were thereafter on the same footing with other citizens of
the United States. They were not entitled to allotments of land. The
court ordered that when the rolls came in, the Chickasaw and Choctaw
nations be given leave to apply for an additional decree to determine the
amount due them for the lands allotted to the freedmen. In May, the
United States and the Chickasaw freedmen appealed the ruling to the
U.S. Supreme Court.[22] Whatever the final outcome, the freedmen were
no longer a people without a country. The Court of Claims confirmed the
deliquency of the United States in failing to remove the freedmen in 1868
and in allowing a segment of its population to struggle in civil and political limbo for thirty-five years.

Although the decree went against the freedmen, their allotments were
not jeopardized. Thus, early in 1903, the Dawes Commission began to
make the final rolls and to transmit them in segments to the secretary for
approval. The first list of 1,031 Chickasaw freedman names was sent on
February 2, to be followed by others through the succeeding years. In
1904 the freedman rolls were adjusted. The names of 1,305 applicants
were transferred to Choctaw freedman rolls because their names had appeared on the 1896 census of Choctaw freedmen. As allotment approached,
those who had been refused enrollment tried desperately to get their names
added, others tried to enroll minors under their care, and still others complained of difficulties in filing because they were unable to procure letters
of guardianship.[23]

Anxiety also beset those freedmen who were anticipating allotment.
They were unsure whether the Atoka Agreement or the supplemental agreement was in effect. Some occupied more land than they would be entitled
to under allotment; they did not know whether to hold on to the excess or
to let it go. Others complained that they had too little. Love Miller of
Purcell held eighty acres and complained that with only forty acres he would

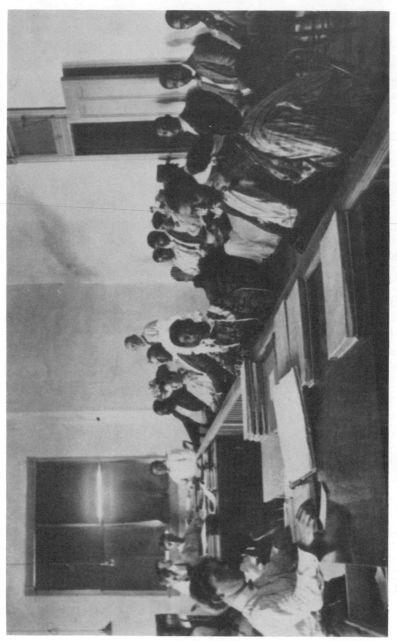

Chickasaw Freedmen Filing on Allotments, circa 1903. Courtesy of Photograph Archives, Division of Library Resources, Oklahoma Historical Society.

not have enough pasture for his herd, and he would be forced to sell his cattle. Some freedmen were beset by other problems. Near Milo, the Chickasaws apparently tried to continue to collect a tax on the livestock of the freedmen, and others had trouble with noncitizens who squatted on the lands they had selected for allotments.[24]

As soon as the secretary of the interior began to approve the partial rolls, allotment got under way. The Dawes Commission established a land office at Tishomingo on April 15, 1903, and during the next fourteen months they received 2,749 applications and allotted 149,701.88 acres to freedmen. In May, 1904, the commission began preparing patents for the Chickasaw and Choctaw allottees, but the work was slow at first. In 1905 an additional 29,280.94 acres were allotted to freedmen. The acreage for each allotment varied according to the quality of the land. If the land was appraised at $6.50 per acre, for example, an allotment of about twenty acres was equal in value to forty acres of the average allottable land. If the land was appraised at $2.00 an acre, an allotment of about sixty-five acres would be made.[25]

On February 23, 1904, the United States Supreme Court affirmed the decision of the Court of Claims; thus the Chickasaw freedmen did not have rights to allotments of land outright. A judgment for the value of the allotments was to be rendered in favor of the Chickasaws and Choctaws, the money to be added to the tribal funds and distributed per capita. There remained only the task of determining the number of freedmen who had received allotments so that the tribes could be repaid the value of the land. By late 1905, the money had not been paid, and the Chickasaw legislature drafted a memorial to Congress asking for it. The United States Court of Claims did not finally render judgment in the case until 1910, when it awarded $606.936.08, less the per-capita amount of any freedman improperly enrolled as a citizen, to the Chickasaws and Choctaws to be paid per capita.[26]

The Dawes Commission's work in the Indian Territory was drawing to a close in 1904. On July 1, 1905, it ceased to exist. The work of completing the process they had begun fell to the commission's chairman, Tams Bixby, whose title was commissioner to the Five Civilized Tribes. Thus ended twelve years of work by one of the most powerful bodies ever organized concerning Indian affairs. They had transformed the Indian Territory from five separate nations of Indians holding the land in common to a new territory on the eve of statehood, populated by individual landholding Indians, blacks, and whites.

According to the Curtis Act, the governments of the Five Civilized Tribes were to end on March 4, 1906, and the Indians and freedmen would become citizens of the United States. As the date drew near, it became apparent that all affairs of the nations would not be closed. A bill to provide for the final disposition of tribal affairs was introduced in Congress, but when it became apparent that the bill would not pass in time, Congress passed a joint resolution that extended the tribal governments until March 4, 1907.[27]

An act of April 26, 1906, authorized the commissioner to the Five Civilized Tribes to consider all applications for enrollment that had been made before December 1, 1905. For ninety days he could receive applications for enrolling children who were minors on March 4, 1906, and whose parents had been enrolled. The act defined the lands allotted to Choctaw and Chickasaw freedmen as homesteads and made them subject to regulations regarding the homesteads of the tribal citizens. It forbade the transfer of any name from the freedman rolls to the rolls of citizens by blood unless the application for transfer was made prior to December 1, 1905. After allotment was completed, the secretary was authorized to sell any unallotted or unreserved lands. In the Chickasaw and Choctaw Nations, the freedmen were granted a preference right to purchase at the appraised value an amount of land equal in value to the allotments they had already received.[28] This important piece of legislation cleared the way for making the final rolls and finally settling the affairs of the Five Civilized Tribes.

Bixby received 754 applications of Chickasaw freedman minors before July 25, 1906. In September the Chickasaw legislature petitioned Congress to exclude the Choctaw and Chickasaw freedman children from the rolls. On November 15, the attorney general's office held that the Chickasaw freedmen were not citizens of the Chickasaw Nation and that the children were therefore not entitled to enrollment. Thus 731 of the cases were dismissed. The remaining twenty-three, who had been born prior to September 25, 1902 and had applied for enrollment before December 1, 1905, were admitted to the rolls. The Chickasaw freedman roll stood at 4,670 in the summer of 1907; it was finally adjusted to 4,662.[29]

Many on the Chickasaw and Choctaw freedman rolls sought to have their names transferred to the roll of Chickasaws and Choctaws by blood. The case that opened the floodgates for applications for change was that of Joe and Dillard Perry. Their mother was Eliza Perry, born about 1874 in the Choctaw Nation. She was half black, one-quarter white and one-

quarter Indian. Her parents were considered freedmen, her mother half
white and her father half Indian. She was first married at fifteen to Mose
James, a Creek, who deserted her, and she then cohabited with Charley
Perry, a Chickasaw. After their son Joe was born in 1892, Eliza and
Charley were arrested for unlawful cohabitation, but the charges were
dropped after they agreed to marry. Then Dillard Perry was born in
1894. The couple lived as husband and wife until Charley's death in
1896. Although the children were five-eighths Chickasaw, they were not
recognized by their father's family. In 1902, their maternal grandmother
enrolled them as freedmen. In November of 1904 the acting commissioner
of Indian affairs recommended the transfer of their names, and it was referred to the attorney general's office for a decision. When the assistant
attorney general reviewed the case in February, 1905, he recommended
that Joe and Dillard Perry be enrolled as Chickasaw citizens. This decision,
in effect, made progeny the basis of citizenship without reference to
legitimacy.[30]

The Chickasaws protested and argued that in applying for admission
to the Chickasaw roll the Perrys were applying for Chickasaw citizenship, the deadline for which applications had passed before they asked
for the transfer. The attorney general recommended that their names be
returned to the freedman rolls in November, 1905, because they had not
applied for enrollment as Chickasaws before December, 1902. The names,
however, were not retransferred until early 1907. In the fall of 1906, Joe
and Dillard Perry made tentative selection of allotments, but the selections were rejected because they had no improvements on the tracts.[31]

Apparently taking their cue from the Perry case, attorneys generated
a number of similar cases. Albert J. Lee of Ardmore, who had handled
the Perry case, represented a number of other applicants. In early November, 1905, he visited Tams Bixby in Muskogee concerning evidence, but
Bixby and Assistant Secretary Thomas Ryan attempted to discourage him
in light of the reversal of the Perry cases. Nevertheless, in early 1906, he
presented the cases of eighteen freedman descendants of Lanie Stevenson, the half-blood Chickasaw daughter of James Colbert. In March, Lee
applied for the transfer of 110 other names. Other lawyers presented cases
during the spring and summer of 1906. Late that year, when a Senate investigating committee came to the Indian Territory to look into the conditions of affairs among the Indians, one of the "matters of greatest immediate concern" was the claims of freedmen to citizenship by right of

their Indian blood. The investigators' questions revealed a huge business in such claims cases, Albert Lee himself handling over nine hundred.[32]

These cases continued into 1907. Claiming to be part Indian, the freedman applicants argued that the Dawes Commission had violated those provisions of the Curtis Act that directed them to make official rolls of the citizens by blood of the Chickasaw and Choctaw Nations by requiring the population to apply for enrollment on a particular roll, making it virtually impossible for anyone who had not been recognized by the tribes before 1898 to apply for citizenship, and by refusing to permit people with mixed Indian and African blood to apply for enrollment as citizens by blood. The freedmen charged that the commissioners recorded only the evidence relative to their black and not their Indian heritage, although they knew of the Indian heritage at the time of enrollment. Conditions at the time had not favored the making of a fair roll. The people were ignorant and may not have understood the questions asked by the commissioners. Others claimed to have asserted their rights to enrollment as Chickasaws but were refused. The freedman appellants presented their case to the Senate Select Committee that visited the Indian Territory in late 1906.[33]

In early 1907 Webster Ballinger, attorney for some of the Chickasaw and Choctaw freedmen, secured a proposed amendment to an Indian appropriations bill directing the secretary of the interior to transfer the name of anyone who appeared on the freedman roll to the blood rolls if he could demonstrate Indian blood on either his mother's or father's side through evidence in the tribal rolls or official records then in the government's files. In hearings before the Senate Committee on Indian Affairs, attorneys for the mixed bloods cast doubt on the validity of the Dawes Commission's work in the field and criticized the government's inattention to the record-keeping process.

It was charged that the Dawes Commission believed that anyone who descended from an ancestor once held in servitude had had his Indian blood polluted by the African. On the other hand, the commissioners did not contend that a child by an Indian man and white woman should be refused enrollment as a Chickasaw by blood. Children who were no more than one thirty-second blood, but one of whose parents was a Chickasaw citizen, were enrolled, but many who possessed a greater measure of Indian blood, but had an African forebear on one side or the other, were excluded. The mixed bloods claimed that some of them had applied to the Commission in the field in 1898 for enrollment as Chickasaws, but at the time of their suit, no records could be found, for, it was alleged, no records of such applications had been kept. Tams Bixby testified before a Senate committee in 1906 that not a single mixed blood who had applied for enrollment as a freedman in 1898 had applied for enrollment at that time as a Chickasaw. Other officials claimed that the mixed bloods willingly applied for enrollment as freedmen despite charges that they were directed from the Chickasaw enrollment tent to the freedman enrollment tent when it was found that they were of Afro-Indian descent.[34]

Apparently, for about two weeks, the commissioners heard the applications of mixed bloods for enrollment as Chickasaws, but were instructed by the Indian Office that if the applicants' mothers were slaves or women who descended from slaves, they were to be enrolled as freedmen. With only a few exceptions after that, the commissioners refused to receive the applications of mixed bloods, no matter what the degree of Indian blood, and enrolled them only if their freedman status could be established. When an applicant came before the commissioners, he was given a preliminary examination. If he claimed Indian rights, the commissioners looked to see if his or his ancestor's name was on one of the tribal rolls, which the Indians had often argued were inaccurate, having been made by careless or corrupt officials. If the name was found, a census card was made. If not, the applicant was allegedly told that it was useless to apply for Indian status. In some cases the commissioners apparently went by appearance of the applicant. If he was black, he was automatically sent to the freedman tent. If he appeared to be Indian, as many of the mixed bloods did, the rolls were checked. There was the case, for instance, of Lydia Jackson, who was probably three-quarters Chickasaw blood and who had never been held in slavery. Because her name was not on the tribal rolls, she was enrolled as a freedwoman. At all costs, it was alleged, the commissioners tried to ferret out African ancestry and enrolled the applicants as freedmen. As A. S. McKennon later said, "No; the one thing they were looking for was negro blood."[35]

An example of how the Dawes Commission worked was the case of Jesse McGee, a Chickasaw who had seven children by his wife, Dora Jackson McGee, a freedwoman. When they appeared before the Commission, the commissioners would not allow Dora and the children to appear for examination with McGee. They sent McGee to the Indian enrollment tent and his wife and children and her father, Joe Jackson, to the freedman tent. Two more children were subsequently born to the couple and added to the freedman roll. Under the act of April 26, 1906, newborns were allowed to apply for enrollment on whichever roll the parents felt they were entitled. Jesse Mc-Gee presented an application for his tenth child as a Chickasaw by blood, and it was placed on the roll of citizens.[36]

There were, however, persons on the Chickasaw and Choctaw rolls who were of Afro-Indian descent. These were the descendants of Indian women who had children by black men and whose names appeared on the tribal roll. While they were not especially proud of these people, the Chickasaws pointed to them as evidence that they did not discriminate against the mixed bloods because of their African blood. It was the source of the blood that concerned the Chickasaws. Most of the mixed bloods were the offspring of Indian men and black women, which offspring the Indians argued were illegitimate because their laws did not recognize the validity of marriages between Indians and blacks. However, no penalties were assessed for violation of the Choctaw laws, and no Chickasaw law could be found on the books. Neither did the tribes recognize common-law marriages between Indians and blacks, although they did recognize them between Indians and between Indians and whites. Those who lived with blacks, they claimed, were socially ostracized. While they recognized the offspring of Indian men and white women as citizens, they fell back on the old custom from slave times and determined the status of Afro-Indians on the basis of the mother's status. Thus, the Indians rejected the mixed blood on the basis of social custom and usage, while the mixed bloods argued for a change in status on the basis of their right as progeny of Indians, basing their argument on the Treaty of 1830, which gave title to the western lands to the Choctaws (and, therefore, the Chickasaws) "and their descendants." Since they were descendants of the Indians, they argued for a share in the tribal domain.[37]

In an effort to put a stop to applications such as that of the Perrys, Congress had written Section 4 of the act of April 26, 1906, which forbade the transfer of names from freedman to citizen rolls unless records in charge of the Commission to the Five Civilized Tribes showed that applications for enrollment as citizens by blood had been made before December of 1902. There then arose the question of what constituted an application. Government officials took it to mean a scrap of paper, a document—in short, anything in black and white—that showed that the applicants were insisting on rights as Chickasaws before late 1902. Thus, the search was on for those scraps of paper, if they existed, and in the search, more questions were raised about the Dawes Commission's procedures.[38]

One of the cases attorney Albert J. Lee had pending at the time of the act of 1906 was that of Calvin, Simon, Willie, and Louis Newberry, Mira Newberry Stevenson, Lula Newberry Stevenson, and their children. These were the descendants of Caldonia Newberry. According to James A. Alexander, a member of the Chickasaw senate, it was often stated by his maternal grandmother that Caldonia was the daughter of Ben Love, the nephew of Alexander's grandmother. Love had about seven-eighths Chickasaw blood. The sons of Caldonia had voted in Chickasaw elections, but when they appeared at Rock Springs to cast their votes in 1890, their right to vote was challenged. Alexander's uncle Frank Colbert told the election judges that the Newberrys descended from Love and "a mixed breed woman" and were eligible to vote, which they were allowed to do. On June 14, 1906, the Commissioner of Indian Affairs denied the Newberrys' petition to transfer their names to the Chickasaw roll because there was no evidence that application had been made for admission to the citizenship rolls before late 1902. In searching the records, however, Lee found evidence on a docket of citizenship cases in the office of the clerk for the United States court for the Southern District of the Indian Territory at Ardmore. It appeared that on August 31, 1896, Caldonia Newberry had applied to have herself and her children enrolled as Chickasaw citizens. The application was apparently denied. But the papers relating to the case could not be found. The courthouse at Ardmore had burned in 1897, and with it burned the court records, presumably among which were those relating to the Newberry case. Indian Office officials, however, refused to recognize the evidence sufficient to be considered an application and denied the Newberrys' application to have their names transferred.[39]

There were allegations early in 1907 that William O. Beall, while secretary to the commissioner to the Five Civilized Tribes, willfully suppressed applications of mixed bloods for enrollment as Chickasaw citizens, specifically the application of Joe and Dillard Perry. In March or April of 1906, a clerk in the office of the commissioner found an application for the Perrys dated August 25, 1896. The document was significant because the Perrys had been rejected because of the absence of an application that predated 1902. When the document was shown to Beall, he took the responsibility of informing Commissioner Tams Bixby, who was in Washington at the time. Bixby denied having received any word of the discovery, and Beall failed to mention it to Bixby until much later. Neither were the Perrys informed of the discovery. While Beall was cleared of charges against him, his actions were questionable because he had sometimes been employed by the attorneys who represented the Choctaw Nation in its opposition to admission of applicants to the tribal rolls. Despite these revelations and the existence of an application, the Perrys' names remained on the freedman roll.[40]

Indian Office officials adopted as their official stand the Chickasaw position that those whose mothers were freedwomen had traditionally been recognized as freedmen, regardless of the amount of Indian blood, that during slavery the status of the child was determined by the status of the mother, that white society had universally classified anyone with any amount of African blood as black, and that the freedmen should be satisfied because the Chickasaws and Choctaws had been much more generous to the freedmen among them than the whites had been to blacks in America. These arguments prevailed in Congress, and the legislation that had proposed to open the rolls failed to pass. In early February, 1907, J. Milton Turner of St. Louis and S. T. Wiggins of Ardmore, attorneys for another group of Chickasaw and Choctaw freedman appellants, sent a memorial to the president with a draft of a bill that would provide for a suit in the Court of Claims against the two Indian nations and the United States, with right to appeal to the Supreme Court. The president did not approve the draft but sent the issue to the attorney general, who ruled, on February 27, that to argue that freedmen who had never been recognized as citizens were now entitled to rights would disregard the "rolls, customs, and usages of the tribes." It would result in endless litigation.[41]

In April, 1907, attorneys for Bettie Ligon, a Choctaw freedwoman, and about two thousand other Choctaw and Chickasaw freedmen (mainly the latter) who claimed Indian blood filed suit in the U.S. Court for the Southern District of the Indian Territory against tribal executives and the secretary of the interior for an undivided interest in the Nations. On May 18, Judge Hosea Townsend dismissed the case for want of jurisdiction. The court of appeals for the Indian Territory sustained the opinion because the judges could not agree on the decree that should be rendered. In June, the case was pending, on appeal, before the U.S. circuit court for the eighth district.[42]

When the case was appealed to the United States Supreme Court, it was dismissed late in 1911 because the appellants failed to file printed briefs. As late as 1928, Chickasaw freedmen were still trying to get their names transferred from the freedman rolls to the Chickasaw rolls. One well-known group was the heirs of Charles Cohee, who had been instrumental in the struggle for freedman rights. Cohee himself had tried unsuccessfully to get his name transferred in 1902, and in 1928 testimony was offered that Cohee, who was part Chickasaw, had applied to be enrolled as a Chickasaw citizen in 1898. But Tams Bixby, it was alleged, had convinced him to enroll as a freedman in order to convince other mixed bloods to enroll as freedmen rather than as citizens; Bixby had allegedly promised to transfer Cohee's name to the tribal rolls at a later date but had failed to do so. In 1928, the Indian Office decided that it was inadvisable to reopen the tribal rolls.[43]

By these actions, the United States excluded from Chickasaw citizenship, forever, hundreds of persons who had more Chickasaw blood than many on the tribal roll. While it might be argued today that people of mixed black-Indian blood had as much right to be considered Indians as did the mixed white-Indians, the theory of "the one fatal drop" that characterized the racial attitudes in the white South prevailed. In rejecting the freedmen, the United States sanctioned the racial bias that had long existed among the Chickasaws. By refusing to rectify its error in not removing the blacks under the Treaty of 1866, the United States penalized the blacks for not removing on their own or for not voluntarily seeking American citizenship. Thus the Chickasaw freedmen lost the long struggle to secure rights in the Chickasaw domain. Whatever victory allotment may have been proved to be a hollow one. As citizens of the new state of Oklahoma, they would find that their lot was not greatly improved.

NOTES

1. *Indian Citizen*, September 20, 1900.
2. W. S. Bennett to Secretary, March 24, 1899, and Ed Colbert to Secretary of the Interior, March 28, 1899, National Archives Record Group 48 (Office of the Secretary of the Interior), Indian Territory Division, *Letters Received*, 836-99, 926-99; A. B. Person to Tams Bixby, October 25, 1898; J. R. Nail to A. S. McKennon, January 2, 1898; Ervin McClain [McCain] to J. George Wright, November 26, 1899, Adge Stephenson to Bixby, January 31, 1899, L. J. Kemp to Dawes Commission, February 13, 1899, R. W. Weddle to Wright, September 8, 1898, McClain [McCain] to Wright, November 27, 1899, Colbert to Secretary, October 27, 1898, and January 10, 1899, and Abram Eastman to McKennon, December 28,

1898, Indian Archives Division, Oklahoma Historical Society, *Dawes Commission–Chickasaw; El Reno News,* October 21, 1898.

3. Gebell Gillespie to Secretary, May 15, 1899, *Dawes Commission–Chickasaw.*

4. Jefferson Goldsmith to Dawes Commission, April 5, 1899, D. P. Brown to Cornelius Bliss, August 17, 1899, M. Cowart to Secretary, February 21, 1899, T. S. Strickland to Dawes Commission, January 6, 1900, and Lucy McKenney to Dawes Commission, June 5, 1900, *Dawes Commission–Chickasaw;* Indian Archives Microfilm Publications, *Records of the Dawes Commission to the Five Civilized Tribes,* DC 9(Letterpress Books, Volumes 20, 21, 22, 23, 25), 22: 445, hereafter cited as *DC9.*

5. Nettie Stephenson to Dawes Commission, June 8, 1899, M. B. Mullins to Dawes Commission, December 4, 1899; Francis Grayson to Bixby, January 9, 1900, and Colbert to Bixby, December 26, 1899, *Dawes Commission–Chickasaw;* Colbert to Bliss, January 18, 1900, National Archives Record Group 48, Indian Territory Division, *Choctaw and Chickasaw Freedmen,* Box 384, 360-00 (subsequent references from this file are from Box 384); Acting Chairman to George Stevenson, December 23, 1899, and McKennon to J. M. Perry, December 20, 1899, *DC9,* 21: 81, 259.

6. E. D. Love to Bixby, January 3, 1900, R. H. McDuffie to Dawes Commission, December 21, 1899, Jesse McGee to Bixby, January 1, 1900, and J. McDonald to Dawes Commission, January 3 and 16, 1900, *Dawes Commission–Chickasaw;* Bixby to Love, January 12, 1900, Acting Chairman to McDuffie, December 27, 1899, and McKennon to McGee, December 27, 1899, *DC9,* 22: 479 and 21: 197, 258.

7. Annual Reports of the Department of the Interior for the Fiscal Year Ended June 30, 1900, 56 Cong., 2 Sess., *House Document 5,* 28-29, 31-32, hereafter cited as *Annual Reports, 1900.*

8. *Ibid.,* 133-135.

9. *Rules and Regulations Governing Mineral Leases, the Collection and Disbursement of Revenues, and the Supervision of Schools in the Indian Territory, Under the General Provisions of the Act of Congress Approved June 28, 1898 (30 Statutes, 495)* and *Regulations Concerning Education in the Indian Territory,* in Indian Territory Division, *Letters Received,* 252-98 Schools; D. C. Carter to Wright, February 21, 1899, Wright to D. H. Johnston, November 2, 1898, and Johnston to Wright, November 7, 1898, *Dawes Commission–Chickasaw; Annual Reports, 1900,* 161.

10. W. A. Jones to Secretary, February 10, 1900, and H. L. Burton, et al. to Secretary, answered February 14, 1900, *Choctaw and Chickasaw Freedmen,* 602-00, 499-00.

11. 56 Cong., 1 Sess., *House Document 221,* 1-2; Thomas Ryan to
Commissioner, April 3, 1900, and May 31, 1900, National Archives
Record Group 75 (Records of the Bureau of Indian Affairs), *Letters
Received,* 16295-00, 26112-00; James K. Jones to E. A. Hitchcock,
May 17, 1900, A. C. Tonner to Secretary, May 24, 1900, and Tonner to
Jones, May 28, 1900, Choctaw and Chickasaw Freedmen, 24513-00,
1677-00, 1700-00.

12. Bennett to Dawes Commission, February 15, 1899, Perry to Commission, February 18, 1899, Nettie Stephenson to McKennon, April 11,
1899, Sam Jones to McKennon, January 14, 1900, Jones to Dawes Commission, February 10, 1900, Charles Cohee to T. B. Needles, February 10,
1900, Cohee to Dawes Commission, January 1, February 26, and August 8,
1900, Acting Chairman to Cohee, March 3, 1900, A. W. Alexander to
McKennon, March 13, 1899, P. P. Dailey to Dawes Commission, February
12, 1900, Kernelius Bacon to McKennon, May 13, 1899, Hardy Colbert
to B. Williams, February 26, 1899 (in B.C. Colbert to McKennon, October
26, 1899), Louis Bennett to Dawes Commission, October 9, 1899, Eastman
Williams to Bixby, January 4, 1900, William Anderson to Dawes Commission, November 1, 1899, William Cohee to Dawes Commission, December
30, 1899, and Bixby to Judge Taylor, December 18, 1899, *Dawes Commission—Chickasaw;* Bixby to Bennett, January 6, 1900, Bixby to Jones,
January 10, 1900, and Acting Chairman to Charles Cohee, January 4, 1900,
DC9, 22: 8, 191, 429, Sam Jones and his daughter Victoria were ultimately
enrolled: numbers 3011 and 4196, respectively. Bacon succeeded in being
placed on the roll: number 4571. The Dawes Commission informed Cohee
that Humday did not appear on their records, and Hardy Colbert does not
appear on the final roll.

13. Frank Wilson to Dawes Commission, November 24, 1899, Fred
Umphrey to Bixby, March 15, 1899, Edmond Colbert to Secretary, October
22, 1898, and Colbert to Commission, March 16, 1899, *Dawes Commission—
Chickasaw.*

14. Thomas Dyer to McKennon, January 29, 1900, Victoria Stephenson
and Charles Cohee to Dawes Commission, January 9, 1900, Cohee to Dawes
Commission, January 1, February 11, 21, and 26, and August 8, 1900,
C. H. Clark to Dawes Commission, February 1, 1900, and Overton Love to
McKennon, March 25, 1899, *Dawes Commission—Chickasaw;* Acting Chair-
man to William Love, December 26, 1899, *DC9,* 21: 141; Bixby to Victoria
Stephenson, January 6, 1900, *DC9,* 22: 167.

15. Bennett to Secretary, May 25, 1900, *Choctaw and Chickasaw Freedmen,* 1844-00; *Indian Citizen,* September 20, 1900; *Purcell Register,* September 14, 1900; Wright to Secretary, December 8, 1900, and Ed M. Dawson to Commissioner, January 4, 1900, Office of Indian Affairs, *Letters
Received,* 60837-00, 732-01.

16. Annual Reports of the Department of the Interior for the Fiscal Year Ended June 30, 1901, 57 Cong., 1 Sess., *House Document 5*, 10, 62-68.

17. *Ibid.*, 18, 20, 32; Annual Reports of the Department of the Interior for the Fiscal Year Ended June 30, 1902, 57 Cong., 2 Sess., *House Document 5*, 17, 166.

18. Commissioner to the Five Civilized Tribes, *Laws, Decisions, and Regulations Affecting the Work of the Commissioner to the Five Civilized Tribes, 1893 to 1906* (Washington, D.C.: Government Printing Office, 1906), 57-70; hereafter cited as *Laws and Decisions; Chickasaw Enterprise,* May 15, 1902, and March 5, 1903; *Cherokee Advocate,* March 28, 1903.

19. Needles and C. R. Breckenridge to Secretary, January 15, 1902, *Dawes Commission—Chickasaw.*

20. W. H. Russell to Hitchcock, January 11, 1902, W. H. Twine to Hitchcock, October 20 and November 15, 1902; W. M. Alexander to Department of the Interior, February 6, 1902, Tonner to Secretary, July 28, 1902, Zack Allen to Secretary, October 18, 1902, Charles Cohee and B. C. Franklin to Secretary, October 29, 1902, and Charles W. Needham to Hitchcock, October 14, 1902, *Choctaw and Chickasaw Freedmen,* 351-02, 6603-02, 7186-02, 1001-02, 4583-02, 6605-02, 6848-02, 6504-02.

21. J. R. Richards to Secretary, December 3, 1902, W. M. Hoyt to Secretary, December 8, 1902, Bill of Interpleader, November 26, 1902, G. G. Gratton and Charley Abram to Secretary, January 15, 1903, Dave McCoy, et al. to Secretary, January 20, 1903, R. H. Bernia to Secretary, January 23, 1903, Ryan to Commissioner, January 23, 1903, *ibid.,* 7461-02, 7573-02, 271-98, 757-03, 777-03, 1149-03, 5259-03; *Daily Oklahoman,* December 24, 1902.

22. Ryan to Commissioner, December 11, 1902, and THE UNITED STATES v. THE CHOCTAW NATION AND THE CHICKASAW NATION AND THE CHICKASAW FREEDMEN (Court of Claims No, 23115), in Secretary to Commission, April 1, 1907, Office of Indian Affairs, *Letters Received,* 73412-02, 31851-07; Needham to Secretary, May 1, 1903, and Needham to Hitchcock, June 2, 1903, *Choctaw and Chickasaw Freedmen,* 4465-03, 5285-03.

23. Tonner to Secretary, March 3, and April 8, 1903, and June 25, 1904; Franklin Winchester to Secretary, January 5 and 23, 1903; Richard Eastman to Secretary, September 3, 1903; Bessie Lee to Department, September 7, 1903; J. H. Blue to Hitchcock, June 30, 1903; and Franklin to Department, July 23, 1903, *Choctaw and Chickasaw Freedmen,* 2322-03, 3362-03, 3672-03, 5220-04, 1903-03, 1251-03, 7307-03, 7855-03,

6079-03, 6555-03; Ryan to Commissioner, April 14, 1903, Hitchcock
to Commissioner, June 28, 1904, Secretary to Commissioner, February 19,
1907, and Commissioner to the Five Civilized Tribes to Secretary, February
20, 1902, Office of Indian Affairs, *Letters Received,* 23116-03, 42753-
04, 17833-07, 19689-07; Annual Reports of the Department of the Interior for the Fiscal Year Ended June 30, 1904, 58 Cong., 3 Sess., *House
Document 5,* 14, hereafter cited as *Annual Reports, 1904.*

24. John Gibbs to Secretary, November 26, 1902; Blue to Hitchcock
June 30, 1903; Love Miller to Secretary, August 1, 1903; George Stephenson to Secretary, June 15, 1903; Adge Stephenson to Secretary, June 17,
1903; and Katie Williams to Department, July 27, 1903, *Choctaw and
Chickasaw Freedmen,* 7399-02, 6079-03, 6793-03, 5703-03, 5739-03,
6663-03.

25. *Annual Reports, 1904,* 42-43; *Chickasaw Enterprise,* December 11,
1902.

26. Needham to Secretary, March 1, 1904, *Choctaw and Chickasaw
Freedmen,* 1713-04; *Chickasaw Enterprise,* February 25, 1904; *Cases
Argued and Decided in the Supreme Court of the United States,* Lawyers'
Edition (Rochester, N.Y.: The Lawyers Co-operative Publishing Company,
1926), Book 48: 640-645; C. F. Larrabee to Secretary, January 25, 1906,
with enclosures, National Archives Record Group 48, Indian Territory
Division, *General Incoming Correspondence, July, 1898-April, 1907,*
1898 File 590, Chickasaw Legislative Acts (Box 466); *Indian Journal,*
January 28, 1910; 61 Cong., 2 Sess., *House Document 920,* 1-2, 8.

27. Joseph B. Thoburn and Muriel H. Wright, *Oklahoma: A History
of the State and Its People* (New York: Lewis Historical Publishing Company, 1929), 2: 622-623.

28. *Laws and Decisions,* 88-97.

29. M. V. Cheadle to Secretary and Congress, September 20, 1906,
Indian Archives Division, *Chickasaw—Citizenship,* 4973; *Annual Reports
of the Department of the Interior for the Fiscal Year Ended June 30,
1907* (Washington, D.C.: Government Printing Office, 1907), 2: 286,
287, 290, hereafter cited as *Annual Reports, 1907;* Angie Debo, *And
Still the Waters Run* (Princeton, N.J.: Princeton University Press, 1972),
47. Allotment did not end with the closing of the rolls. Allotment to
freedmen was still continuing in early 1908. *See,* for example, Report
of Chickasaw Land Office, December 10, 1907, January 2 and 3, 1908,
Dawes Commission—Chickasaw.

30. *Laws and Decisions,* 165-168; 59 Cong., 2 Sess., *Senate Document 257,* 54, hereafter cited as *Document 257.*

31. *Laws and Decisions,* 168-179; Bixby to Secretary, October 30,
1906, Office of Indian Affairs, *Letters Received,* 96250-06.

32. 59 Cong., 2 Sess., *Senate Report 5013,* 1: ii, 272-291, and 2: 1514-1517, hereafter cited as *Report 5013;* Department of Justice to Commissioner, July 6, 1906, with enclosures, Bixby to Secretary, July 25 and 27, and August 17, 1906, with enclosures, and January 30, 1907, Office of Indian Affairs, *Letters Received,* 57046-06, 64730-06, 64844-06, 71810-06, 71816-06, 11039-07; William O. Beall to Bixby, February 21, 1906, *Dawes Commission–Chickasaw.*

33. *Report 5013,* 2: 1497, 1511-1531.

34. *Document 257,* 19, 20, 21, 34-39.

35. *Ibid.,* 9, 11, 12, 20, 40, 48, 49.

36. *Ibid.,* 10.

37. *Ibid.,* 3, 13, 19, 22, 23, 50; 59 Cong., 2 Sess., *Senate Document 298,* 8-9.

38. *Document 257,* 61.

39. *Ibid.,* 1, 5, 6, 7, 32-33.

40. *Ibid.,* 1, 5, 6, 7, 32-33.

41. *Annual Reports, 1907,* 106-107; *Muskogee Cimeter,* February 22, 1907.

42. *Annual Reports, 1907,* 107.

43. *Muskogee Times Democrat,* December 14, 1911; Franklin to Secretary, October 29, 1902, *Choctaw and Chickasaw Freedmen,* 6848-02; Charles H. Burke to Wilburn Cartwright, April 9, 1928, National Archives Record Group 75, *Central Classified Files,* 95003-1922 Chickasaw 053, with enclosures.

9

Transition to Citizenship

For forty years, the Chickasaw freedmen had tenaciously clung to the Chickasaw Nation as their home and had sought, by what means they knew and the best they could afford, to establish a right to a share in the Chickasaw domain comparable to that held by their counterparts in the other Civilized Tribes. The extent of their participation in the final disposition of the Chickasaw Nation fell far short of their desires and by no means compensated for the decades of deprivation they had suffered as a result of their exclusion from both Chickasaw and American citizenship.

In retrospect, the freedmen might have believed that their lot would have been better had they sought United States citizenship when the Chickasaws failed to adopt them in 1868. To have done so, however, would have meant the severing of nationalistic ties. By the time of the Civil War, many black families had lived among the Chickasaws for generations. They lived like Chickasaws and spoke the language. As slaveholding increased and more blacks came into the Indian country from the states, they became important in the process of acculturation of the Chickasaws. While the blacks were learning new ways of life in the Chickasaw Nation, they brought into Chickasaw society ideas and ways of life they had acquired during slavery among the whites. By mid-nineteenth century, the cultural ties were bolstered by blood ties to the Chickasaws. Although members of the Chickasaw mixed-blood elite insisted that the Chickasaws were for the most part free of African blood, many of those that the Chickasaws designated as freedmen had more Chickasaw blood than African, and in some instances the blood was that of the Chickasaw elite. Thus the freedmen's insistence that the Chickasaw Nation was their home was not based entirely on economic or political motives but resulted from a sense of national identity based on blood and cultural ties.

Had the Chickasaws not been beset by constant threats to their national integrity in postwar years, matters might have gone differently for the freedmen. But after the railroads crossed the Chickasaw Nation, bringing with them economic growth and thousands of United States citizens, the Chickasaws slowly lost control of their country. They viewed the freedmen as an internal threat. The freedmen's numbers rapidly increased after the war, and they freely intermarried with blacks from the states, after a time making it difficult to determine which blacks belonged to the Chickasaw Nation. The Chickasaws dared not adopt the freedmen because they feared the black vote. That fear was sustained by an intense racial prejudice, especially on the part of the mixed bloods. The Chickasaws were not willing to risk the hastening of the demise of their nation by giving political power to a people they distrusted.

Had the United States fulfilled its treaty obligations to the Chickasaws and Choctaws, the freedmen undoubtedly would have fared differently. The treaty stipulations were clear enough. If the Chickasaws and Choctaws did not adopt the freedmen within two years following the Treaty of 1866, the United States would remove them. The Chickasaws refused to adopt them and demanded their removal. Despite the freedmen's insistence that they wished to remain in the Chickasaw Nation, the United States could have removed them. The question first became one of location, and as that matter was debated, the only possibility seemed to be the Oklahoma lands. But by the time official policy seemed to favor removal, the American public was putting pressure on Congress to open those lands to Americans. The pressure prevailed.

When the debate over treaty obligations was going on between the Chickasaws and the United States, the freedmen for the most part lived in grinding poverty and under the constant fear that they would be dispossessed of the improvements they had made on the Chickasaw domain. They lived without civil rights, the right to vote, and, for the most part, educational privileges. Their condition was extremely dismal by the time Congress took control of affairs in the Indian Territory in the early 1890s.

Unfortunately, the American public's desires once more took precedence over the obligations to the freedmen. The Dawes Commission, sent to negotiate the dissolution of the tribal status, at first appeared concerned with the freedmen's rights but later became so intent on obtaining agreements from the Chickasaws and Choctaws that it let the tribes have their way regarding the freedmen and left the final decision concerning their rights to the United States courts. Although the freedmen were enrolled and received allotments, in the final judgment they were denied what they had so long sought: recognition as rightful citizens of the Chickasaw Nation. The freedmen retained their allotments of land, but the courts ruled that they had no legal right to them and that the Chickasaws should receive indemnity. The freedmen, many of whom by blood and appearance were more Chickasaw than African, were legally cut off from what they claimed as their rightful birthright and heritage.

As the prospect of American citizenship became a reality, the freedmen no doubt had great hopes that they would at last belong to a society from which they would not be excluded. However, whatever expectations, hopes, and aspirations they may have had faded quickly as they found themselves a part of a society that was in most ways more hostile to them than Chickasaw society had been.

There was, for instance, no respite from their poverty. Many of the freedmen found themselves "land poor." Each freedman received the equivalent of forty acres of the average allottable land. Thus, those who received lower grades of land sometimes held several hundred acres. Since freedman families were large, they sometimes held four hundred or more acres of good land. Heads of families found it impossible to improve the land and put it into cultivation because they lacked the teams and agricultural implements to do so. The owners could not fence their property. They had no cash, and they could borrow but little. While they realized the necessity of retaining the title to their lands, they were in an economic stalemate without the right to sell or mortgage part of their lands to obtain the cash necessary to improve their lot.[1]

The freedmen found themselves placed on the same level with the full-blood Indians. They resented being placed so. The full bloods in many cases did not speak English, but all of the freedmen did. The full bloods for the most part were not literate. The freedmen, however, had tried all along to seek an education. Many could read and write, and the last generation had "fair educations," they maintained.[2]

The closer the Indian Territory moved toward statehood, the more extensive were the educational opportunities that the Chickasaw freedmen had long sought. In 1902, it was estimated that one-sixth of the male population over twenty-one in the Indian Territory was illiterate, as was a much greater percentage of youth, because federal schools had been so long in coming.[3] Despite their protests to the contrary, the rate of illiteracy was no doubt even higher among the Chickasaw freedmen.

Although the tribal schools of the territory had been placed under federal control in 1898, the Atoka Agreement, as incorporated in the Curtis Act, excluded provisions for the use of coal royalties, which constituted the school funds, for education of the Choctaw and Chickasaw freedmen. They were too poor to support private schools. Inquiries concerning federal schools came from the freedmen in the Chickasaw Nation. Ed Colbert reported 200 children of school age near Colbert, where there was a building eighty by forty feet ready for use as a school. From Wiley, Isaac Kemp asked for schools, stressing that 90 percent of the people there were illiterate. By 1902 there were only two schools admitting freedmen in the Chickasaw Nation. At Ardmore there were 193 black children in school, and at Chickasaw there were 104. These were public schools, which were established in incorporated towns and not under the supervision of the superintendent of schools in the Indian Territory.[4]

To supplement the schools maintained by the tribal funds, Congress appropriated $100,000 on April 21, 1904, to maintain, strengthen, and enlarge the tribal schools and to provide for the attendance of the children of noncitizens. That fall, some Indians of the Five Civilized Tribes threatened to boycott any schools that blacks were permitted to attend. The Chickasaws argued that the money was intended to be spent on Indian children alone, but they apparently had no objections to attending school with whites.[5]

At the time, the government was conducting twelve day schools for the blacks, enrolling 739 students. The following were some of the schools. Near Colbert was Central Union, taught by John Colbert, Roberta Williams, and S. C. Counter and enrolling 69 students. A. Harrison taught the school at Wiley. Just north of Berwyn was Dawes Academy, which enrolled 32 children and was taught by J. W. Spencer and another teacher. And D. J. Counter taught 22 students at Mead. There were as well 300 blacks enrolled in public schools at Ardmore, 183 at Chickasha, 104 at Purcell, 29 at Tishomingo, and 125 at Wynnewood.[6]

The Act of April 21, 1906, authorized the secretary of the interior
to assume control of the schools of the Five Civilized Tribes along with
school lands and property. John D. Benedict, superintendent of schools
for the territory, had direct control, and his policies were carried out by
the supervisor of schools in each tribe. The Act of 1906 limited the amount
of tribal funds expended for education to that expended by each tribe during the 1904-05 school year, or $145,471.89 in the Chickasaw Nation.
Congress appropriated an additional $300,000 for "the maintenance,
strengthening, and enlarging of tribal schools" and for providing schools
for children not of Indian blood. Throughout the Indian Territory, about
a thousand schools operated during 1906-07, enrolling about 8,600 blacks.
Of the 216 day schools maintained in the Chickasaw Nation during the
1906-07 year, 25 were for blacks. In the public schools of Chickasha and
Marietta, there were enrolled 209 and 62 blacks, respectively.[7] During the
1906-07 year, twenty schools for blacks were conducted in the Chickasaw
Nation. Blacks were also enrolled in public schools in Ardmore (493),
Chickasha (107), Marietta (62), and Wynnewood (127). The Act of June 21,
1906, provided for reserving one acre from allotment for schools maintained for the Chickasaw and Choctaw freedmen. In the summer of 1906,
E. K. Kemp, Birthet Harper, Oscar Tutter, and Arthur Willis asked that an
acre of land be reserved from allotment for the establishment of the Brown
Spring Colored School near Wynnewood. The commissioner, however,
recommended against the reservation because no school was at the time
located or maintained on the tract.[8]

On March 1, 1907, Congress appropriated $300,000 for schools during
the 1907-08 school year. Records of twenty-one day schools for blacks in
the Chickasaw Nation show that, in several, Indians and blacks attended
school together—Athens, near Ada; Leader, near Conway; Lone Isle, near
Woodville; and Jehova, near Milo.[9] Upon statehood, maintainance of the
tribal schools was assumed by the local governments of the State of Oklahoma, at which time they became public schools. Throughout the half-
decade preceding statehood and the years following, only those Chickasaw
freedmen who lived in towns large enough to maintain high schools for
blacks had the opportunity to pursue an education beyond the elementary
grades.

Before statehood, blacks in the Chickasaw country began to experience
discrimination in education. In April, 1906, the City of Ardmore held an
election to approve the issuance of bonds for the construction of sewers,

waterworks, and schools. The bond issue was passed, including $35,000 for the construction and equipping of new school buildings. After the election, the black community was informed that the two new brick buildings would be used by the whites and that the blacks were to have two old frame buildings that the whites had used for several years. Black leaders protested that since they would be paying taxes to support the bonds, they should have one of the new buildings and that the two frame buildings constituted discrimination against them. The blacks were conducting school for up to seventy students in a room fifteen by twenty-eight feet. The board of education planned to move one of the frame buildings formerly used by the whites to a new site for the blacks to use. However, the site selected was near the cesspool of the city's sewer system. The blacks objected, brought suit in federal court, and won an injunction to prevent location of the school at the new site. In the fall of 1907, the unoccupied building rested on blocks, and the board had not determined any further action to take. Another case of discrimination had arisen at Pauls Valley. In November, 1906, Judge J. T. Dickerson of the Southern District of the Indian Territory issued a writ of mandamus against the Pauls Valley school board, directing them to admit black children to the public schools. The judge said it was up to the board to decide if separate schools would be provided.[10]

The freedmen's lack of education made them easy prey for opportunists, speculators, and swindlers. They knew little about deeds, titles, or contracts. There were instances in which freedmen agreed to lease their allotments for mining stone and other minerals in and above the ground for ten years with options for ten years more. Near Maxwell, some freedmen leased their allotments for five years for very little, and others sold their allotments, although they were restricted from sale, for no more than what they would ordinarily receive for a year's rent. In the spring of 1906, freedman A. B. Kemp appealed to the secretary of the interior for help. He had bought the improvements on a place in 1899, at which time no one else claimed it. Since then, he said, "the frauds and grafters" had allowed him to make only $45 by renting the place that had sixty acres in cultivation and produced about fifteen bales of cotton a year. In 1906 he was dispossessed through an allotment contest by a person who was allegedly not in the Chickasaw Nation and never had been. Kemp had a large family that, although enrolled as freedmen, showed more Chickasaw blood, he claimed, than seven-tenths of those on the Chickasaw rolls. With a large family to support, he was "broke down worrying over this financially and physically." His right was contested by a person who could not be found, and he could not get a clear title to his allotment "without a lawyer tricking with it." In some instances, administrators of estates of incompetent freedmen sold the improvements of their charges. There was also fraud concerning town lots. In 1906, a number of black citizens of Chickasha, among them some Chickasaw freedmen, presented their case to the secretary of the interior. In 1900-01 they had bought lots east of the Rock Island tracts on land that belonged to a Chickasaw citizen, who signed their deeds under the assumption that the lots were included in the plat of the city of Chickasha. They were forced to buy them because blacks were not allowed to buy anywhere else in the city. Thus they had settled, built homes and churches, paid city taxes, worked on the streets, and otherwise supported the public enterprises. Then in 1906, a Chickasaw citizen informed them that the section of land was not in the city, contested the allotment of the citizen from whom they had purchased the lots, and threatened to dispossess the estimated 250 persons living east of the tracks.[11]

For the most part, however, the alienation restrictions on allotments protected the freedmen for a few years. At least some of the freedmen realized that the restrictions stood between them and disaster. As one freedman put it, if the restrictions were not removed, "they can't run us off but if moved they will run us off and kill us and take our home over." However, land speculators had early begun to work to have the restrictions removed. It was racial prejudice that made it possible for land speculators to take advantage of the ignorant freedmen and divest them of their allotments. Late in 1903, bills were introduced into Congress to remove restrictions on the sale of allotments of all freedmen and black citizens of the Indian Territory. An act passed in 1904 had provided for removal of restrictions on freedmen's surplus allotments but not on homestead allotments. Land speculators such as the Indiahoma Realty Company of Ardmore went to work. Buyers purchased freedman land, many freedmen selling their holdings for "a song," even though in the Choctaw and Chickasaw Nations the allotments were inalienable for twenty-one years. Too, the freedmen of the Choctaw and Chickasaw Nations were exempted from the law because they had no surplus allotments, but their allotments were not classified as homesteads at that time. The land speculators sought clarification of the law in the federal

courts of the territory and, in the summer of 1905, obtained a ruling
that the lands were inalienable and that all sales were null and void.
But pressure from whites and some Indians continued for the removal
of restrictions.[12]

When the freedmen learned that a Senate Select Committee planned
to visit the Indian Territory, the Choctaw and Chickasaw Freedmen
Association met at South McAlester in October, 1906. They resolved
to present a memorial to the committee and elected J. Fletcher Morris,
Wesley McKinney, A. J. Johnson, William Glover, William Seitz, and
Edmond Colbert to present it. They asked the committee to recommend
legislation that would extend the time for receiving applications for freedmen minors. They also asked for the removal of restrictions from the sale
of all lands of the adult Chickasaw and Choctaw freedmen. They argued
that their slavery had not been as rigorous as that among the whites,
that a larger percentage of them were educated than were the blacks of
"the plantation districts of the South," that they had always tried to
improve themselves, that in comparison to the full-blood Indians they
were more capable of handling their property, that the younger generation was becoming educated, and that many were land poor. Removal
of restrictions would allow them to sell or mortgage part of their land
in order to improve the rest and buy badly needed implements.[13]

The Senate Select Committee heard a great deal of testimony regarding the matter during the winter of 1906-07. Federal Judge John Thomas
of Muskogee, for instance, believed that restrictions on sales thwarted the
economic development of the country. One way to stimulate the economy
and get money in circulation was to shake the freedmen loose from their
land. Speaking of the Creek freedmen, Thomas said, "Those negroes won't
work if they can avoid it and as long as they have one hundred and sixty
acres of land, they won't work." Indian leaders such as Creek Chief Pleasant
Porter knew that the freedmen's ignorance of legal matters would result in
a loss of their land, yet he saw no reason to protect them. Because agitation
was so great for removal of restrictions on homestead allotments of the
freedmen and citizens without Indian blood, the Senate Select Committee
recommended legislation to remove those restrictions.[14]

Besides creating opportunities for graft and fraud, the freedmen's ignorance of matters relating to land titles had in other ways resulted in dis-
ruptions in the freedman communities. In the process of choosing allotments, they sometimes forgot to make provisions for the lands on which
their churches sat. They sometimes found that cemeteries they had used

for thirty or forty years were filed on by Chickasaw citizens. In 1906, the
secretary of the interior ruled on such cases. The ruling was occasioned
by the request of Clifton Mayes and other freedmen near Washington, Chickasaw Nation, for an allotment for the Jerusalem Church and cemetery. Most
of the land they sought had been allotted, as was common in such cases, but
the secretary ordered the allotment of a smaller tract nearby and set down
rules that were to be used thereafter by the commissioner to the Five Civilized Tribes in handling such cases. If the commissioner found that a church
organization existed and meetings were held regularly or that a building
existed and was used by or under the control of the freedmen, he was to
allow a reservation of not more than one acre. If he found a school building in which school had recently been conducted by the freedmen, he was
to allow one acre. If a cemetery existed, he was to determine the probable
needs of the community and reserve a sufficient quantity of land.[15]

This ruling, however, did not solve all problems. A prime example was
Dawes Academy, which had been built by the freedmen in the 1880s about
three miles north of Berwyn. After allotment, it sat in the northeast corner
of freedman Eddie Eastman's allotment. In late 1907, the commissioner to
the Five Civilized Tribes visited the community to locate school and cemetery lands and set aside one acre in the northwest corner of the adjoining
forty acres, making it necessary to move the building about thirty yards.
Eastman's father had told the freedmen that they could hold and use the
building where it stood until other arrangements could be made, but in
early January, 1908, Eddie Eastman nailed the doors shut and forbade
anyone to enter it. His fellow freedmen offered to pay him rent, but he
refused it. Veteran freedman leader Charles Cohee appealed to the Indian
inspector for assistance because for the first time in thirty years the Dawes
Academy had closed and the educational life of the community was dis-
rupted.[16]

By the time the Chickasaw Nation was dissolved, the freedmen must
have realized that their change in status was not necessarily a change for
the better. As American citizens, they found themselves faced with a
brand of racial hatred that was more intense than that the Chickasaws
had felt toward them. While the Chickasaws had not given them rights,
they had not passed legislation against the blacks. Now, the racial discrimination would become more systematic as the whites assumed political power in the new state.

Racial hatred was a basic issue in the founding of the State of Oklahoma. Delegates were elected from Oklahoma Territory and Indian Ter-

ritory to attend a state constitutional convention in Guthrie, Oklahoma
Territory, in November of 1906. The race issue was paramount in the
campaign for seats in the convention. The Democrats campaigned for
separate schools, coaches, and depots and against mixed marriages and
the election of blacks to public office. They favored institutionalizing
segregation by the insertion of a Jim Crow provision in the constitution.
The Republicans split over the race issue, and the result was the election
of ninety-nine Democrats, twelve Republicans, and one Independent. Perhaps the hardest fought issue of the convention was the Jim Crow provision. Fearing that President Roosevelt would veto a document contain-
ing such a provision southern politicians urged the Democratic leaders of
the delegates not to insert it and instead pass a Jim Crow law in the first
legislature of the new state. The Democrats followed the advice. When
the first legislature convened on December 2, 1907, a Jim Crow bill was
introduced immediately in both houses, and a law was passed on December 5. It went into effect, attended by racial violence, on February 16,
1908. In subsequent months, new laws were passed prohibiting marriages
between whites and blacks and segregating public institutions.[17] In 1910,
Oklahoma adopted the grandfather clause, which effectively disfranchised
the black population of the state.

In the fall of 1910, some of the Chickasaw and Choctaw freedmen took
advantage of a provision of the Act of 1906 that had given them the right
to purchase surplus lands of the nations at the appraised value. Despite
strong opposition from the Indians, they bought 21,134.95 acres. Meanwhile, many freedmen had been divested of their land holdings. Congress
had finally enacted legislation on May 27, 1908, removing restrictions
from all allotments of not only whites and freedmen but of Indians with
less than half blood, removing restrictions on the surplus allotments of
Indians of one-half to three-quarters blood, and maintaining restrictions
on all allotments of Indians with more than three-quarters blood. Historian
Angie Debo has graphically described the means by which land speculators
took advantage of the weak and ignorant and divested them of their property through flattery, fraud, and deceit. She has also described the bewilder-
ment and fear with which the unassimilated Indians entered the new society.
But, she writes,

The most unfriended were the freedmen, coddled by speculators eager to
protect their "rights" in the division of tribal property, and regarded by

the general populace with hate and envy while they owned their allotments, and with hate and contempt after they lost them.[18]

Thus, after forty years, the Chickasaw freedmen at last were citizens of the State of Oklahoma and of the United States of America. But the state to which they belonged disfranchised most of them and subjected all of them to a system of land laws that they little understood and were ill equipped to deal with. Because of the prevailing racial hatred on the part of whites, who controlled the political and legal processes, they were afforded no protection. As a result, they were systematically divested of their land, to which they had at least had access under the Chickasaw government. In many respects, their lot as American citizens was worse than it had been during the forty years that they were a people without a country.

NOTES

1. 59 Cong., 2 Sess., *Senate Report 5013,* 1: 965, hereafter cited as *Report 5013.*

2. *Ibid.,* 1: 965.

3. *Chickasaw Enterprise,* April 17, 1902.

4. Ed Colbert to Secretary, December 28, 1898; Isaac Kemp and L. C. Kemp to Secretary, January 17, 1899, National Archives Record Group 48 (Records of the Office of the Secretary of the Interior), Indian Territory Division, *General Incoming Correspondence, July 1898-April 1907,* 1898 File 252, Schools, Box 383(54D), 1247-98, 206-99; Annual Reports of the Department of the Interior for the Fsical Year Ended June 30, 1902, 57 Cong., 2 Sess., *House Document 5,* 2: 247.

5. *Report of the United States Indian Inspector for the Indian Territory to the Secretary of the Interior for the Year Ended June 30, 1906* (Washington, D.C.: Government Printing Office, 1906), 10, hereafter cited as *Inspector's Report, 1906; New York Times,* September 12, 1904.

6. Monthly Report of George Beck, October 1904, and January 31, 1905, and Beck to John D. Benedict, January 4, 1905, Indian Archives Division, Oklahoma Historical Society, *Dawes Commission—Chickasaw;* Annual Reports of the Department of the Interior for the Fiscal Year Ended June 30, 1905, 59 Cong., 1 Sess., *House Document 5,* 1: 749, 751.

7. *Reports of the Department of the Interior for the Fiscal Year Ended June 30, 1907* (Washington, D.C.: Government Printing Office, 1907), 2: 336, 350, 353, hereafter cited as *Annual Reports, 1907.*

8. *Inspector's Report, 1906,* 73-75; C. F. Larrabee to Secretary,

December 4, 1906, *General Incoming Correspondence,* 1898 File 252, Schools, Box 383(54D): 22414-06.

9. *Annual Reports, 1907,* 2: 336; National Archives Record Group 75 (Records of the Bureau of Indian Affairs), *Attendance Books for Choctaw and Chickasaw Neighborhood Schools in Indian Territory, 1900-1901, 1906-1907.*

10. J. D. Springer, et al. to Secretary, April 29, 1906, and Frederick H. Umholtz to Benedict, October 7, 1907, *Dawes Commission – Chickasaw; Muskogee Cimeter,* November 16, 1906.

11. Dana Kelsey to Secretary, August 15, 1906, W. L. Bennett to Secretary, April 19, 1907, and Nero Perry to Secretary, April 15, 1907, National Archives Record Group 75, *Letters Received,* 71918-06, 40180-07, 40181-07; Jesse E. Wilson to U.S. Indian Inspector, August 31, 1906, J. Titus Fleming to Secretary, April 25, 1906, A. B. Kemp to Secretary, April 17, 1906, and E. C. King, et al. to Secretary, February 22, 1906, *Dawes Commission – Chickasaw. See also* Larrabee to U. S. Indian Inspector, May 20, 1907, *ibid.*

12. Frank Love to Secretary, February 28, 1906, *Dawes Commission – Chickasaw;* Angie Debo, *And Still the Waters Run* (Princeton, N.J.: Princeton University Press, 1972), 136, 157; *Indian Chieftain,* December 24, 1903 and April 7, 1904; *Pauls Valley Enterprise,* April 28, 1904, and July 20, 1905; *Report 5013,* 1: v.

13. *Report 5013,* 1: 964-965.

14. *Ibid.,* 1: v; Debo, 136, 157.

15. Adge Stephenson to Tams Bixby, July 5, 1899, Robbart Stevenson, et al. to Secretary, April 26, 1906, and E. A. Hitchcock to Commission to the Five Civilized Tribes, December 14, 1906, *Dawes Commission – Chickasaw.*

16. Charles Cohee to J. George Wright, January 5, 1908, *Dawes Commission – Chickasaw.*

17. *Purcell Register,* September 13, and October 18, 1906; "Address by Hon. E. J. Giddings, Oklahoma City, O. T., September 22nd, 1906," Oklahoma Historical Society Library, *Fred S. Barde Collection,* Vertical File, "Negroes"; *Muskogee Cimeter,* September 19 and 27, 1906; *Shawnee Daily Herald,* September 27 and October 19, 1906, February 27 and December 4 and 19, 1907; *Muskogee Times Democrat,* January 10 and 16 and December 3, 1907; *Journal of the Constitutional Convention of Oklahoma* (Muskogee, Indian Territory: Muskogee Printing Co., 1907), 222; *Weekly Times-Journal,* January 27, 1907; *Journal of the House of Representatives of the First Session of the First Legislature of Oklahoma* (Guthrie, Okla.: Leader Printing and Manufacturing House, 1908), 12, 14; *Atoka Indian Citizen,* December 26, 1907.

18. Debo, 260; chapters 4, 8, especially pages 181-183.

Bibliography

MANUSCRIPTS

Records of the Bureau of Indian Affairs (National Archives Record Group 75)
  Attendance Books for Choctaw and Chickasaw Neighborhood Schools
    in Indian Territory, 1900-1901, 1906-1907
  Central Classified Files
  1839 Chickasaw Census Roll
  Letters Received
  Letters Received Relating to Choctaw and Other Freedmen, 1878-84
  Letters Sent
  Letters Sent by the Choctaw and Chickasaw Agency, 1867, 1870-73
  Rolls of Choctaw Freedmen, 1885
Records of the Chickasaw Nation (Indian Archives Division, Oklahoma
    Historical Society)
  Chickasaw—Citizenship
  Chickasaw—Federal Relations
  Chickasaw Volume 53
Records of the Dawes Commission (Indian Archives Division, Oklahoma
    Historical Society)
  Dawes Commission—Chickasaw
  Dawes Commission—Choctaw
Records of the Department of the Interior, Office of the Secretary (National Archives Record Group 48)
  Indian Territory Division: Chickasaw Freedmen
  Indian Territory Division: Choctaw and Chickasaw Freedmen
  General Incoming Correspondence, July, 1898-April, 1907
  Letters Received
Records of the United States Army Continental Commands, 1821-1920
    (National Archives Record Group 393)
  District of Indian Territory: Letters Received, 1867-68
  Frontier District: Seventh Army Corps and Department of Arkansas,
    Letters Received, 1865-66

MICROFILM

Office of Indian Affairs, Letters Received (National Archives Microfilm
Publications, *Microcopy M234*), Rolls 138, 139, 142, 180, 181,
182, 836, 837, 838, 865, 866, 867, 868, 869, 870, 871, 872, 873,
875, 877
Office of Indian Affairs, Letters Sent (National Archives Microfilm Pub-
lications, *Microcopy M21*), Rolls 79, 80, 89, 97, 114, 116, 118,
123, 124, 130, 132, 133, 136, 138, 142, 150, 160, 155, 157
Office of Indian Affairs, Report Books (National Archives Microfilm
Publications, *Microcopy M348*), Rolls 14, 17, 22, 23, 24, 29
Office of the Secretary of the Interior, Letters Sent (National Archives
Microfilm Publications, *Microcopy M606*), Rolls 9, 17
Records of the Bureau of Census, Population Census Schedules, 1860:
Arkansas Slave Schedules (National Archives Microfilm Publica-
tions, *Microcopy M653*), Roll 54
Records of the Dawes Commission to the Five Civilized Tribes (Indian
Archives Microfilm Publications), Roll DC9
Records of the Chickasaw Nation, Minute Book of the District Court:
Chickasaw Volume 23 (Indian Archives Microfilm Publications),
Roll CKN16
Special Files of the Office of Indian Affairs, 1807-1904 (National Archives
Microfilm Publications, *Microcopy M574*), Roll 76

FEDERAL DOCUMENTS

United States Congress
  *American State Papers: Documents, Legislative and Executive of the
  Congress of the United States, from the First Session of the First
  to the Third Session of the Thirteenth Congress, Inclusive, Commencing March 3, 1789, and Ending March 3, 1815.* 38 vols. Washington, D.C.: Gales and Seaton, 1832-61.
Congressional Record
    25 Cong., 3 Sess., *Senate Document 1*
    26 Cong., 1 Sess., *Senate Document 1*
    26 Cong., 2 Sess., *Executive Document 2*
    27 Cong., 2 Sess., *Executive Document 2*
    29 Cong., 2 Sess., *Executive Document 4*
    31 Cong., 1 Sess., *Executive Document 5*
    38 Cong., 1 Sess., *House Executive Document 1*
    38 Cong., 2 Sess., *House Executive Document 1*
    39 Cong., 1 Sess., *House Executive Document 1*

40 Cong., 2 Sess., *Senate Executive Document 82*
41 Cong., 2 Sess., *House Executive Document 1*
41 Cong., 2 Sess., *Senate Executive Document 71*
41 Cong., 3 Sess., *House Executive Document 1*
42 Cong., 2 Sess., *House Executive Document 1*
42 Cong., 2 Sess., *House Report 95*
42 Cong., 3 Sess., *House Executive Document 1*
42 Cong., 3 Sess., *House Executive Document 207*
42 Cong., 3 Sess., *House Miscellaneous Document 46*
42 Cong., 3 Sess., *House Report 98*
43 Cong., 1 Sess., *Senate Miscellaneous Document 118*
43 Cong., 2 Sess., *House Executive Document 1*
45 Cong., 3 Sess., *Senate Report 744*
47 Cong., 1 Sess., *Senate Miscellaneous Document 117*
48 Cong., 1 Sess., *Senate Executive Document 51*
49 Cong., 1 Sess., *Senate Report 1278*
50 Cong., 1 Sess., *Senate Executive Document 166*
53 Cong., 3 Sess., *Senate Miscellaneous Document 24*
54 Cong., 1 Sess., *Senate Document 12*
54 Cong., 1 Sess., *Senate Document 182*
55 Cong., 1 Sess., *Senate Document 93*
55 Cong., 1 Sess., *Senate Document 157*
55 Cong., 1 Sess., *Senate Document 183*
56 Cong., 1 Sess., *House Document 5*
56 Cong., 1 Sess., *House Document 221*
56 Cong., 2 Sess., *House Document 5*
57 Cong., 1 Sess., *House Document 5*
57 Cong., 2 Sess., *House Document 5*
58 Cong., 3 Sess., *House Document 5*
59 Cong., 1 Sess., *House Document 5*
59 Cong., 2 Sess., *Senate Document 257*
59 Cong., 2 Sess., *Senate Document 298*
59 Cong., 2 Sess., *Senate Document 357*
59 Cong., 2 Sess., *Senate Report 5013*
60 Cong., 1 Sess., *Senate Document 505*
61 Cong., 2 Sess., *House Document 920*
United States Census Office. *The Five Civilized Tribes in Indian Territory: The Cherokee, Chickasaw, Choctaw, Creek, and Seminole Nations.* Washington, D.C.: U.S. Census Printing Office, 1894.
United States Commissioner to the Five Civilized Tribes. *Laws, Decisions, and Regulations Affecting the Work of the Commissioner to the Five Civilized Tribes, 1893-1906.* Washington, D.C.: Government Printing Office, 1906.

United States Department of the Interior

Annual Report of the Commissioner of Indian Affairs to the Secretary of the Interior for the Year 1876. Washington, D.C.: Government Printing Office, 1876.

Annual Report of the Commissioner of Indian Affairs to the Secretary of the Interior for the Year 1877. Washington, D.C.: Government Printing Office, 1877.

Annual Report of the Commissioner of Indian Affairs to the Secretary of the Interior for the Year 1882. Washington, D.C.: Government Printing Office, 1882.

Annual Report of the Commissioner of Indian Affairs to the Secretary of the Interior for the Year 1883. Washington, D.C.: Government Printing Office, 1883.

Annual Report of the Commissioner of Indian Affairs to the Secretary of the Interior for the Year 1884. Washington, D.C.: Government Printing Office, 1884.

Annual Report of the Commissioner of Indian Affairs to the Secretary of the Interior for the Year 1885. Washington, D.C.: Government Printing Office, 1885.

Annual Report of the Commissioner of Indian Affairs to the Secretary of the Interior for the Year 1887. Washington, D.C.: Government Printing Office, 1887.

Annual Report of the Commissioner of Indian Affairs to the Secretary of the Interior for the Year 1888. Washington, D.C.: Government Printing Office, 1888.

Annual Report of the Commissioner of Indian Affairs to the Secretary of the Interior for the Year 1889. Washington, D.C.: Government Printing Office, 1889.

Annual Reports of the Department of the Interior for the Fiscal Year Ended June 30, 1907. Washington, D.C.: Government Printing Office, 1907.

Annual Reports of the Secretary of the Interior for the Fiscal Year Ended June 30, 1897. Washington, D.C.: Government Printing Office, 1897.

Annual Reports of the Secretary of the Interior for the Fiscal Year Ended June 30, 1898. Washington, D.C.: Government Printing Office, 1898.

Report of the Secretary of the Interior. Washington, D.C.: Government Printing Office, 1866.

Report of the Secretary of the Interior. Washington, D.C.: Government Printing Office, 1868.

Report of the Secretary of the Interior. Washington, D.C.: Government Printing Office, 1869.

Report of the United States Indian Inspector for the Indian Territory to the Secretary of the Interior for the Year Ended June 30, 1906. Washington, D.C.: Government Printing Office, 1906.

Reports of the Department of the Interior for the Fiscal Year Ended June 30, 1907. Washington, D.C.: Government Printing Office, 1907.

United States Supreme Court. *Cases Argued and Decided in the Supreme Court of the United States.* Lawyers' Edition. 100 vols. Rochester, N.Y.: The Lawyers Co-operative Publishing Company, 1901-1956.

BOOKS AND PAMPHLETS

Abel, Annie Heloise. *The American Indian as Slaveholder and Secessionist.* Cleveland, Ohio: The Arthur H. Clark Company, 1915.

——. *The American Indian under Reconstruction.* Cleveland, Ohio: The Arthur H. Clark Company, 1925.

Address by P. P. Pitchlynn, Principal Chief of the Choctaw Nation and Winchester Colbert, Governor of the Chickasaw Nation to the Choctaws and Chickasaws. Washington, D.C.: Joseph L. Pearson, 1866.

Britton, Wiley. *The Civil War on the Border.* 2 vols. New York: G. P. Putnam's Sons, 1890-1904.

Constitution, and Laws of the Chickasaw Nation, together with the Treaties of 1832, 1833, 1834, 1837, 1852, 1855, and 1866. Parsons, Kans.: The Foley Railway Printing Company, 1899.

Constitution and Laws of the Choctaw Nation. New York: William P. Lyon & Son, 1869.

Constitution, Laws, and Treaties of the Chickasaws. Tishomingo City, Chickasaw Nation: E. J. Johnson, 1860.

Debo, Angie. *And Still the Waters Run.* Princeton, N.J.: Princeton University Press, 1972.

——. *The Rise and Fall of the Choctaw Republic.* New ed. Norman: University of Oklahoma Press, 1967.

——. *The Road to Disappearance.* Norman: University of Oklahoma Press, 1941.

Flickinger, Robert Elliott. *The Choctaw Freedmen and the Story of Oak Hill Industrial Academy.* Fonda, Iowa: Journal and Times Press, 1914.

Foreman, Grant. *The Five Civilized Tribes.* Reprinted. Norman: University of Oklahoma Press, 1966.

Fritz, Henry E. *The Movement for Indian Assimilation, 1860-1890.*

Philadelphia: University of Pennsylvania Press, 1963.

Gibson, Arrell M. *The Chickasaws.* Norman: University of Oklahoma Press, 1971.

Goode, William H. *Outposts of Zion, with Limnings of Mission Life.* Cincinnati, Ohio: Poe and Hitchcock, 1864.

Hawkins, Benjamin. *Letters of Benjamin Hawkins, 1796-1806.* Collections of the Georgia Historical Society, Vol. 9. Savannah, Ga.: The Morning News, 1916.

Hitchcock, Ethan Allen. *A Traveler in Indian Territory: The Journal of Ethan Allen Hitchcock, Late Major-General in the United States Army,* ed. Grant Foreman. Cedar Rapids, Iowa: The Torch Press, 1930.

Johnson, Neil R. *The Chickasaw Rancher.* Stillwater, Okla: Redlands Press, 1961.

Journal of the Constitutional Convention of Oklahoma. Muskogee, Indian Territory: Muskogee Printing Co., 1907.

Journal of the House of Representatives of the First Session of the First Legislature of Oklahoma. Guthrie, Okla.: Leader Printing and Manufacturing House, 1908.

Mills, Lawrence. *Oklahoma Indian Land Laws.* St. Louis: Thomas Law Book Company, 1924.

Rawick, George P., ed. *The American Slave: A Composite Autobiography.* 19 vols. Westport, Conn.: Greenwood Publishing Company, 1972.

Shirley, Glenn. *Law West of Fort Smith: Frontier Justice in the Indian Territory, 1834-1896.* New York: Collier Books, 1957.

Swanton, John R. *The Indians of the Southeastern United States.* Bureau of American Ethnology Bulletin 137. Reprint ed. New York: Greenwood Press, 1969.

Thoburn, Joseph B., and Wright, Muriel H. *Oklahoma: A History of the State and Its People.* New York: Lewis Historical Publishing Company, 1929.

Wardell, Morris L. *A Political History of the Cherokee Nation, 1838-1907.* Norman: University of Oklahoma Press, 1938.

Wright, Muriel H. *A Guide to the Indian Tribes of Oklahoma.* Norman: University of Oklahoma Press, 1951.

ARTICLES

Brown, Loren N. "The Dawes Commission," *Chronicles of Oklahoma,* 9 (March, 1931), 71-105.

Chapman, Berlin B. "Freedmen and the Oklahoma Lands," *The Southwestern Social Science Quarterly,* 29 (September, 1948), 150-159.

Doran, Michael F. "Population Statistics of Nineteenth Century Indian Territory," *Chronicles of Oklahoma*, 53 (Winter, 1975-76), 492-515.

Hiemstra, William L. "Early Presbyterian Missions among the Choctaw and Chickasaw Indians in Mississippi," *The Journal of Mississippi History*, 10 (January, 1948), 8-16.

"Journal of the Adjourned Session of the First General Council of the Indian Territory," *Chronicles of Oklahoma*, 3 (June, 1925), 120-140.

"Journal of the General Council of the Indian Territory," *Chronicles of Oklahoma*, 3 (April, 1925), 33-44.

Laracy, John. "Sacred Heart Mission and Abbey," *Chronicles of Oklahoma*, 5 (June, 1927), 234-250.

Littlefield, Daniel F., Jr., and Underhill, Lonnie E. "Negro Marshals in Indian Territory," *Journal of Negro History*, 54 (April, 1971), 77-87.

McAdam, Rezin W. "An Indian Commonwealth," *Harper's New Monthly Magazine*, 87 (November, 1893), 884-897.

Meserve, John Bartlett. "Governor Jonas Wolf and Governor Palmer Simeon Mosely," *Chronicles of Oklahoma*, 18 (September, 1940), 243-251.

Morton, Ohland. "Confederate Government Relations with the Five Civilized Tribes," *Chronicles of Oklahoma*, 31 (Summer, 1953), 189-203.

———. "The Confederate States Government and the Five Civilized Tribes," *Chronicles of Oklahoma*, 31 (Autumn, 1953), 299-322.

"Okmulgee Constitution," *Chronicles of Oklahoma*, 3 (September, 1925), 216-228.

Parsons, John E., ed. "Letters on the Chickasaw Removal of 1837," *The New-York Historical Society Quarterly*, 37 (July, 1953), 273-283.

Phelps, Dawson A. "The Chickasaw Mission," *The Journal of Mississippi History*, 13 (October, 1951), 226-235.

———, ed. "Excerpts from the Journal of the Reverend Joseph Bullen, 1799 and 1800," *The Journal of Mississippi History*, 17 (October, 1955), 259-281.

Rainwater, Percy L. "Indian Missions and Missionaries," *The Journal of Mississippi History*, 28 (February, 1966), 15-39.

"Report of the Board of Indian Commissioners to the Secretary of the Interior for the President, for the Year 1870," *Chronicles of Oklahoma*, 5 (March, 1927), 91-92.

Trickett, Dean. "The Civil War in the Indian Territory," *Chronicles of Oklahoma*, 18 (December, 1940), 266-280.

Warren, Harry. "Missions, Missionaries, Frontier Characters and Schools,"
     Publications of the Mississippi Historical Society, 8 (1904), 571-
     598.
Williams, Nudie E. "Bass Reeves: Lawman in the Western Ozarks,"
     Negro History Bulletin, 42 (April-June, 1979), 37-39.
Wright, Muriel H. "American Indian Corn Dishes," *Chronicles of Okla-
     homa,* 36 (Summer, 1958), 155-156.

NEWSPAPERS AND PERIODICALS

Alliance Courier (Ardmore)
Atoka Independent (Atoka, Choctaw Nation)
Cherokee Advocate (Tahlequah, Cherokee Nation)
Chickasha Express (Chickasha, Chickasaw Nation)
Daily Ardmoreite (Ardmore, Chickasaw Nation)
Daily Oklahoman (Oklahoma City, Oklahoma Territory)
Edmond Sun-Democrat (Edmond, Oklahoma Territory)
El Reno News (El Reno, Oklahoma Territory)
Indian Champion (Atoka)
Indian Chieftain (Vinita, Cherokee Nation)
Indian Citizen (Atoka)
Indian Journal (Muskogee and Eufaula, Creek Nation)
Missionary Herald (Philadelphia)
Muskogee Phoenix (Muskogee)
Muskogee Times Democrat (Muskogee)
New York Times
Oklahoma Star (Caddo, Choctaw Nation)
Pauls Valley Enterprise (Pauls Valley)
Purcell Register (Purcell, Chickasaw Nation)
Shawnee Daily Herald (Shawnee, Oklahoma Territory)
Stillwater Gazette (Stillwater, Oklahoma Territory)
The Vindicator (Atoka)
Weekly Times-Journal (Oklahoma City)

Index

About the Author

DANIEL F. LITTLEFIELD, JR. is professor of English at the University of Arkansas at Little Rock. His earlier books include *Africans and Seminoles* (Greenwood Press, 1977), *The Cherokee Freedmen* (Greenwood Press, 1978), and *Africans and Creeks* (Greenwood Press, 1979).